A WORLD FOR

Butterflies

A WORLD FOR

Butterflies

THEIR LIVES,
BEHAVIOR AND
FUTURE

PHIL SCHAPPERT

FIREFLY BOOKS

A FIREFLY BOOK

Published by Firefly Books (U.S.) Inc., 2005

First Printing

Publisher Cataloging-in-Publication Data (U.S.)

Schappert, Phillip Joseph, 1956-
A world for butterflies : their lives, behavior and future / Phil Schappert.
[320] p. : col. photos. ; cm.
Includes bibliographical references and index.
Summary: Guide to butterflies, including their physical characteristics, behavior, migration, life cycle and environment.
ISBN 1-55407-065-1 (pbk.)
1. Butterflies. I. Title.
595.78/9 22 QL542.S35 2005

Published in the United States by
Firefly Books (U.S.) Inc.
P.O. Box 1338, Ellicott Station
Buffalo, New York 14205

Published in Canada by Key Porter Books Limited

Electronic formatting: Jean Lightfoot Peters
Illustrations: John Lightfoot
Design: Peter Maher
Frontispiece: John Tennent
Photograph (front cover): Mario Maier
Photographs (back cover): (left) Mario Maier; (right) J.M. Fengler

www.aworldforbutterflies.com

Printed and bound in Canada

Dedicated to

REUBEN AND PAULINE SCHAPPERT,

for instilling a deep abiding love for "all creatures, great and small,"

and

DR. W. JOHN D. EBERLIE,

who shared the benefits of the wisdom gained in a lifetime
of studying, rearing and photographing butterflies
through all of their stages.

I hope there are many butterflies wherever they are...
and that they think of me half as often as I think of them.

Acknowledgments

This book would simply not have been possible without the help of a great many friends, colleagues, acquaintances and Lepidopterists of all sorts. First and foremost, I wish to thank my wife, Pat, for putting up with me for the last fifteen years while I made a sharp right turn in the course of my life. Pat also read the entire manuscript (more than once) and, as usual, served as a capable foil for my many explanations, reasonings, meanderings and other foibles. My undying gratitude to Larry Gilbert at the University of Texas at Austin for fostering me and allowing us to live at the Stengl "Lost Pines" Biological Station during the writing of this book. My special thanks to Laurence Packer at York University in Toronto for reading the entire manuscript, catching one major blunder and providing useful insights on many other aspects of the text. Also, Dr. Packer and M. Brock Fenton were the original co-conspirators that introduced me to the folks at Key Porter Books in Toronto and thus provided me with the opportunity to write the book that I'd often thought of writing.

Thanks are due also to the many people that read all or part of the manuscript during its preparation and were brutally frank with their comments. They are (in addition to those already mentioned) Sharon Bramblett, Nicole Gerardo, Carla Guthrie, Durrell Kapan, Marcus R. Kronforst, David Millard and Brian Wee. The readability of the text was greatly improved by Beverley Beetham Endersby and Patrick Crean. Thanks also to the "crew" at Key Porter Books in Toronto (Anna Porter, Clare McKeon, Janice Zawerbny, Peter Maher and Susan Renouf). What is correct is due to their careful diligence, what may still be wrong is entirely my own fault.

Many wonderful people, most of whom I've never met but have only corresponded with via email, have taken the bulk of the photographs herein. They are James Adams (USA), Corina Brdar (Canada), Marcio Zikan Cardoso (Brazil), Peng Chai (USA), Chris Durden (USA), Alana Edwards (USA), Jeff Fengler (USA), Nelson Guda (USA), Bill Hark (USA), Durrell Kapan (USA), Tooru Kawabe (Japan), Oleg Kosterin (Russia), George Krizek (USA), Takashi Kumon (Japan), John Landers (USA), Torben Larsen (Africa), Mario Maier (Germany), David Millard (USA), Patti Murray (USA), Paul Opler (USA), Camille Parmesan/Mike Singer (USA), Kenelm Philip (USA), Emil Pignetti (USA), Mike Quinn (USA), Hub Reumkens (Netherlands), Gary Ross (USA), Leroy Simon (USA), Andrei Sourakov (USA), Ann Swengel (USA), Richard Tanner (Canada), John Tennent (UK), Norbert Ulmann (Germany), Jane Yack (Canada), and Cor Zonneveld (Netherlands). Without their spectacular photos the book would've been much more difficult...a photo *is* worth a thousand words. I remain convinced that the best photos are taken by those that spend the time in the field with the creatures that they so obviously adore. I'm sure that a quick perusal of the many unusual and beautiful photos that they have taken will convince you as well.

Writing this book is the hardest thing that I have ever done. It's easy to communicate science to other scientists but exceedingly difficult, as I have found out, to do the same for non-scientists. As much as I hate to admit it, being able to do so is probably the difference between a "teacher" and a "researcher." I hope that I have bridged that gap but you, the reader, will be the ultimate judge of that.

Contents

Acknowledgments 7

Preface 12

1. Why Butterflies? 18

A BUTTERFLY'S HERITAGE 20

THE LIFE CYCLE 22

BODY FORM AND STRUCTURE 29

BUTTERFLIES OR MOTHS? 38

LEPIDOPTEROLOGY: SCIENCE OR ART? 41

WHY CONSERVE BUTTERFLIES? 45

2. Butterflies of the World 48

THE ORIGIN OF BUTTERFLIES 50

TAXONOMY, CLASSIFICATION AND NOMENCLATURE 51

BUTTERFLIES OF THE WORLD 56

3. A World of Butterflies 82

THE GEOGRAPHIC DISTRIBUTION OF BUTTERFLIES 84

POPULATION BIOLOGY 100

4. A Butterfly's World 116

BEING A GOOD EGG 117

GROWING UP BIG AND STRONG 123

THE BIG SLEEP 141

CHANGES IN LIFESTYLE 150

SEX, SURVIVAL AND THE SINGLE BUTTERFLY 152

LIFE AND DEATH: GAMES BUTTERFLIES PLAY 156

STAYING AHEAD OF THE GAME 189

MATING RITUALS 215

COMPLETING THE CYCLE 244

5. A World for Butterflies? 248

CAUSES OF BUTTERFLY ENDANGERMENT 250

SELECTED CASE STUDIES 265

WHAT CAN I DO? 289

Resources 303

Glossary 304

Bibliography 309

Index 317

Preface

BUTTERFLIES ARE THE "CHARISMATIC MEGAFAUNA" OF THE INSECT world. Their relatively large size, brilliant colors and ability to fly; their complex behavior and relationships with plants and other animals; and their occurrence in a wide variety of habitats have fascinated us for centuries. Recently, their decline in numbers and potential use as determinants of habitat and ecological health—butterflies may be the "canaries in coal mines" of modern times—have provided both an impetus and a focus for conserving them and, more importantly, their habitats.

The questions that the mere existence of butterflies poses are varied and interesting. Why are there so many kinds of butterflies? And why aren't there more? What purpose do their bright colors and patterns serve? Where did they come from? How do they live? How will they survive in a world that is increasingly dominated by the effects of mankind? This book will help you to find answers to many of these questions, but it also asks many other questions for which we do not yet have answers. This is part of the joy that I find in butterflies—there's always something new to learn about them.

I hope that this book will interest a wide readership. The unique color photos—all of living butterflies *doing* something—have been taken by some of the world's finest lepidopterists and photographers. The narrative is tailored to those with an interest in butterflies and I have tried to keep jargon or "biospeak" to a minimum. Where it is necessary to use scientific terms and nomenclature, I've tried to explain their meaning wherever possible. (You will also find a useful glossary at the end of this book.) Together, the text, photos and captions should provide hours of enjoyment for everyone—from the amateur naturalist to the undergraduate studying life sciences. Later, you can visit www.aworldofbutterflies.com for further insights, information, and links to sites around the world.

The book is divided into five chapters, each of which focuses on a major question: What are butterflies? How many kinds of butterflies are there? Where do they live? How do they live? What can we do to help them survive into the twenty-first century? While the questions might seem simple, the answers to them—and the additional questions that the answers raise—are sometimes difficult, often surprisingly complex and, in almost all cases, filled with wonderment and joy.

Chapter 1, "Why Butterflies?" introduces the book and provides the background knowledge you will need to get the most from the chapters that follow. In this chapter, you will learn about the history of the study of butterflies (lepidopterology); butterflies and man; the life cycle of the butterfly, including developmental patterns, body form and structure, and

LEFT: **Butterflies, like this female Japanese swallowtail,** *Sericinus montela* **(Papilionidae), have six jointed legs, three segmented body divisions and an external skeleton like all other insects yet we treat them differently.**

A courting pair of sleepy orange butterflies, *Eurema nicippe* (Pieridae), reminds us that not only do species have to survive to be conserved, they need to be able to reproduce.

how they move about; and why butterflies aren't moths (and vice versa). Questions that we seek answers to here include how long people have been studying butterflies; why butterflies have four stages in their life cycle; how caterpillars grow and become butterflies; why butterflies are insects; what features comprise a butterfly; and why we should conserve butterflies and other insects.

Chapter 2, "Butterflies of the World," provides a survey of the different kinds of butterflies, their evolution and their historical relationships. Here you will learn about butterfly diversity; butterfly names and nomenclature; the butterfly family tree and the evolutionary origins of butterflies. Questions that we will address include how many different kinds of butterflies there are, how long ago butterflies evolved, who their nearest relatives are, and why there aren't more kinds of butterflies.

Chapter 3, "A World of Butterflies," places the diverse kinds of butterflies into geographical context. Here we examine reasons for the worldwide distribution of butterflies, and various aspects of butterfly ecology, including population biology, kinds of habitats needed and used by butterflies, and butterfly migration and dispersal habits. The questions

OPPOSITE: **Variation among the more than 18,000 species of butterflies provides abundant diversity for us to consider. Many butterflies also vary within species, like these two naturally occurring forms of *Argynnis paphia* (Nymphalidae) shown here (nominate form, left; form *valesina*, right).**

The atala, *Eumaeus atala* (Lycaenidae), once considered endangered due to loss of habitat in Florida, is now more common than it once was.

examined include what factors determine the geographic range of butterflies, why butterflies are more common in the tropics, why some butterflies are rare, which places are most likely to have butterflies, why some butterflies are found exclusively in one region of the world, and how butterflies get to faraway places.

Chapter 4, "A Butterfly's World," is the heart of the book. It examines how butterflies live, how they perceive the world, how they reproduce, what they eat and what eats them—in other words, what it would be like to live in a butterfly's world. In this chapter, we explore the relationships between butterflies and plants, butterflies and other insects, and butterflies and their predators; caterpillars and butterflies that have unusual diets; important ecological distinctions between stages of the butterfly life cycle; strategies that butterflies use to find mates, court and reproduce, or to avoid being eaten by predators; aspects of butterfly behavior that have important implications for their success; and butterfly senses. Some of the

16

many questions include what butterflies and caterpillars eat, how they eat, what eats butterflies, why butterflies don't grow (or why caterpillars don't reproduce), how butterflies manage to avoid being eaten but still attract mates; what butterflies see, smell or hear; what factors are most important in the day-to-day lives of butterflies; and how butterflies reproduce.

Chapter 5, "A World for Butterflies?," examines the interaction between butterflies and people. Here you'll learn about causes of butterfly endangerment, including habitat loss; the effects of humans and the protective measures that can be or have been taken; examine six selected case histories that illustrate some conservation principles and successes; and what you can do to aid in butterfly conservation, through observing and studying butterflies, rearing and life-history studies, and butterfly gardening and other habitat restorations.

When was the last time that you stopped and watched a butterfly? Most people are surprised to learn that much of what we know about the biology of animal populations, the evolution of animal behavior and of flowering plants, and the ecology of insects is based on the study of butterflies. Many of the world's best-known biologists and scientists have studied butterflies (even if they do it surreptitiously, in their backyards). Like you, they wonder why there are so many kinds of butterflies, why their wings are so boldly colored and patterned, why they flutter when they fly, why they choose particular plants to lay their eggs on, and a thousand or more questions besides.

Why write a book about butterflies? I think you may already know the answer...

Butterflies that are usually considered striking or bold, like this *Parnassius actius* (Papilionidae), can be surprisingly cryptic in their habitat. Many Parnassians are endangered or threatened by human activities.

PHIL SCHAPPERT
Smithville, Texas
September 1999

Why Butterflies?

BUTTERFLIES ARE INSECTS. THIS SIMPLE STATEMENT COMES AS something of a shock to many people. Surprisingly large numbers of people have a knee-jerk, insecticidal response to insects—including caterpillars, the immature growth stage of butterflies and moths—but few feel this way about butterflies, the adult reproductive stage of these same insects (although moths are a whole other story). If butterflies are insects, why don't people feel the same aversion to them that they do to, say, cockroaches, bumblebees, even some moths?

Unfortunately, we do perceive the vast array of insect species, comprising more than 60 percent of all of the species with which we share this planet, as our enemies. They bite or sting, compete with us for food, eat our possessions, and generally bother us when we least want to be "bugged." Many people see them as small, drab, ugly little creatures that creep around at night doing unspeakable things. But contrary to popular belief, insects are really not that bad. In fact, of the more than one million species of insects that are known to science (and this likely represents only a fraction of the 30 million or so insect species thought to exist), much less than one-tenth of one percent are really pests. We conveniently forget—or just fail to recognize—the essential services that they provide. After all, they pollinate virtually all of the plants and crops that make our lives possible, they recycle themselves (and much of our garbage), and provide the essential links in the natural food web that sustains us.

The reason may be that butterflies are to insects as baby mammals are

18

to animals in general: they appeal to us on a visceral or subconscious level. Contrary to what we think of most insects, butterflies are large, colorful and boldly patterned; they fly during the day, many of them with a distinctive "flutter" that evokes the gentleness we ascribe to them; and they visit flowers. Of course, bees can be surprisingly large, are colorful and boldly patterned and visit flowers during the day, but they do not instill in us the same awe and wonder we feel when we watch a butterfly. Is it because bees are noisy, pugnacious and armed, and butterflies are silent and appear defenseless? I'll leave it for you to decide.

Another reason may be the miracle of the lowly caterpillar's transformation into the fragile beauty of a butterfly. Metamorphosis (a change in form) has come to symbolize the transfiguration of the human soul or spirit, the *psyche*, at the moment of death. Many other insect groups, certainly the most commonly encountered, also undergo similar awe-inspiring metamorphoses, yet do not evoke the same wonder. What is it about the aesthetics of the butterfly that we see as inherently spiritual? Is it that they represent the warm, sunny days of our youth? The celebrated author and accomplished lepidopterist Vladimir Nabokov once lamented that "it is astonishing how few people notice butterflies." I think that he really meant "adults," because children are inordinately fascinated by butterflies (and by insects in general). I hope this book will rekindle the interest that may have been extinguished by entomophobic parents.

So, why write another book about butterflies? In part, because of all these things, but also because they need our help and protection.

A Butterfly's Heritage

Butterflies (and moths) are members of the insect order Lepidoptera (from the Greek words *lepis*, meaning "scale," and *pteron*, meaning "wing") because they share a single defining characteristic: scales cover their bodies and their wings. The scales, which are really modified hairs, give the wings their colors and patterns, overlapping like roof tiles or shingles to, in most cases, cover the wings completely. It is thought that scales evolved from hairs to allow butterflies and moths to escape from spiders' webs: the scales are loosely anchored in the wing membrane and are easily detached. Anyone who has ever handled a butterfly or moth knows that the wings are "dusty" and leave "powder" on the fingertips. The "powder" is the scales from their wings.

The Lepidoptera, comprising about 165,000 species, are the second-largest single group of similar organisms in the world (only the beetles, Coleoptera, have more species). There are almost ten times as many species of Lepidoptera as there are of all birds and all mammals combined, but butterflies, or the Rhopalocera, as they are also sometimes known, constitute only about 11 percent of the order. The remaining 89 percent of Lepidoptera are moths, collectively known as the Heterocera. The Rhopalocera generally include only the "true" butterflies, or Papilionoidea, and, the somewhat moth-like skippers, or Hesperioidea. But relatively recent developments in the study of the Lepidoptera, colloquially known as "lepidopterology," have suggested that a couple of primitive groups of "butterfly-moths" should really be considered as butterflies.

The wings of butterflies are colored and patterned in such a way that the majority of species can be identified on sight. Think about this for a second. The vast majority of the 18,000 or so species of butterflies have completely unique, recognizable upper, or dorsal, wing patterns, but—and here's the kicker—the dorsal and ventral (underside) patterns are, in almost every species, completely different. The ease with which we can recognize the many species of butterflies may be another part of their attraction for us. Moths, of course, also have wing scales and exhibit a marvelous diversity in wing color patterns, but, since they are mostly nocturnal, and because many are brown or gray, and small, they are far more difficult to identify. Take into consideration also that there are eight to nine times as many moths as butterflies, many of which are encountered infrequently, and it is more obvious why there are fewer guides to moth identification.

Butterflies, like many insects, are holometabolous. This means they undergo complete metamorphosis; that is, they have four distinct stages in their life cycle: *egg*, or ovum (plural: ova), *caterpillar*, or larva (plural: larvae), the *chrysalis*, or pupa (plural: pupae), and *adult*, or imago (plural:

imagines). Also, like other insects, butterflies (and caterpillars) have three major body divisions (head, thorax and abdomen), six segmented "true" legs and an external skeleton, or exoskeleton, made of chitin.

The Life Cycle

Since the life cycle of a typical butterfly is a continuous process, the choice of a starting point is entirely arbitrary—we could debate which came first, the butterfly or the egg, without resolution for many years. I find it useful

A female Mexican fritillary, *Euptoieta hegesia* (Nymphalidae), nectaring at the flowers of a *Lantana camera* shrub (Verbenaceae) in Jamaica.

An egg ready to hatch (on leaf at upper right) and a freshly hatched caterpillar of the Mexican fritillary, *Euptoieta hegesia* (Nymphalidae).

to begin with the act of an adult female butterfly laying an egg because fertilization of the egg—that is, the formation of the embryo that will develop into a caterpillar—occurs as the egg is laid. Also, many species, especially in temperate regions, undergo diapause (remain in a state of arrested development) as eggs, and this fact becomes an important component of their biology.

The species that I know best is the Mexican fritillary, *Euptoieta hegesia* (Nymphalidae), from the island of Jamaica, so I will describe its life cycle. The life cycle of this species is not very different from that of the spicebush swallowtail, *Papilio troilus* (Papilionidae) shown in the photo essay (see pages 24, 25). The number of variations on the simple theme of a four-stage life cycle, even among a relatively consistent group such as the butterflies, staggers the imagination. As we will see, the variety in size, shape, texture, and color of eggs, caterpillars and chrysalids; duration of the egg stage; number and length of each larval instar or growth period and

The life cycle of a "typical" butterfly, the spicebush swallowtail, *Papilio troilus* (Papilionidae). The caterpillars of this species vary remarkably between growth stages, from resembling a bird dropping when small to looking like the head of a snake as they get larger.

25

By the time the caterpillar of the Mexican fritillary, *Euptoieta hegesia* (Nymphalidae), is full-grown it will be more than 3,000 times larger than it was when it hatched.

duration of the pupal stage is as astonishing as the variations in the adult butterflies themselves. However, the process of metamorphosis is essentially similar, so this species is as good an example as any.

The eggs of the Mexican fritillary are laid one at a time, primarily on the tissue between the veins on the undersides of leaves of either the preferred host plant, *Turnera ulmifolia*, or any of the small number of passion vines (*Passiflora* sp.) that are used as alternate hosts. The female butterfly fixes the egg to the leaf with adhesive "cement" to prevent it from falling off. Eggs are conical in shape, less than 1 millimeter tall and about 25 percent taller than they are wide, white to light green in color; darkening to red-brown with age as the head capsule of the developing larva begins to fill the egg. When the eggs hatch, five days after being laid, the caterpillar's first meal is often the remaining eggshell. The newly hatched caterpillar (see the photo on page 23) is light tan or orange, but, soon after it is exposed to the air and begins feeding on the green plant tissue, its color darkens to red-brown, and then to brick red. Young larvae of this species feed only on the tissue on the underside of the leaf of the host plant, causing readily recognizable "windows" in the leaves. They probably dine selectively because the upper side of the leaf has a thick waxy coating that can "gum up" the small mandibles and mouth parts of the tiny caterpillars.

As caterpillars feed and grow, they must periodically molt, or shed their skin. The period between each molt is called an instar. At these times, they may change their appearance drastically (the photos of the life cycle of the spicebush swallowtail show a wonderful example of this). The Mexican fritillary is not nearly so dramatic; however, the color of the Jamaican larva deepens from brick red to almost blood-red maroon, and black-edged white lines on the top and sides of the body appear between the second and third instars (see photo on page 132). This new color pattern coincides with a change in caterpillar feeding behavior: caterpillars begin to feed and spend more of their time on the tops of leaves instead of on the bottom. The larval stages develop in twelve to eighteen days in this species, depending on temperature and host plant used, but larval stages can take as long as two or three years in arctic or high-altitude species that simply do not have enough time in one season to complete their growth.

The pupae of Nymphalids, like this Mexican fritillary, *Euptoieta hegesia* (Nymphalidae), hang head-down (or tail-up if you prefer).

More often than not, in the last stage, or "prepupal stadium," the caterpillar wanders away from its host plant, searching for a place to undergo its final molt into a chrysalis. The final instar larva of the Mexican fritillary spins a silk pad, fastens its terminal legs in the pad, lets go of the substrate with the remainder of its legs so that it hangs free, and begins its final molt into a pupa (see photo on this page). Other species, such as the spicebush swallowtail, may spin a "girdle" of silk to support them upright, or simply rest on the ground or some other substrate. Late on the seventh day of the eight-day pupation period of the Mexican fritillary, the

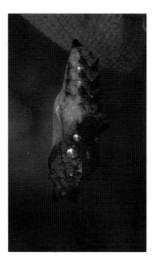

The emergence, and subsequent expansion of the wings, of a female *Damora sagana* (Nymphalidae). No matter how many times one witnesses a butterfly's emergence into the world, it is always an unbelievably magical process.

exoskeleton becomes almost transparent, and the wing pattern and details of the external anatomy of the butterfly can be seen. On the eighth day, the butterfly uses the intake of air to expand its body, until a suture or seam opens near the head of the pupal case that allows the butterfly to eclose (emerge), or slide out.

The butterfly looks very small and shrunken at this point because the wings are wet and not yet expanded. Before the fresh butterfly can fly off to pursue its life, the wings must be expanded. Haemolymph, or body fluid, is pumped through the veins to expand the wings while the butterfly hangs on to its pupal case or the substrate on which it pupated. However, the body fluid must be withdrawn from the veins before the wings can dry. If you watch closely you can see the abdomen pump as the butterfly takes in air to displace the fluid from the wings. Blood-red meconium, the waste products of metamorphosis and the final larval meal, is ejected from the anus and this blood-like appearance may be a useful defense for the butterfly if it is disturbed during this vulnerable period of its life.

One of the major events that has occurred during pupation is the development of the reproductive system. Butterflies are reproductive engines while caterpillars are eating machines. Caterpillars do not reproduce and butterflies do not grow. Butterflies do feed, usually on the energy-rich, sugary nectar of flowers (but also on a wide variety of other substances as we will see), to fuel the muscles that allow them to fly, but

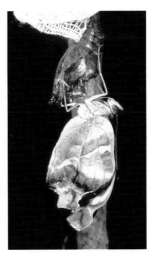

they do not grow any larger. The strategies that butterflies and caterpillars use to survive, avoid being eaten, find mates and reproduce are many and varied, and are discussed in Chapter 4. For now, it's sufficient to realize that, a day or so after a male and female mate, the female begins searching for host plants and begins to lay her eggs. And the cycle begins anew.

Body Form and Structure

There are entire volumes devoted to the form and function of the body parts of the various stages of insects or butterflies, so it stands to reason that I cannot do justice to the subject in a few pages. Here I offer a simplified, and somewhat selective, summary of the major features of the external anatomy of the stages of the butterfly life cycle.

EGGS

The variation in the size, shape, texture and color of the eggs of butterflies (see plate 1) is astounding. A typical egg may be spherical, conical, spindle- or barrel-shaped; have a smooth or sculptured appearance; be solid-colored or patterned, depending on species-specific characteristics of the eggshell, or chorion (actually they are appearance or pattern characteristics of the female ovarioles in which the eggs develop). The egg is usually fixed to a

A mating pair of Mexican fritillaries, *Euptoieta hegesia* (Nymphalidae), photographed near Mammee Bay, Jamaica in June 1991.

surface by an adhesive secreted by the female when the egg is laid, and may be partially or completely coated in hairs from the female's abdomen. The egg is fertilized as it is laid, by sperm stored by the female, through a small opening, or micropyle, at the top of the egg. Eggs may be laid singly or in groups, depending on the species.

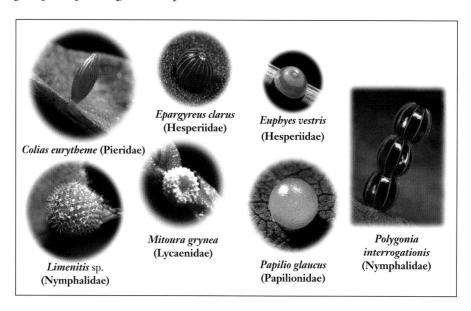

Colias eurytheme (Pieridae)

Epargyreus clarus (Hesperiidae)

Euphyes vestris (Hesperiidae)

Limenitis sp. (Nymphalidae)

Mitoura grynea (Lycaenidae)

Papilio glaucus (Papilionidae)

Polygonia interrogationis (Nymphalidae)

PLATE 1 Variation in the appearance of typical butterfly eggs. All of the illustrated species are from North America.

30

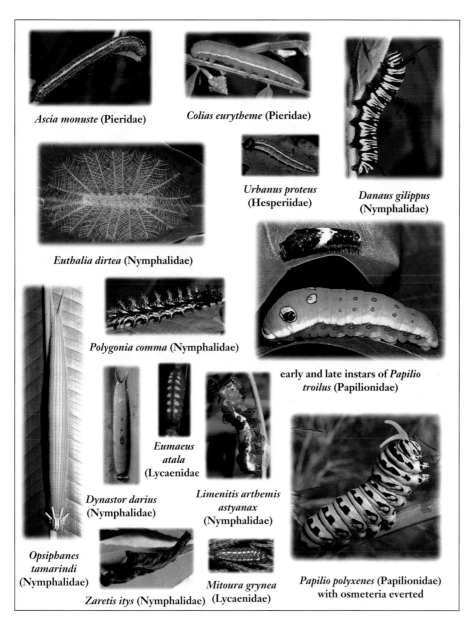

Ascia monuste (Pieridae)

Colias eurytheme (Pieridae)

Urbanus proteus (Hesperiidae)

Danaus gilippus (Nymphalidae)

Euthalia dirtea (Nymphalidae)

Polygonia comma (Nymphalidae)

early and late instars of *Papilio troilus* (Papilionidae)

Eumaeus atala (Lycaenidae

Dynastor darius (Nymphalidae)

Limenitis arthemis astyanax (Nymphalidae)

Opsiphanes tamarindi (Nymphalidae)

Zaretis itys (Nymphalidae)

Mitoura grynea (Lycaenidae)

Papilio polyxenes (Papilionidae) with osmeteria everted

PLATE 2 **Variation in the appearance of typical butterfly caterpillars. All of the illustrated species are from North America except *Z. itys*, *D. darius* and *O. tamarindi* from Costa Rica and *E. dirtea* from Malaysia.**

CATERPILLARS

Caterpillars also vary considerably in size, shape and texture, but also in color pattern and the presence and location of hairs, spines, glands, fleshy tentacles and various other kinds of protuberances from the body (see plate 2). A butterfly caterpillar is an eating machine. All it really does is eat, defecate and grow—and it does it very well. This lifestyle has profound implications for its body shape: a caterpillar is, in essence, an open-ended

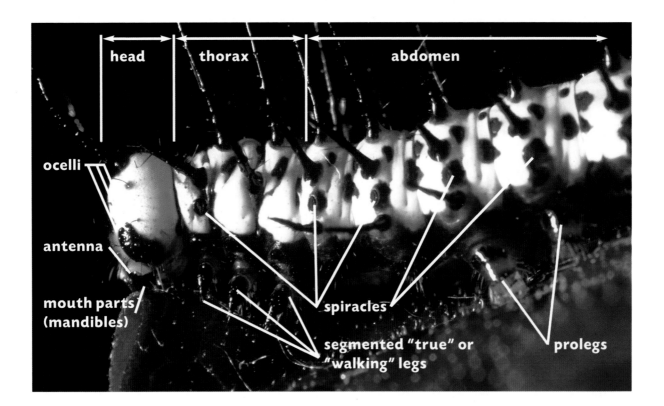

The image is labeled with: head, thorax, abdomen (top), ocelli, antenna, mouth parts (mandibles), spiracles, segmented "true" or "walking" legs, prolegs.

The major anatomical features of the head and thorax of a zebra longwing caterpillar, *Heliconius charithonia* (Nymphalidae).

tube (the mouth, gut system and anus) surrounded by a long fluid-filled sac that contains the internal organs. In a caterpillar, what goes in one end does, truly, come out the other.

The body of a caterpillar has a recognizable head and thirteen body segments. The head capsule contains the mouth parts, including the hard mandibles that are used for chewing, six pairs of tiny simple eyes, or ocelli (usually six eyes on each side of the mouth parts), miniature antennae and a spinneret for spinning silk. In contrast to the head, or the bodies of most other insects, the caterpillar body is a relatively soft cylinder whose shape is maintained by internal body pressure. There are three thoracic segments, each with a pair of segmented "walking" legs, and a pair of spiracles, openings that allow for gas exchange or breathing, on each side. Then there are ten abdominal segments, half of which each contain a pair of unsegmented grasping prolegs (there are a pair of prolegs on the last, or terminal, segment, and four other pairs on other segments). Each of the walking legs has a claw for grasping, and each proleg has a multitude of crochets, or tiny hooks—very similar to the hook side of a Velcro strip—which allow the caterpillar to cling to the surface of the leaf or its own silk.

Even though the cuticle or skin tissue is relatively soft, the stretching ability or expandability of the exoskeleton is limited. Caterpillars, however, are extremely efficient at turning plant material into caterpillar tissue, so they grow extremely rapidly—almost exponentially—and may gain as much as 3,300 times their hatching weight by the time they begin to pupate. The consequence of this prodigious growth and the limited expandability of their skin is that they must molt or shed their skin in order to get bigger. Most caterpillars have three to five molts, thus three to five instars. One of the ways in which caterpillars capitalize on what, at first, may seem like a severe limitation—molting is a hazardous process—is to use the molts to change their appearance.

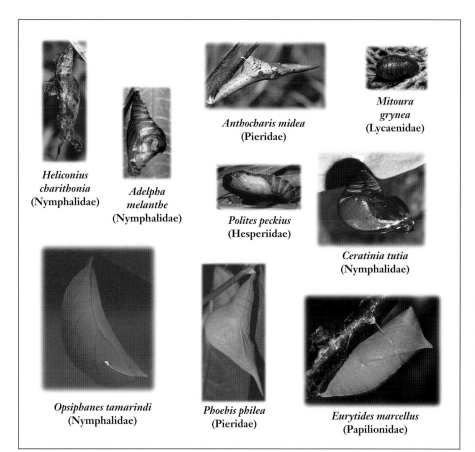

Heliconius charithonia (Nymphalidae)

Adelpha melanthe (Nymphalidae)

Anthocharis midea (Pieridae)

Mitoura grynea (Lycaenidae)

Polites peckius (Hesperiidae)

Ceratinia tutia (Nymphalidae)

Opsiphanes tamarindi (Nymphalidae)

Phoebis philea (Pieridae)

Eurytides marcellus (Papilionidae)

PLATE 3 **Variation in the appearance of the pupae of butterflies. All of the illustrated species are from North America except** *A. melanthe, C. tutia* **and** *O. tamarindi* **from Costa Rica.**

The major anatomical features of a pupa of the zebra longwing, *Heliconius charithonia* (Nymphalidae).

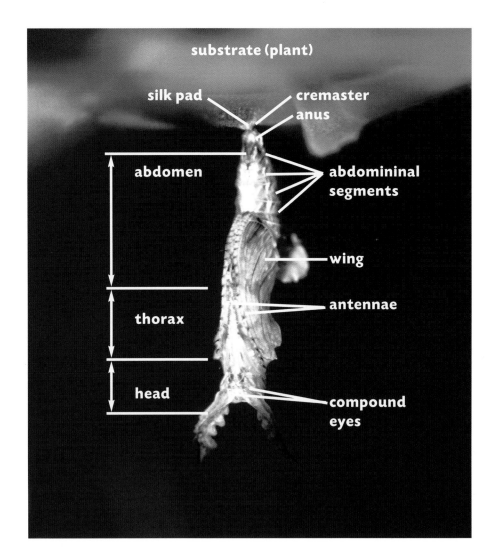

CHRYSALIS

It will come as no surprise that the butterfly chrysalis also varies in size, shape, texture and color, but also in orientation, the locations chosen and the use of girdle-like guide wires and crude cocoon-like structures, similar to those used by their relatives the moths (see plate 3 on previous page). In the exoskeleton of the chrysalis, you can see many of the features and appendages of the adult butterfly, including the forewings, antennae, abdominal segments and spiracles, and eyes. On the final day, the butterfly begins to expand its body (by taking in air) and pushes against the pupal case until it opens and the butterfly emerges.

The pupal stage is really just the final instar of a developing caterpillar, but inside the chrysalis is where "metamorphosis" becomes more than just a word. Inside the pupal exoskeleton, the complete disassembly, or chemical dissolution, of the larval body occurs, and areas of undifferentiated cells that have persisted through all of the molts of the larvae, called "imaginal disks," begin to form the tissues of the adult butterfly. The complete re-creation of the body of a caterpillar into the body and wings of a butterfly is, without doubt, one of the wonders of life on Earth. Much like the birth of a child, the process of butterfly emergence, or eclosure, is a wonder beyond description. Watch the face of

The major anatomical features of the head of a zebra longwing, *Heliconius charithonia* (Nymphalidae).

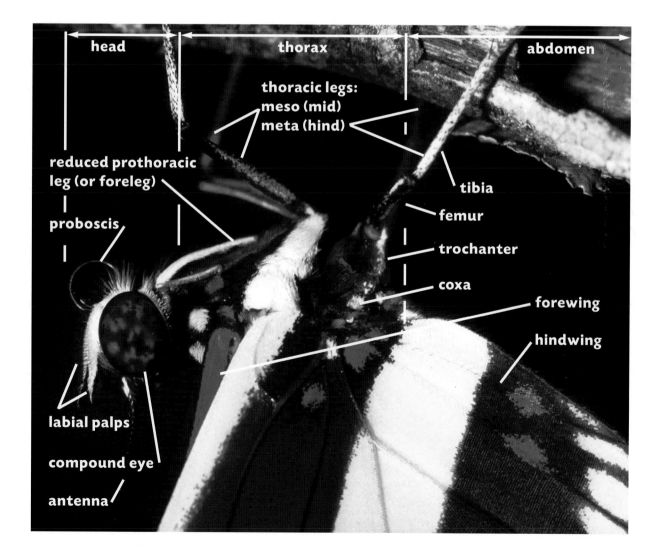

Nomenclature for the identifying features of the (i) wing veins and (ii) areas of a typical butterfly. After Smith *et al.*, 1994.

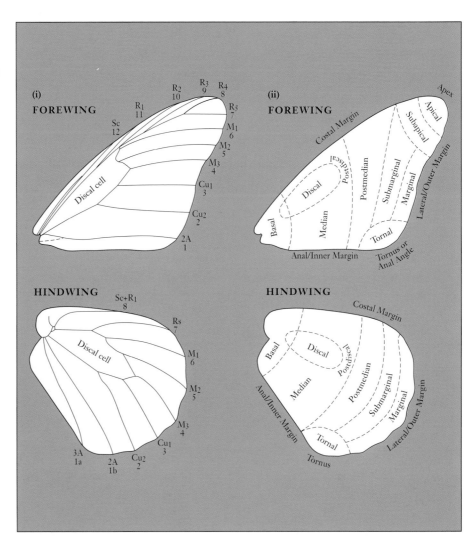

a small child as a boldly colored butterfly slides out of the pupal case and begins to expand its wings. The rapture on the child's face will say it all.

BUTTERFLIES

Butterflies are, for me, the quintessential expression of the variety and diversity of life. Here, a relatively simple body plan, similar in almost every respect to that of the adults of the vast majority of insects, is clothed in a seemingly boundless array of colors and patterns. The butterfly's head contains pairs of extremely large compound eyes and elongated, clubbed antennae, and unique mouth parts modified into the coiled, extensible, straw-like proboscis that is so highly suited to sucking up liquid nourishment from flowers. The three-segmented thorax has three pairs of long "walking" legs, one pair per thoracic segment, and two pairs of extremely large wings on the posterior two segments, the meso- and metathorax. Some families have reduced or vestigial forelegs and thus appear to have only four legs. As one might expect from the presence of the legs and wings, the thorax contains the muscles that allow the butterfly to walk and fly.

The wings consist of a membrane, stretched to form a dorsal (upper) and ventral (under) surface over a skeleton of "veins," or nervures that is, like the body, covered in scales and fine hairs. The veins are tubes within tubes, and are not what we normally consider to be veins, because they don't transport fluids through the wings (except when the wings are being expanded after eclosing from the pupa). After the wings are fully expanded, the fluid (haemolymph) is withdrawn and the tubes stiffen as the wings dry. The veins are more like structural members, joists in a house frame, in that they support the intervenal membrane and scales.

As you already know, the wings of butterflies are colored and patterned in such a way that the majority of species can be identified on sight. It should not be surprising that a complete system for identifying the various areas and "veins" of the wings has been developed (see previous page). The system of veins has some taxonomic implications; as you might expect, species whose venation systems are similar to those of species A but not those of species B are more likely closely related to species A. One of the things that I find especially intriguing about butterfly wings is their size: they are much larger than is necessary for flight. While assessments of wing coloration and pattern—including changes in either of these between generations or species—or even the shape of the wings, have been undertaken, curiously little attention has been paid to wing size.

The abdomen of butterflies, like that of caterpillars, consists of ten segments: eight pre-genital segments that contain spiracles and two segments that bear the genitalia. Butterflies are reproduction engines; their purpose (if they could be said to have one) is to reproduce. The reproductive organs, along with the digestive and excretory systems, are housed in the long tapering abdomen. The females have paired ovaries that contain the ovarioles which develop individual eggs; the corpus bursae, where the sperm is stored until needed; and the accessory glands necessary to secrete the egg adhesive. The males have a pair of valvae, or claspers, with which to hold on to the female while they insert their aedeagus, or penis, into the duct leading to the corpus bursae. Here the male deposits a spermatophore, a package of sperm and nutrients that the female will need in order to lay her eggs. The position of the sex organs at the terminus of the abdomens means that butterflies mate "back-to-back" or abdomen to abdomen, facing away from each other.

Butterflies or Moths?

Without a doubt, the most common question that I am asked is "What's the difference between a butterfly and a moth?" The problem is that recent discoveries have made giving an easy definitive answer almost impossible. About all I can promise is that you can be 99 percent certain that a butterfly is not a moth by noting the differences below (approximately in order of importance).

Butterflies tend to have clubbed antennae; that is, each antenna ends in a thickened knob, although in skippers (Hesperioidea) the club may be recurved or hooked; moths have antennae that taper to a point, look "saw-

BELOW LEFT: **The head and antennae of a butterfly.**

BELOW RIGHT: **The head and antennae of a moth.**

edged" or toothed, or are plumose like a feather. Butterflies are able to fold their wings up, vertically, over their "back," although many butterflies will typically rest with their wings spread out horizontally; moths either hold them in a "tent" that hides the abdomen or hold them spread out like a butterfly does. Butterflies tend to have larger, more colorful or more boldly patterned wings than the usually drab moths, although many moths are quite large and have large wings. Many day-flying moths, such as the beautiful *Urania*, are even more brightly colored and patterned than the most audacious of butterflies. Butterflies and moths differ in the way that the fore and hind wings are coupled together; moths have a device called a "frenulum" but butterflies do not (this is difficult to see and, unless you're a taxonomist, or carry around a hand lens, the wing-coupling mechanisms are relatively uninformative).

   Butterflies are primarily diurnal—that is, they fly during the day—

Moths are not necessarily small, drab or confined to a nocturnal existence. Some day-flying moths, such as these green Urania, *Urania leilus* (Uraniidae), rival butterflies in wing color and pattern, behavior and migratory tendencies.

OPPOSITE: **Butterflies like this 88 butterfly,** *Diaethria cemdrera* **(Nymphalidae), from Argentina, beg the question: Is Lepidopterology a science or an art ? Or both?**

although some rainforest species are crepuscular (i.e., they fly at dawn and/or dusk). Moths are mostly nocturnal; that is, they fly at night. However, there are a number of day-flying moths, including hummingbird sphinx moths, some clearwing moths, and buck moths. This difference between day-flying and night-flying is linked to their reliance on sight (most butterflies) or odor (most moths) for navigation and mate-location. Butterflies also tend to have thinner, more elongated and less hairy bodies than moths, although some, for example, many skippers, have very robust and quite hairy bodies. Butterflies tend to have "naked" pupae, meaning that they don't spin a silken cocoon around the chrysalis or pupate in the soil or under leaves like most moths do; however, some butterflies spin a rudimentary cocoon, and some pupate in the soil or under leaves. So you can begin to see the problem: the division between moths and butterflies is one of evolution and accumulated adaptation, not necessarily of appearance. The characteristics used to differentiate them are not sharply defined but appear to blend from one into the other. In short, not all of the characteristics are entirely reliable at all times.

This problem has been compounded recently by the discovery of so-called butterfly-moths. As you might expect from their name, they exhibit many of the characteristics, or sometimes a mix of the characteristics, of both groups. The giant butterfly-moths (Castniidae), found in the neotropics, Indonesia and Australia, are large diurnal, boldly colored and patterned "moths" with clubbed antennae; they do not spin a cocoon around the pupae, but they have very moth-like caterpillars. The primitive butterfly-moths (Hedylidae), found exclusively in the neotropics and Caribbean, are smaller, drab-appearing moths that are both nocturnal and diurnal, rest with their wings spread, and do not spin a cocoon (they girdle the pupa like the swallowtails; Papilionidae) and do not have clubbed antennae. They have very butterfly-like eggs and caterpillars. So, as long as you stay away from these two groups, and follow the few simple rules outlined above, you can be *almost* certain—*most of the time*—of being able to tell a moth from a butterfly.

Lepidopterology: Science or Art?

Author, and butterfly aficionado, Jo Brewer once wrote that, "in approaching the study of butterflies, one is always faced with a dilemma"— namely, should butterfly study be considered a science or an art? Should we

Butterflies have been incorporated into the legends and myths of many ancient civilizations including the Aztecs of Mexico. This photo shows an ornament from an incense burner found at Teotihuacan, Mexico. The butterfly is believed to be one of the manifestations of the god of the Aztecs and the Nahuatl (Aztec) name is Xochiqetzalpapalotl (which means flower-plumed-serpent-butterfly). Notice the similarity of "papalotl" to "papilio."

subject butterflies to dispassionate scrutiny in order to understand them, or should we approach them as something to be admired more than comprehended? The two positions are deemed mutually exclusive, but Jo goes on to frame my own feelings when she says that "the science of butterflies is neither dull nor dogmatic. It is like the unfolding of a mystery, the ending of which is not known until the last page is turned. It is much, much more than a detailed knowledge of taxonomy, which, for the majority of people, is not relevant to what they see or how they live. What is relevant is an appreciation of the consummate beauty of a living butterfly…"

Lepidopterology is the study of butterflies and moths in much the same way that entomology is the study of insects, or biology is the study of life. The discipline has many facets, as one might imagine, and is really a microcosm of the study of biology or entomology, with the primary focus being—obviously—the study of the lives of these charismatic insects. In the chapters that follow, we examine various aspects of the science of lepidopterology, including butterfly diversity and evolution, geographic distribution and habitats, biology and ecology, and conservation. But the artistic *appreciation*, rather than the study, of butterflies is, unfortunately, beyond the scope of this book, so I will offer what little attention I can to this subject here.

The study of butterflies is currently undergoing a resurgence. Butterflies are now almost as popular as they were under the patronage of the wealthy aristocrats of the nineteenth century. During this period, almost every noble house in Britain and continental Europe included a conservatory and glasshouse for the keeping of a wide variety of tropical plants and, of course, butterflies. But the appreciation of butterflies, and their association with the symbolism of the soul or the dying, goes back 5,000 or more years, to the ancient Egyptians, Greeks and Romans. Butterflies can be found decorating the tombs of Egyptian pharaohs, where they were depicted as being present in the afterlife, but it was the Greeks and Romans who elevated the butterfly to symbolic "high art." The ancient Greek word for butterfly, *psyche*, meant "soul" or "breath" and has now come to be associated with the mind.

A Roman legend tells of the romance of the god Cupid and the mortal woman Psyche, who was admonished to never look at the face of her lover. But her human curiosity would not be contained; she looked, and Cupid fled, leaving Psyche to search endlessly for her lost love. Finally, the father of the gods, Jupiter, makes her immortal so that she may be reunited with Cupid. Thus, butterflies have become associated with the immortal souls of the dead, and the Latin word *papilio* or *papilionis* (butterfly) connotes that the soul of a dead person returns in the form of a butterfly. The symbolic association of butterflies with the soul, resurrection and purity continued to grow.

The advent of the Industrial Revolution, and the remnants of a repressive cultural feudalism, provided nineteenth-century aristocrats and nobles with the time to indulge their fascination for "God's creations." Their interest became monumental when they began financing expeditions to the tropics to bring back new and interesting plants and animals; the writings of Charles Darwin, Alfred Wallace, H.W. Bates, the Müller brothers and other early scientists are based on such expeditions. Needless to say, they returned from the tropics with many new and wonderfully

The tropics of the world are home to most butterfly diversity. The Indoaustralia region is home to the clipper, *Parthenos sylvia* **(Nymphalidae).**

beautiful butterflies. The twentieth century has seen lepidopterology grow from being the province of the wealthy, educated noble to become an everyday interest of a wide variety of people. But this century has also posed a threat to butterflies: humanity has been so prolific, and so uncaring in its quest to have "dominion" over nature, that butterfly numbers are now declining dramatically. My hope is that, in the twenty-first century, we will have the foresight to begin to mitigate the losses of the last hundred years.

44

Why Conserve Butterflies?

Michael Samways, author of *Insect Conservation Biology*, calls butterflies the "flamboyant flagships" of insect conservation. Insects have such a bad reputation, undeservedly so, that the concept of insect conservation is of little concern to many people. Yet insects are a vital part of the world around us. They are the most numerous of the world's fauna, in terms of both the numbers of species and numbers of individual organisms. These

"Flamboyant flagships" seems especially appropriate for this summer form of the Question Mark, *Polygonia interrogationis* (Nymphalidae), from North America.

Is the orange sulfer or alphafa butterfly, *Colias eurytheme* (Pieridae), the insect equivalent of a "canary in a coal mine?" Often we notice the loss of such a flamboyant flag before we see the damage to its habitat.

large numbers mean that their combined "biomass" represents an important food resource for other animals and that they contain much of the raw materials for the energy and nutrients that are cycled through ecosystems. But, because of their small size, appearance and behavior—and our cultural biases and misconceptions—insects are either accidentally overlooked or intentionally ignored when it comes to setting or enacting conservation policy. Thankfully, the concept of conserving butterflies does not generate the same lack of sympathy.

People are finally beginning to think about the importance of insects in the natural world. Some would argue that insects have an "intrinsic value," an incontrovertible right to exist. Unfortunately, arguments based on such ideas carry little persuasive power and we are forced to revert to anthropocentric utilitarian arguments, such as the monetary value of the pollination services that they provide, to justify their "worth." We still have a long way to go to generate the kind of enthusiasm that is accorded to the conservation of vertebrates. Very few animal-rights organizations consider the inherent right of a mosquito, cockroach or any other insect to exist, nor do they actively support their conservation. This is where butterflies can help: their charisma, as well as the long history of their study, can be put to work to raise awareness about all insects.

Butterfly conservation is important for three main reasons. First, as noted above, butterflies represent the hundreds of thousands of other neglected insects that we do not work toward conserving. Second, because certain groups of butterflies have been relatively well studied, we know that they are far less abundant, and many are more narrowly distributed, than they once were. Importantly for butterflies, some of these declines have been studied and we have useful knowledge about why they declined. Finally, butterflies are, because of their close relationship to plants and sensitivity to disturbance, the modern-day equivalent of "canaries in coal mines;" that is, they can be important indicators of habitat or ecosystem health. An additional reason is that butterflies are one of the few groups of insects for which we have reasonably accurate knowledge of their diversity, geographic distribution and biology.

The conservation of any organism, be it plant or animal, requires that we know three major kinds of information about it. First, we need to know its place in the "scheme of things," that is, how it is related to the other similar or dissimilar organisms around it. Second, we need to know the geographic range and the habitat requirements or preferences of the organism. This frame of reference is essential because habitat is the template upon which the evolution of diversity is hammered out. Finally, we need to know as much as we can of the biology and ecology of the organism. Specifically, we need to know how the organism interacts with the world around it: how it survives and reproduces.

So that is where this book will take you: on a journey through the butterfly kingdom, visiting butterfly diversity, habitat requirements, and aspects of biology and ecology, to give you an understanding of why and how butterflies should and can be conserved. One of the reasons I wrote this book is to plead unabashedly for and promote the need for insect conservation. The organisms that I, and many other conservation-minded or ecological entomologists, know best are butterflies. They are worth getting to know, worth saving and are worthy representatives for the conservation of insects. The question remains: Do we have the motivation and incentive to ensure that there is a world for butterflies?

Butterflies of the World

THERE ARE APPROXIMATELY 18,000 SPECIES OF BUTTERFLIES IN THE world. At first glance, this might seem like a lot, but it's only about 11 percent of the Lepidoptera. In other words, more than 89 percent of all of the scale-winged insects are moths, not butterflies. Why would this be so? Why are there so many species of moths, or alternatively, why are there so few species of butterflies?

The Lepidoptera are, for the most part, phytophagous insects, meaning that they're one of the orders of insects that have a large proportion (more than 99 percent) of species that feed on plants (the other predominantly plant-eating orders are the sucking bugs, Hemiptera; the grasshoppers, Orthoptera; the beetles, Coleoptera; and the flies, Diptera). Plant-eaters account for almost 46 percent of all insects and more than 26 percent of all plant and animal species on Earth. Only the Orthoptera have as large a proportion (better than 99 percent) of species that feed on plants; the others have fewer plant-eating species: Hemiptera, 91 percent; Coleoptera, 35 percent; and Diptera, 29 percent. These translate roughly into 163,000 species of moths and butterflies, 105,000 beetles, 82,000 sucking bugs, 29,000 flies, and 20,000 grasshoppers and their kin that feed exclusively on plants. Obviously, moths and butterflies are the most numerous, and potentially the most significant, insect herbivores in the world.

All plant-eating insects have had to overcome some difficult barriers in order to use plants as food. Plant tissues are hard to digest because they are primarily composed of carbohydrates; further, they lack the high energy

Almost 99% of all butterfly and moth caterpillars feed on plants, like this *Opsiphanes tamarindi* (Nymphalidae) larva feeding on a leaf of a bird of paradise plant (*Heliconia*).

content of the proteins found in animals, and possess some necessary nutrients in very limited quantities (e.g., nitrogen and salts), which, as we shall see later, have profound effects on butterfly biology and ecology. Many plants also have significant physical (e.g., hairs, spines, tough waxy leaves) and chemical defenses that are barriers to casual plant-eaters. Other issues, common to all plant-eating insects, include the need to avoid desiccation—that is, to limit water loss through activity schedules and resting postures, body-structure modifications (e.g., a thick, water-resistant cuticle), or by acquiring supplemental water—and to stay attached to plants that have smooth, waxy or hairy parts, using modified legs and appendages (such as the crochets on the prolegs of caterpillars). Despite these obstacles, more than 99 percent of all Lepidoptera feed on plants (the remaining 1 percent are primarily carnivorous—more on this later), so a plant diet does not explain why there are fewer species of butterflies than of moths.

There are remarkably few differences between the immature stages of moths and butterflies. Both lay eggs on plants, thereby subjecting them to much the same risks and benefits. This is also true of the caterpillar and the chrysalis stages, although moths generally conceal the pupa within a cocoon, and moth caterpillars may be highly modified and extremely cryptic. No, the real differences—at least ecological ones that may explain why there are now more species of moths than butterflies—lie in the flying, adult or reproductive stage. It comes down to differences due to nocturnal versus diurnal living; namely, the use of odor (olfaction) or sight (vision) for orientation, species recognition and behavioral response. Suffice it to say that living in the dark has more going for it than being diurnal and more visible to your enemies! But, if diurnal living is so much more difficult, where do butterflies come from?

The Origin of Butterflies

Fossil evidence for the origin of butterflies is sparse; there are only about four dozen known butterfly fossils, because butterflies are relatively "soft-bodied" and do not preserve well when rocks are being formed. This means that much of the evolutionary history of the butterfly is sheer speculation anchored by inferences made from infrequent observations of other insects in the fossil record. With that in mind, we can say that the insects are thought to have appeared in the Devonian period of the Paleozoic era, about 380 million to 400 million years ago. Interestingly, winged insects appear about 50 million years before *Archaeopteryx* and other early reptile-like birds; that is, insects were the first masters of the air.

The Lepidoptera appear in the fossil record together with the Trichoptera, or caddisflies (believed to be the closest living relatives of the moths and butterflies), and seem to be descended from an ancestor that superficially resembles the larvae of modern-day scorpionflies (Mecoptera). In Queensland, Australia, fossils of the earliest Trichoptera, a primitive moth, *Agathiphaga*, and a primitive butterfly, *Euschemon*, all occur together in the same rocks. *Agathiphaga* is reminiscent of modern moth genera in the superfamily Eriocranioidea, and the Pyrgine (Hesperiidae) butterfly genus *Euschemon* is still represented by modern relatives. Interestingly, the Australian skipper *Euschemon rafflesia* (Hesperiidae: Pyrginae) is the only living butterfly that still retains the coupling mechanism of the fore and hind wing that occurs in moths. The oldest known Lepidoptera fossil is of *Archaeolopsis*, a moth, found near Dorset, England, which dates from the Jurassic period (the "Time of the Dinosaurs"), about 208 million years ago.

Generally, however, the butterflies are much more recent, first appearing in Cretaceous rocks of the Mesozoic era, approximately 66 million to 144 million years ago, although the vast majority of the known fossils date from Eocene (Tertiary) deposits, which are less than 50 million years old. The oldest "true" butterflies (as distinct from skippers) are swallowtails (Papilionidae) from Texas that are uncannily similar to the modern-

A fossil of *Praepapilio* sp. (Papilionidae) from middle Eocene deposits in Texas. A butterfly very much like this fossil is the likely ancestor of *Baronia brevicornis* (Papilionidae; Baroniinae) and the Parnassiinae.

day monotypic species *Baronia brevicornis* (Papilionidae: Baroniinae) that is still found in Mexico. This fossil and another swallowtail, a Satyrine (Nymphalidae), and a primitive Riodinine (Lycaenidae) from shale deposits in Texas and Colorado, date back to 48 million years ago.

A number of larvae, preserved in Baltic amber, have also been found— including a Lycaenid and two Papilionids—from about 37 million years ago. The shale beds of Florissant Fossil Monument in Colorado, dating from 36 million to 44 million years ago, have produced fossil butterflies that represent the modern Pieridae, Nymphalinae and Libytheinae (Nymphalidae) families. Together, all of the fossil evidence suggests that all of the modern families of butterflies were already well developed and differentiated by the beginning of the Cenozoic era, some 66 million years ago. This coincides with the development of the flowering plants, the angiosperms, that are the hosts of the vast majority of butterflies today.

Taxonomy, Classification and Nomenclature

The name given to any organism, including butterflies, tells something about its relationship with other organisms, that is, how it is classified in relation to others. These relationships are based on a step-down hierarchy of similarities between organisms; eventually you arrive at the very small differences by which two or more similar organisms can be differentiated. A taxonomic hierarchy of categories denotes the relationship between all organisms, proceeding from all-inclusive, broad categories in which many organisms are considered similar to one another, to extremely specific categories in which no other organism is considered similar. Here's an example of the classification of one butterfly, the Mexican fritillary:

Kingdom: Animalia
  Phylum: Arthropoda
    Class: Insecta
      Order: Lepidoptera
        Family: Nymphalidae
          Genus: *Euptoieta*
            Species: *hegesia* (Cramer), 1775

The Kingdom Animalia includes all organisms that are not plants, fungi, single-celled organisms or bacteria—in other words, all of the animals. But a mammal such as a mouse is not very similar to a lobster or a butterfly, so the Phylum Arthropoda includes only the invertebrates (lacking an internal skeleton) that have jointed legs and a segmented body plan covered by an external skeleton. Similarly, the Class Insecta includes only those arthropods that have six legs (thus excluding the spiders and the crustaceans). An easy way to remember this hierarchy is the mnemonic "King Phillip Came Over From Greece Sunday." A genus (the generic name is always capitalized) is the smallest or most specific category by which organisms are classified due to their similarity, while each species (the specific name is never capitalized) differs from every other in the genus; in other words, all species in a genus are very similar, but each species is different.

This system of nomenclature, commonly called "Binomial Nomenclature," or the Linnean system, dates from 1758 and the tenth edition of Carolus Linnaeus's *Systema Naturae*. The genus and species (the "binomial" or "two names") are always italicized or somehow offset from the body of a text (in much the same way as proper names are always capitalized). In the Linnean system, all organisms have an original description that justifies its placement within the hierarchy, a type specimen (true for all but *Homo sapiens*!) and must have been published in a recognized book or journal. The name of the "authority" that named the species becomes a part of the classification, as does the year of the description (brackets denote that a species has been moved to another genus). The International Code of Zoological Nomenclature contains the modern rules regarding the naming of animals.

There are many intermediate categories, such as suborders, superfamilies, subfamilies and tribes within subfamilies, and even subspecies (a genus, species and subspecies is called a "trinomial"), and these intermediate categories are important components of Lepidoptera classification. An expanded classification for the Mexican subspecies, as opposed to the Jamaican subspecies, of *Euptoieta hegesia*, the Mexican fritillary might look like this:

Kingdom: Animalia
  Phylum: Arthropoda
    Subphylum: Hexapoda
      Class: Insecta
        Order: Lepidoptera
          Suborder: Rhopalocera
            Superfamily: Papilionoidea
              Family: Nymphalidae
                Subfamily: Nymphalinae
                  Tribe: Argynniini
                    Genus: *Euptoieta* Doubleday, 1848
                      Species: *hegesia* (Cramer), 1779
                        Subspecies: *hoffmanni*, Comstock, 1944

Note that the endings of the upper-category names provide clues to the position within the classification: superfamilies end in -oidea, families in -dae, subfamilies in -nae, and tribes in -ini.

People are often confused, or even afraid, of binomial nomenclature because of its use of Latin or Greek words. Part of the problem, I'm sure, is the lack of stability in nomenclature—taxonomy is not "set in stone" but is always subject to revision as we learn more about the relationships among species. But most of the fear/confusion seems to be over the potential for mispronunciation or just because the names "look hard" but this shouldn't be an excuse to not learn the "true" names of organisms.

Many people insist on using common or local names (which, not surprisingly, are almost never common and often cause more problems then they are thought to solve). They can be useful for some easily recognizable organisms, including butterflies, *in some places and times*—but I believe that the only "true" system for naming organisms is the good old Linnean binomial system. Here's an example of why using only common names can be a problem: The very common, temperate Nymphalid butterfly *Nymphalis antiopa* is called the mourning cloak in North America, and the Camberwell beauty in the United Kingdom. Someone from Britain would not understand what you were talking about if you mentioned a "mourning cloak" butterfly, but *Nymphalis antiopa* is universally recognizable. Still "common name" committees are rife, as are the official lists they put forward, but standardization is useful only when everybody agrees on the standards.

BUTTERFLY CLASSIFICATION AND DIVERSITY

Current estimates of the numbers of genera and species (two sources) of the families and subfamilies of the Rhopalocera, or the butterflies, are listed below. Taxonomy is after Ackery (1984), Heppner (1991) and Scoble (1992).

TAXONOMIC CATEGORY	NO. OF GENERA	NO. OF SPECIES (SHIELDS 89)	NO. OF SPECIES (HEPPNER 91)
Class: Insecta			
Order: Lepidoptera			
Suborder: Rhopalocera	1,231	17,320	19,445
Superfamily: Castnioidea			
Family: Castniidae	4	–	167

TAXONOMIC CATEGORY	NO. OF GENERA	NO. OF SPECIES (SHIELDS 89)	NO. OF SPECIES (HEPPNER 91)
Superfamily: Hedyloidea			
Family: Hedylidae	1	35	40
Superfamily: Hesperioidea			
Family: Hesperiidae	445	3,592	3,658
Subfamily: Pyrrhopyginae	20	155	180
Subfamily: Pyrginae	150	1,193	1,195
Subfamily: Trapezitinae	10	67	84
Subfamily: Hesperiinae	255	2,048	2,044
Subfamily: Megathyminae	2	49	49
Subfamily: Coeliadinae	7	80	80
Subfamily: Heteropterinae	–	–	26
Superfamily: Papilionoidea			
Family: Papilionidae	28	566	572
Subfamily: Baroniinae	1	1	1
Subfamily: Parnassiinae	8	54	54
Subfamily: Papilioninae	19	511	517
Family: Pieridae	71	1,215	1,222
Subfamily: Pseudopontiinae	1	1	1
Subfamily: Dismorphiinae	3	95	95
Subfamily: Pierinae	56	905	910
Subfamily: Coliadinae	11	214	216
Family: Lycaenidae	350	5,440	6,564
Subfamily: Lepteninae	50	527	–
Subfamily: Poritiinae	6	52	536
Subfamily: Lyphrinae	1	20	–
Subfamily: Miletinae	4	111	169
Subfamily: Curetinae	1	22	43
Subfamily: Theclinae	74	2,128	–
Subfamily: Lycaeninae	6	97	4,414
Subfamily: Polyommatinae	48	1,132	–
Subfamily: Riodininae	160	1,365	1,402
Subfamily: Styginae	1	1	–

TAXONOMIC CATEGORY	NO. OF GENERA	NO. OF SPECIES (SHIELDS 89)	NO. OF SPECIES (HEPPNER 91)
Family: Nymphalidae	334	6,445	7,222
Subfamily: Brassolinae	6	81	81
Subfamily: Amathusiinae	6	55	200
Subfamily: Satyrinae	100	2,400	2,240
Subfamily: Morphinae	3	100	55
Subfamily: Calinaginae	1	16	1
Subfamily: Charaxinae	16	431	–
Subfamily: Nymphalinae	124	2,500	2,512
Subfamily: Heliconiinae	9	155	72
Subfamily: Acraeinae	4	240	366
Subfamily: Danainae	9	157	162
Subfamily: Ithomiinae	40	305	305
Subfamily: Tellervinae	1	6	–
Subfamily: Libytheinae	1	12	12

Dashes (–) denote a taxonomic category not considered, or subsumed, within other categories, by the respective authors. Numbers of genera based on Smart 1975, except Nymphalidae, based on Ackery 1988.

Butterflies of the World

Within the formal classification system, the approximately 18,000 species of butterflies are classified in three superfamilies: the Hedyloidea, or primitive butterfly-moths; the Hesperioidea, or skippers; and the Papilionoidea, or "true" butterflies. Some researchers also include the Castnioidea, another group of butterfly-moths, although their immature stages suggest that they are most closely related to some families of moths. Here, I offer a systematic survey of the butterflies to provide examples of each of the major families and subfamilies, with general notes and descriptions of the characteristics that are used to differentiate the groups. Of course, it is impossible to attempt a comprehensive or exhaustive survey in a book of this size, so here I try only to give you an overall impression of the taxonomic diversity of butterflies.

Collectively, these superfamilies comprise the Rhopalocera. I find it amusing that the term Rhopalocera had fallen into disrepute—its use was actively discouraged—because of the advent of phylogenetic systematics. Modern systematics bases groups of organisms on "natural assemblages" of organisms that are thought to contain their common ancestor and it was believed that the Hesperioidea and Papilionoidea did not include their common ancestor, that is the Rhopalocera was not a monophyletic assemblage. But the recent studies of Annette Aiello and Malcolm Scoble provide good evidence that, together with the Hedylids, the Rhopalocera are, once again, a "natural" group. I include the Castnioidea out of interest, lack of consensus—there is considerable dispute over their true position in the taxonomic hierarchy—and their resemblance to skippers (Hesperiidae).

SUPERFAMILY: CASTNIOIDEA; *Family Castniidae*

The Castnioidea, represented by a single family, the Castniidae, are a tropical group of medium- to large-sized moths with a 1- to 5-inch (3- to 13-cm) wingspan that exhibit a number of butterfly-like characteristics.

The Castniidae are often considered moths yet are diurnal, have clubbed antennae and resemble the Hesperiidae in many respects. This giant sugarcane-borer, *Castnia licus*, was photographed in the Rondonia region of Brazil in 1992.

ABOVE: **Despite the moth-like antennae, the butterfly-moths of the Hedylidae, like this** *Macrosoma heliconiaria* **from Panama, are thought by some to be the common ancestor of the Hesperioidea and Papilionoidea. Inclusion of the hedylids resurrects the Rhopalocera as a phylogenetic unit.**

RIGHT: **This rainbow skipper,** *Phocides urania* **(Hesperiidae), photographed in Mexico, shows the spread-wing posture and elongated forewings typical of many species in the hesperiid subfamily Pyrginae.**

They are diurnal, brightly colored and boldly patterned; have the clubbed antennae of butterflies (often flattened and somewhat hooked); and do not spin a cocoon around the pupa, but have very primitive caterpillars. There are some 165 species found in three subfamilies, the largest of which, the Castniinae, contains 81 percent of the species and is exclusively neotropical. The Neocastniinae contains only 3 very rare species found in the islands of Indonesia, while the Synemoninae, with approximately 30 species, are exclusively Australian. Like some Hesperiids, the larvae are borers of stems and roots, and are commonly associated with grassy-leaved plants. A great deal of controversy surrounds the classification of Castniids. Some researchers have suggested that their closest relatives are the diurnal, brightly colored

moths of the Zygaenoidea, while others suggest that they are most closely related to the Sesioidea or the Cossoidea. It seems possible that some modern-day butterflies may be descended from a Castniid-like ancestor.

SUPERFAMILY: HEDYLOIDEA; *Family Hedylidae*
The Hedyloidea are represented by a single family, the Hedylidae, containing a single genus, *Macrosoma*, of some thirty-five to forty species that are found in the neotropics. These "butterfly-moths" are, as you

A pair of fiery skippers, *Hylephila phyleus* (Hesperiidae; Hesperiinae). The female (above) is interested in the flowers but the male (below) is more interested in the female.

Two dull firetip skippers,
Pyrrhopyge araxes
(Hesperiidae; Pyrrhopgyinae)
foraging on seep willow
flowers, *Baccharis* sp.
(Compositae), in Arizona.
Together with the
Coeliadinae, these species
are commonly called "mimic
skippers" due to the difficulty
we have identifying many of
them.

might expect, unusual "butterflies." They do not have the typical clubbed antennae of butterflies and are very moth-like in appearance. Still, they do share a number of broad characteristics with the rest of the Rhopalocera, including upright eggs, similar to many Pieridae, and a full complement of prolegs in the caterpillars and a cocoon-less pupa with a posterior spiny pad, (a cremaster), that is girdled with silk in much the same manner as many Papilionidae. The adults are brown to gray, with a few off-white or mostly white species, often marked with semi-translucent areas in the centers of the wings. They are both nocturnal and diurnal, and rest with their wings slightly raised but spread.

SUPERFAMILY: HESPERIOIDEA; *Family Hesperiidae*

The Hesperioidea are also represented by a single family, the Hesperiidae, but differ from the previous two superfamilies by having a number of discernible subfamilies with as many as 445 genera and approximately 3,600 species. Slightly more than 20 percent of all butterflies are Hesperiids. There are five to seven subfamilies. The skippers, as they are colloquially known, are widespread, small to medium-sized butterflies (the largest species has a wingspan of slightly more than 3 inches [7.5 cm]) with thick, heavy bodies and large heads; their antennae have widely separated bases and hooked clubs. The caterpillars live and pupate in shelters constructed from tied or folded leaves, or live inside plant tissues as borers of stems and leaves, and the pupae are often concealed within weakly woven cocoons. They are fast, erratic flyers (giving rise to their common name, "skippers") and often rest in characteristic poses, with the forewings held almost vertically and the hindwings horizontally.

About 90 percent of the species are found in two subfamilies, the Pyrginae and the Hesperiinae. The Pyrginae, or open-winged skippers, rest, as their common name suggests, with their wings outspread, often looking much like true butterflies. The caterpillars feed on Dicotyledons

This awl king, *Choaspes benjaminii* (Hesperiidae; Coeliadinae) from Japan, where it is called Aoba-seseri (*aoba* means "blue wing") is a member of the mimic skipper group that is sometimes called the "awls."

(broad-leafed plants) of many families and live in nests of rolled leaves that are tied together with silk. The Hesperiinae, or branded skippers, are named for the patch (brand) of specialized scales on the forewings of males. The caterpillars feed primarily on Monocotyledons (mostly grasses) and live in nests of leaves tied together with silk. The less diverse families include the Pyrrhopyginae, or, together with the Coeliadinae, the mimic skippers, and the Megathyminae, or giant skippers; with the Trapezitinae, or Australian skippers; and Heteropterinae, or intermediate skippers, sometimes being considered as full subfamilies.

The Pyrrhopyginae and Coeliadinae are closely related, being found in the New and Old World tropics, respectively. It has been suggested that they have diverged separately only since the African and South American continents divided and drifted apart. The Megathyminae, as both the subfamily and common names suggest, are the largest skippers and are often also called Yucca skippers since the majority of the species feed on succulents in the Yucca family (Agavaceae). The Megathyminae are

61

This Strecker's giant-skipper, *Megathymus streckeri* (Hesperiidae; Megathyminae) is one of the yucca or giant skippers. Note that the large abdomen of this female makes the skipper appear gigantic.

sometimes elevated to family status, for example, as the Megathymidae. The Trapezitinae are almost exclusively Australian, with a few species found elsewhere in the Australasian region, while the Heteropterinae, considered to be intermediate between the Pyrginae and the Hesperiinae, are neotropical. Both the Trapezitinae and Heteropterinae are often combined with, or included as part of, the Hesperiinae.

SUPERFAMILY: PAPILIONOIDEA

The "true" butterflies are represented by four families, possibly more (although here I treat them, conservatively, as subfamilies), which are well delineated: the Papilionidae, or swallowtails and parnassians; the Pieridae, or whites and sulfurs; the Lycaenidae, including the blues, coppers, hairstreaks and metalmarks; and the Nymphalidae, commonly called the brushfooted butterflies. Together, the four families are extremely diverse and contain more than 780 genera with between 14,000 and 15,000 species. They are colorful, range in size from very small to very large, and are characterized by antennae that terminate in very defined clubs.

Some of the characteristics that define the families are the presence/absence of an epiphysis (a moveable lobe on the tibia of the foreleg that is probably used to clean the antennae), the size and development of the foreleg itself, the presence/absence of a cremaster and use of a silken thread or girdle in the pupa, and the arrangement of crochets on the prolegs of larvae. The Hesperiidae and the Papilionidae possess an epiphysis, the cremaster is absent in the Lycaenidae while the Nymphalids hang freely and do not use a girdle during pupation, and the forelegs are reduced in Nymphalids and in the males of Libytheids and Lycaenids. Proleg crochets are arranged in a circle in Hesperiidae, in one or two series divided by a fleshy lobe in the Lycaenidae, and otherwise in the rest.

Family: Papilionidae

The Papilionids are divided into three subfamilies containing 28 genera with about 570 species. Eggs of Papilionids are generally spherical, the caterpillars possess an eversible forked osmeterium (plural: osmeteria), a gland found on the prothorax that is used in defending the larva, and the pupae are exposed, generally upright on the cremaster, and attached by a silken thread or girdle around the thorax, although the pupae of parnassians lie horizontally on the ground. The adults range from small (with a 1.25 inch [3.2 cm] wingspan) to very large (see below), are often sexually dimorphic (often with mimetic females) and are mostly slow, apparently meandering flyers. They rarely stop flying to feed, preferring to nectar on the wing. Many swallowtails and parnassians are considered threatened or endangered.

The vast majority of Papilionid species (more than 90 percent) are found in the Papilioninae or swallowtail subfamily. Swallowtails are characterized by the presence of hindwing tails (hence their common

Butterflies, like this arctic skipper, *Carterocephalus palaemon* (Hesperiidae; Heteropterinae), that visit orchids (*Orchis militaris* in this case), hold a special place in my heart. This species is holarctic, meaning that it can be found in the northern hemisphere of both the Old and New Worlds.

The North American zebra swallowtail, *Eurytides marcellus* (Papilionidae; Papilioninae), is one of the most beautiful of the charismatic swallowtails.

appellation)—although many species lack tails—and their large to very large size. They contain the largest butterflies in the world, the Troidine or birdwing butterflies, females of which often attain wingspans of 8 inches (20 cm) or more, although males, and most other species, are considerably smaller. The swallowtails reach their greatest diversity in the Old World tropics. Their major host-plant families include pipevines (Aristolochiaceae), laurels (Lauraceae), magnolias (Magnoliaceae) and carrots (Rutaceae).

In contrast, the other two subfamilies, the Parnassiinae, or apollos, and the Baroniinae, are species poor. The Baroniinae contains only a single genus with a single species, *Baronia brevicornis*, believed to be the most primitive of swallowtails. Its host plant is an acacia. The Parnassiinae

64

contain some eight genera with 54 species and are found predominately in north temperate regions. Their coloration and patterns are distinct and very recognizable. Their larval hosts include pipevines (Aristolochiaceae), poppies (Papaveraceae), stonecrops (Crassulaceae) or saxifrages (Saxifragaceae).

Family: Pieridae

The Pierids are almost instantly recognizable in almost any form. The "whites and sulfurs," as they are most commonly known, are (as you might expect) predominately white, yellow and orange, a coloration resulting from the incorporation of specific pigments in the scales of the wings. The eggs are almost always upright, taller than they are wide. The caterpillars

The Parnassiianae lack the tails that characterize the swallowtails but have their own charm. This male *Parnassius eversmanni* (Papilionidae), visiting alpine flowers in its native western Siberia in Russia, is unusual for its yellow coloration.

This Canadian olympia marblewing, *Euchloe olympia* (Pieridae), is typical of the "whites," the subfamily Pierinae. The underside of the hindwing has a distinctive marbling, due to individual yellow and brown scales that trick the eye into seeing green.

are cylindrical, tapering at both ends, and, while they may be pubescent, generally lack long external hairs, spines or tentacles. The pupa is also usually long and tapered, attached by a cremaster, and usually, but not always, with a silk girdle in a manner similar to Papilionids.

There are four subfamilies with a total of 71 genera and about 1,220 species. The largest proportion of species (almost 75 percent) is found in the Pierinae, with more than 17 percent of the rest of the family placed in

LEFT: The sulfurs, subfamily Coliadinae, are predominately yellow, although this Caribbean yellow angled sulfur, *Anteos maerula* (Pieridae), appears to be almost green.

BELOW: The European wood white, *Leptidea sinapsis* (Pieridae; Dismorphiinae), is the best known of a relatively small group of Pierids. Here a female is depositing an egg in the influorescence of a *Lathyrus* sp. (Leguminosae).

the Coliadinae. The Pierinae are the "whites," although some species such as the jezabels, *Delias* sp., are brilliantly colored, while the Coliadinae are the "sulfurs," or "yellows." The Pierines are cosmopolitan—some of the most widespread of butterflies belong to this group—with larvae feeding predominately on plants of the mustard or cabbage and pepper families (Cruciferae and Capparidaceae). Some Pierines have a pest-like fondness for cultivated crops and garden plants, and often gather in incredible numbers in aggregations on damp sand. The Coliadinae, not to be outdone, are almost as widespread, but feed

The hairstreaks, subfamily Theclinae, like this red-banded hairstreak, *Calycopis cecrops* (Lycaenidae), typically have hair-like tails that imitate antennae. Together with patterns on the wings and the placement of brightly colored eyespots at the anal angle of the hindwing, these suggest a "false head" that draws predators to attack less critical parts of the butterfly.

on plants in the aster and legume families (Compositae and Fabaceae). The Pseudopontiinae are monotypic with a single species, *Pseudopontia paradoxa*, found in West Africa. The 95 species of Dismorphiinae are primarily neotropical (although there is one Palearctic genus, as shown on the previous page), feeding on legumes.

Family: Lycaenidae

The Lycaenids are acknowledged to be polyphyletic, meaning that they are derived from multiple ancestors. This is immediately apparent even upon consideration of the common names of the group: the blues, coppers, hairstreaks and metalmarks. The number and division of subfamilies are in dispute. Some authors consider there to be as many as ten subfamilies, while others reduce this number to eight, or even as few as five. One recent development, probably correct, is that the Riodinines be given family status as the Riodinidae (including the monotypic Styginae). I've chosen the conservative approach and here consider the metalmarks as a subfamily of the Lycaenidae.

The subfamilies of the Lycaenidae contain approximately 32 percent, that is, some 5,500 to 6,500 species, of butterflies, regardless of how many subfamilies there are. The largest subfamilies are the Theclinae, or hairstreaks, with 39 percent (approximately 2,100 species); the Riodininae, or metalmarks, with slightly more than 25 percent (about 1,400 species); and the Polyommatinae, or blues, with almost 21 percent (slightly more than 1,100 species). The coppers are found in the Lycaeninae and comprise fewer than 2 percent of the species in the family. Surprisingly, the

Metalmarks, subfamily Riodininae, are often decorated with, as the name suggests, metallic markings. The little metalmark, *Calephelis virginiensis* (Lycaenidae), of North America has them.

This butterfly, the North American western pygmy blue, *Brephidium exilis* (Lycaenidae; Polyommatinae) is quite possibly the smallest butterfly in the world. It is usually less than the size of a small coin with an average wingspan of only ½ inch (13 mm).

The coppers, subfamily Lycaeninae, are often burnished brown or orange on top of their wings but, like this bronze copper, *Lycaena hyllus* (Lycaenidae), reveal their obvious relationship to the "blues" on their undersides.

The North American harvester, *Feniseca tarquinius* (Lycaenidae; Miletinae), is aptly named: its larvae, like many in its subfamily, do not feed on plants but "harvest" wooly aphids.

This butterfly, *Mimeresia libentina* from Ghana, is a member of the small Leptininae subfamily of the Lycaenidae.

The second largest subfamily of the Nymphalidae, the Satyrinae are often considered to be a separate family. The creamy-white color of this mating pair of *Melanargia russiae* is unusual and not really typical of these "brown eyespot" butterflies.

Miletinae, an aphytophagous (that is, not plant-eating) group that includes the North American harvester, contains more species than the Lycaeninae, but its members are not canonized in the group of common names given to the family!

Lycaenids are small- to medium-sized butterflies (maximum 2 ¾ inches [7-cm] wingspan), often with anal tails or projections on the hindwings. Eggs are slightly flattened to spherical, often decorated with pits or projections. The caterpillars are "slug-like," flattened (usually broader than they are tall), often with a retractable head, and usually contain a dorsal gland, a pair of extensible and retractable organs and small "pore cupola" organs on the abdomen. These glands, organs and pores are associated with the often-symbiotic relationship that Lycaenid larvae have with

OPPOSITE: The largest subfamily of butterflies, the Nymphalinae, contains some of the most beautifully colored species, like this male banded peacock, *Anartia amathea* (Nymphalidae), from Grenada.

The Charaxinae, like this *Charaxes eupale* (Nymphalidae) from Kenya, are known for their attraction to fallen, rotting or fermenting fruit. This photograph was taken when the butterfly was attracted to a bait trap containing week-old rotting fish and shrimp.

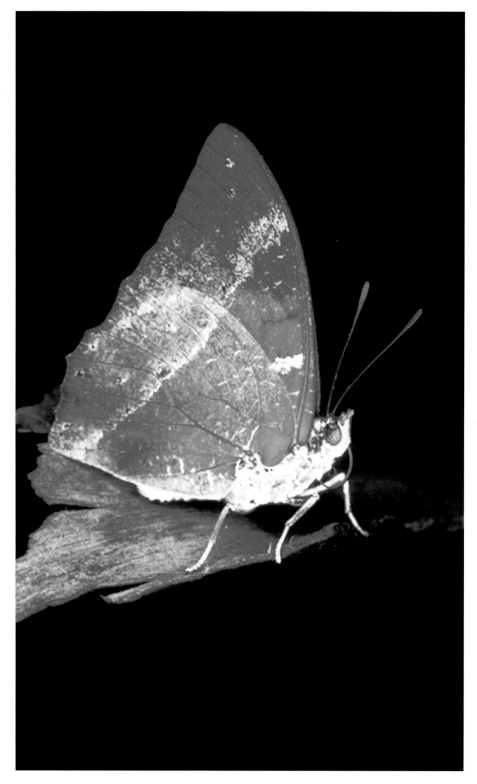

ants (Hymenoptera). Pupae are variable and may be girdled, like those of Papilionids; loose on the substrate, like Hesperiids; or suspended upside-down, like Nymphalids. The diet of Lycaenids is the most diverse among butterflies and ranges from lichens and fungi to flowering plants (often legumes, Fabaceae). Many groups are partially or entirely carnivorous—often feeding on Homoptera (Hemiptera) or ant larvae—and are opportunistically cannibalistic.

Family: Nymphalidae
Like the Lycaenids, the Nymphalids, often called the "brushfoots" because the forelegs are reduced to brush-like pads, are polyphyletic. A number of putative "families" have been proposed in the past, including the Danaidae, the Satyridae, the Heliconiidae and the Libytheidae. Only the Libytheids,

The large, reflective upper wings of many "Morphos," subfamily Morphinae, seen in this basking *Morpho peleides* (Nymphalidae), are rarely open like this. Instead, their relatively slow, flapping flight in the dark understory of the tropical rainforest pulses their metallic blue reflective upper wings.

7 5

The Brassolinae, or owl butterflies (named for the large owl-like eyespots on the underside of the hindwing), like this Costa Rican *Caligo atreus* (Nymphalidae), are large butterflies of the tropical rainforest understory.

or snouts, possess an acknowledged "family-level" difference since females do not exhibit the reduced forelegs that are so characteristic of the Nymphalids. Interestingly, the presence of normal forelegs in females allies the Libytheids with the Lycaenids. However, the multiple origins of the Nymphalidae indicate that the family will be divided into multiple families in the not too distant future. As with the Lycaenids, I have chosen the conservative approach to the taxonomy of this group and recognize 13 subfamilies.

Most of the thirteen subfamilies, with the exception of the Satyrinae and the Nymphalinae, are quite small, possessing in total fewer than 24 percent of the species in the family. The largest subfamily, the Nymphalinae, contains some 2,500 species (almost 39 percent of the total), while the Satyrinae account for about 2,300 species (37 percent). The Nymphalinae are, undoubtedly, themselves polyphyletic, since the range of variation within even this subfamily is quite large. Included here are, among others, the fritillaries (Argynnini); the familiar painted ladies, tortoiseshells and

The Heliconiinae are largely characterized by their elongated forewings, as seen in this *Heliconius numata* (Nymphalidae). Together with the Argynnini tribe of the Nymphalinae, and the Acraeinae, this group is on the verge of being elevated to family status.

The Acraeinae are found in Africa and South America but have evolved in isolation from each other over a long enough period of time to have distinctive differences in their host preferences and chemical defenses. This mating pair of *Actinote ozomene* (Nymphalidae) was photographed in Ecuador.

buckeyes (Nymphalini), the admirals (Limenitini) and the checker and crescentspots (Melitaeini). One of the few characteristics uniting this varied assemblage is the branched spines of the caterpillars, giving rise to the extended common name, the spiny brushfooted butterflies.

The Satyrinae, or eyespots and browns, are, as their names suggest, often brown with rows of marginal eyespots on the wings, although there are some truly beautiful species. Many are shade lovers, preferring forested situations, or crepuscular (flying at dawn and dusk). The larvae are smooth, often with horns on the heads, and many sport "forked" tails and feed primarily on grassy-leaved plants. Close relatives of the Satyrines include the Charaxinae, Morphinae and the Brassolinae. The Charaxines, forest dwellers, can often be found feeding on dung or carrion, and are attracted to rotting fruit; they have larvae with one or two pairs of horns on the head. They are fast, powerful flyers, and often have underside patterns that resemble dead leaves. The Morphinae, or Morphos, are among the most colorful of tropical butterflies and are justifiably famous for the bright, metallic coloration of their upper wings; however, their underside pattern is recognizably a variation on the Satyrid plan. The Brassolinae, or owl butterflies, are quite large, with large eyespots on the under hindwings, which, when displayed upside down and spread (an unnatural pose) are vaguely reminiscent of the head of an owl. The larvae are often large, with horned heads and forked tails, and feed exclusively on Monocots. The Amathusinae are often included with the Brassolines or Morphos, and are forest or crepuscular species found in Australia and the islands of Indonesia. Brassolines and Amathusines are often pests in banana plantations.

The Heliconiinae, Acraeinae and Ithomiinae have similar wing and body shapes—long, tapering narrow wings with thin, elongated bodies and long antennae. The Heliconiines and Acraeines are, in many ways, parallel, occurring in South and Central America, on the one hand, and mainly in Africa, on the other. Both groups feed on closely related plants—the passion vines, Passifloraceae and the Flacourtiaceae, respectively—although some Acraeines feed on *Passiflora* or nettles (Urticaceae) and asters (Asteraceae). The Heliconiines are of special interest, due to the

The characteristically scaleless wings of some species of Ithomiinae have provided them with the common name clearwings or glassy wings. Here *Hypoleria cassotis* (Nymphalidae) nectars at a flower in Costa Rica.

79

The usual example used for the Danainae is the almost universally recognized monarch but I much prefer the delicate black and white markings of the Australasian large tree nymph, *Idea leucone* (Nymphalidae).

prevalence of mimetic species, their long reproductive lives, use of pollen in addition to nectar, and coevolution with their host plants. The Ithomiines, often called glasswings (although not all species are transparent), occupy similar habitats as Heliconiines and often mimic them. They feed on plants of the Apocynaceae and Solanaceae, from which they acquire an unusual class of protective chemicals. The monogeneric Tellervinae are often combined with the Ithomiinae.

The Danainae, or milkweed butterflies, are well known, primarily because of the unique migratory behavior of the widely distributed monarch, *Danaus plexippus*. They are mostly tropical in origin, and are boldly patterned in brown, orange and black, with some strikingly marked in black and white. The larvae feed almost exclusively on members of the milkweed and dogbane families (Asclepiadaceae and Apocynaceae), which provide them with protective chemicals, and are smooth and brightly colored and have pairs of fleshy tentacles. The Libytheinae, often called snouts or beaks, are a very small group, with only twelve species in a single genus, but are nonetheless very widely distributed. They get their common name from the characteristic way that they hold their labial palps extended in front of them, like a long nose. The larvae are almost featureless, resembling Pierids, and they feed exclusively on hackberries (Ulmaceae).

The beaks or snouts, subfamily Libytheinae, named for the resemblance of their distinctively forward-thrust labial palps to a long nose or "beak," are almost certainly worthy of family status. Here an American snout, *Libythea bachmanii* (Nymphalidae), basks in the sun.

A World of Butterflies

BUTTERFLIES ARE FOUND ALMOST EVERYWHERE EXCEPT FOR
Antarctica, within about six degrees of the North Pole, and on very high
(more than 18,000-foot [5,500-meter]) mountains. However, their
abundance and diversity are by no means uniform everywhere they occur.
For example, there are many more butterfly species in the tropics than in
temperate regions. The rather simple realization that numbers of species
vary from one place to another leads to questions: Why are some families
or subfamilies more common in one region than they are in others? Are
there patterns in the geographic distribution of butterflies? How is
butterfly diversity related to distribution? Why are some species endemic,
that is, found nowhere else, to particular places, or found only at particular
times? Why when you see butterflies in one place, such as a park, don't you
see them in other nearby places, such as your backyard? Questions like
these take you to the realms of biogeography and population biology.

Biogeography (or biological geography) is the study of the large-scale
distribution of plants and animals. It combines the formerly separate
studies of plant distribution, or phytogeography, and animal distribution,
or zoogeography. Population biology, as you might expect, is concerned
with how many individuals of a species are present in some defined area or
region, large or small, and with how their abundance changes over time.
The range of available habitat types and habitat preferences that butterflies
have, is largely responsible for why individuals are present or absent in
some (usually smaller) defined area or region. Together, biogeography,

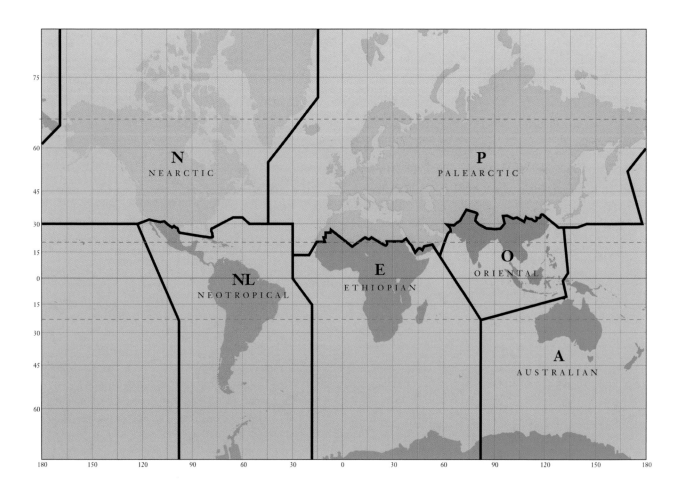

The six zoogeographic regions for butterflies and moths. The regions are differentiated not by geography but by biological similarities shared by the taxa within them. After Heppner, 1991.

population biology and habitat preferences provide insights into large-scale patterns of distribution, the commonness or rarity of individuals and species, and potential explanations for the small-scale distribution of individuals.

The Geographic Distribution of Butterflies

The butterflies of the world can be usefully considered to occur in six zoogeographic regions: the Neararctic, Neotropic, Palearctic, Ethiopian, Oriental, and Australian realms (see map above). These realms parallel recognized phytogeographic regions, or floristic provinces, as they're also

84

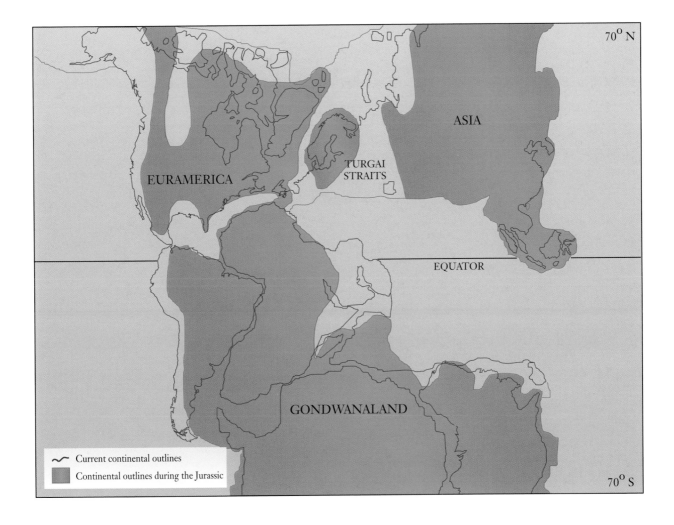

known, rather closely. Two questions spring to mind: Why are there differences between the butterfly faunas of these regions (or, conversely, why are there similarities within each region)? Why should there be an association between the flora and butterfly fauna of these regions? Surprisingly, we have to go back a long way to find answers to these questions. The answers, however, are important in explaining the evolution of, and faunal distribution of butterfly diversity. The answers also play a large role in planning potential conservation measures for butterflies and other insects.

A reconstruction of the ancient supercontinent of Pangea with the shapes and approximate locations of the modern continents. After Heppner, 1991. The continents as we now know them drifted apart or were pushed together, carrying butterflies and other animals and plants, with them

An unusual, but strikingly beautiful, Acraeine, *Acraea leucographa* (Nymphalidae), from Kenya. The Acraeinae subfamily has a disjunctive distribution, occurring both in Africa and South America, which suggests that the group evolved before the continents drifted apart.

CONTINENTAL DRIFT AND BUTTERFLY DIVERSITY

Two hundred million years ago, during the Jurassic period, all of the land area on Earth was found in one large continent called Pangea. Since our best evidence suggests that the modern butterfly families originated somewhere between 66 million and 144 million years ago, it makes sense that we have to go back at least this far to learn something about the origins of their current distribution and diversity. The supercontinent of Pangea began to break apart, through a process known as continental drift, about 165 million years ago (see the map on page 85).

Continental drift is the ongoing result of plate tectonics. Briefly stated, the continents are part of the crust of the Earth and, because the underlying core is less solid than the crust, thermal currents within the

Earth move the continents around. The movements are extremely slow, taking hundreds of thousands to hundreds of millions of years to travel significant distances. As the continents are pulled apart or pushed together, areas of subduction (where the earth sinks; for example, in deep ocean trenches) and areas of uplift (where the earth is pushed up; for example, mountain ranges) are formed.

Pangea split into two portions: Laurasia, the northern continent, and Gondwanaland, the southern continent. Laurasia consisted of portions of modern North America, northern Europe and eastern Asia, including most of the Indochinese peninsula. The southern continent of Gondwanaland included portions of modern South America, Africa, India, Antarctica and Australia. Slowly, over the next 150 million years or so, the continents as we now know them drifted apart or were pushed together, carrying butterflies and other animals and plants, with them.

Laurasia separated into North America and eastern Asia. In Gondwanaland, Antarctica and Australia were pulled southwards, gradually separating, while India was driven northwards into the southern coast of Asia, resulting in the uplift of the Himalayas. South America and Africa separated, with Africa being driven northwards into what is now southern Europe, resulting in the uplift of the Alps. Similarly, the western mountains of North and South America were uplifted in the process of the breakup and the moving apart of the former Laurasia and Gondwanaland.

The end result of continental drift and its effects on the evolution of butterflies can be seen in the affinities or similarities between the faunas of areas that are now widely separated. One example, among many, is found in the modern-day Acraeinae that occur in both Africa and South America; it appears that their common ancestor evolved before those two land masses separated. Similarly, the almost entirely northern distribution of the many species in the Argynninae is likely due to their original development and subsequent species radiation in Laurasia-associated land masses. The relatively few Argynnines that are now found in southern regions have probably colonized these areas relatively recently.

Another example is the Gondwanaland origin of the Castnioidea. The effect of these processes can also be seen, at least on the family level, in the

This endemic Jamaican skipper, Schaus' tawny skipper, *Pyrrhocalles jamaicensis* (Hesperiidae), illustrates the extreme diversity of skippers in the neotropical region. There are at least four times as many skipper species in the neotropics as there are in any of the other biogeographic realms.

relative diversity of each region (see the table on the next page), because the longer the time since a taxonomic group originated, the greater the potential for it to have evolved into many species during that time. Still, while knowledge of plate tectonics and continental drift provides great insight into the affinities of modern regional butterfly faunas, it does little to explain much of the modern-day species diversity of butterflies.

For further insight we must turn to more "recent" history. Almost everyone knows that the ages of glaciation during the Pleistocene periodically cloaked the northern hemisphere with ice. What do you suppose the consequences of these glacial periods were? Where did the water come from for all of that ice to form? The ocean levels declined, which changed the coastlines of the continents. The presence of all of that ice also meant that the climate changed dramatically. The extent of tropical rainforests (and temperate forest regions too) were reduced, and since more species of butterflies occur in tropical rainforests than anywhere else on Earth, the distributions of these species had to contract with their habitat. This led to small isolated "islands" of rainforest that became the last refuge of many species.

BUTTERFLY DIVERSITY BY ZOOGEOGRAPHIC REGIONS

TAXA				REGION			
	N	NL	P	E	O	A	TOTAL
Castnioidea							
Castniidae	–	135	–	–	3	29	167
Hedyloidea							
Hedylidae	–	40	–	–	–	–	40
Hesperioidea							
Hesperiidae	290	2,016	155	437	569	191	3,658
Papilionoidea							
Papilionidae	33	120	84	87	178	70	572
Pieridae	64	323	167	174	307	187	1,222
Lycaenidae	164	2,611	407	1,413	1,540	429	6,564
Nymphalidae	214	2,857	1,083	1,156	1,563	349	7,222
Total	765	8,102	1,896	3,267	4,160	1,255	19,445
Species Richness (%)	(3.9)	(41.7)	(9.8)	(16.8)	(21.4)	(6.4)	
Sp./million km^2	51	674	61	200	633	214	224

Regions: N: Neararctic; NL: Neotropic; P: Palearctic; E: Ethiopian; O: Oriental; A: Australian
Note: The same taxa may occur in more than one region, thus the grand total does not sum to the number of species reported in "Butterflies Classification and Diversity on page 54, "After Heppner, 1991."

THE THEORY OF ISLAND BIOGEOGRAPHY

Islands, whether tracts of land surrounded by water or single butterfly host plants in a field of different kinds of plants, or rainforest refugia during a period of glaciation, have two interesting physical properties: their dimensional area and their distance from other islands. Together, these two properties largely determine how many species occur in or on an island. Let's consider species–area relationships. Would you expect to find more species of butterflies on an island that is one square mile (2.6 kilometers) in area or one that is 100 square miles (259 square kilometers) in area?

One would think that the larger island could support more species

Caribbean islands have generally been isolated from each other for a long time, allowing for the development of endemic species, like Jamaica's Miss Perkins' blue, *Leptotes perkinsae* (Lycaenidae).

because it probably has more resources and more kinds of habitat than a smaller island. Now, let's say that we have two islands that are identical in size (both 10 square miles/26 square kilometers) but one is 10 miles (16 kilometers) and the other 100 miles (160 kilometers) from the mainland. If the "mainland" is a source of potential colonists, which of the two equal-sized "islands" is more likely to be colonized by a butterfly? The nearer of the two islands will, on average, be colonized more easily than the one that is farther away.

This is due not only to the distance between the colonist source and the island, but also to the "angular area" of the island. Picture this in your

Another endemic from Jamaica, the Jamaican pygmy fritillary, *Phyciodes (Antillea) proclea* (Nymphalidae), is a Nymphalid that is smaller than many Lycaenids.

mind's eye: both our islands have an area of 10 square miles (26 square kilometers), one 10 miles (16 kilometers) and the other 100 miles (160 kilometers) away. From any given point on the "mainland," the nearer island occupies a much larger portion of the horizon. Any prospective colonist setting out from the "mainland" has a better chance of finding the nearer island.

So, islands that are close to a source of potential colonists will, on average, have more species than a smaller island that is the same distance from the source of colonists, *or* an island of the same size that is farther from the source of colonists. Together these two facets, species–area relationships and area–distance relationships, are the physical basis of the theory of island biogeography.

Now, what happens when we add the element of time? Let's consider a

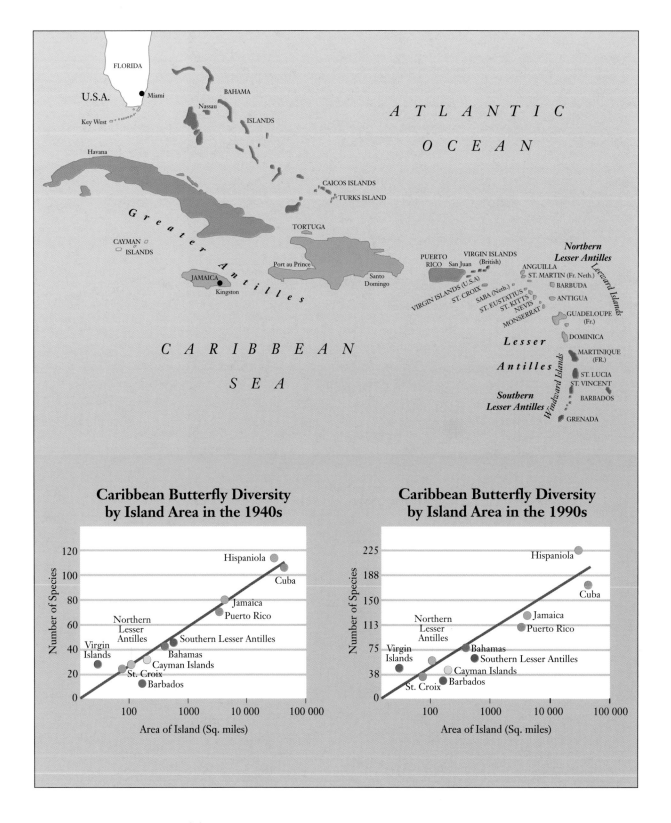

Caribbean Butterfly Diversity by Island Area in the 1940s

Caribbean Butterfly Diversity by Island Area in the 1990s

small island that is far away from a source of colonists. We've already established that the island will contain relatively few species, but, because it is a small island, and thus has fewer resources, it will also support fewer individuals of those species. In other words, the population sizes of the species that are there will also be small. We've also established that a small distant island will receive colonists less frequently because the chance that a colonist will find the distant island is small.

If we put these two ideas together and add a sufficient amount of time, say 5,000 years, what happens? Because the length of time is relatively long (as butterflies measure time), the chance that an unusual event, such as a climatic disturbance (for example, a drought, a flood or a hurricane), will occur on the island is relatively high. Since population sizes are small, it's quite possible for a sufficiently strong disturbance to cause a species to become extinct and, because the island is distant from the source of colonists, another species is unlikely to fill the vacant space. Our conclusion? Species on small islands far away from a source of colonists, given a sufficient period of time, may become extinct; species on larger, closer islands are more likely to survive.

This is all well and good, but why should you care about island biogeography theory? Because it's important to realize that these considerations apply equally well to a woodlot surrounded by fields, a hedgerow between a road and a field, or a small population of butterfly host plants surrounded by vegetation that does not include the host plant. Sources of potential butterfly colonists might include another woodlot "island" in a "sea" of fields or a forested "mainland" that is more or less continuous, or a neighboring host-plant population. As you might imagine, in this day of habitat fragmentation and outright habitat loss due to human activities, island biogeography becomes a very important consideration in conservation planning.

RAINFOREST REFUGIA AND BUTTERFLY DIVERSITY

What happens when major climatic shifts brought about by glaciation cause the contraction of rainforests into islands? These events are thought to have occurred many times in the relatively recent history of the Earth

The relationship between species diversity and area in the butterfly fauna of the islands of the Caribbean. As island size increases so does the number of butterflies that each supports. Originally noted by Canadian entomologist Eugene Monroe, and illustrated in his thesis in the 1940s (although his contribution to island biogeographic theory was unrecognized until the early 1980s), the relationship between island size and species numbers has not changed significantly in the 1990s, despite a vast increase in our taxonomic knowledge of these islands.

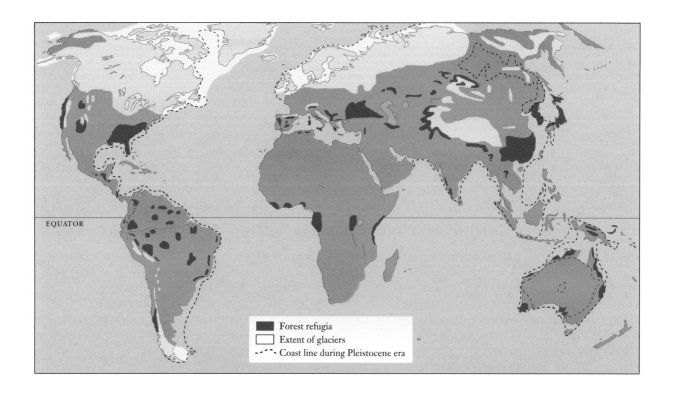

EQUATOR

Forest refugia
Extent of glaciers
- - - Coast line during Pleistocene era

Hypothesized locations of forest refuges during the Pleistocene ice ages. These "refugia" islands of forest in seas of less hospitable habitats, became centers of speciation for butterflies and many other species of plants and animals. After Heppner, 1991.

(see map above). You'll recall that the large-scale distribution of butterfly families and subfamilies is already in place due to continental drift and the processes, such as island building and the uplift of land bridges, that accompany it. What concerns us here is the diversity of butterfly species within the larger taxonomic categories: Why do some families contain many species (they are speciose) while others are species depauperate? As we've just seen, answers to questions like these depend not only on the distribution of the families after continental drift, but also on the size of rainforest refuges, the distances between these islands of livable habitat, and the amount of time that they were isolated from each other.

We know, from our look at the ramifications of island biogeography theory, that large islands support more species, that islands that are close together are more likely to exchange individuals, that the combination of these factors affects colonization rates, and that species on small islands are more likely to go extinct over extended periods of time. The consequences of living in rainforest or temperate-region habitat refuges varied

94

considerably. Undoubtedly some of the refuges were too small, and many butterfly species, perhaps entire lineages, went extinct, but some were large enough that species were able to thrive, despite being isolated from other refuges.

In fact, given the amount of time that these larger refuge "islands" were isolated from each other, it's almost certain that species continued to adapt and evolve within them, generating new, often quite similar, species in the process. When climatic conditions improved, and the refuges gradually expanded, this process continued, even accelerating as new opportunities—perhaps a change in the chemistry or form of a host plant or maybe the colonization of an area with more seasonal tendencies—to exploit arose. The end result was many new species.

Evidence for these effects of "islandizing" of rainforest refugia is relatively easy to find. The speciosity of some groups, and the remarkably close subfamily relationships among groups like the Nymphalinae, Heliconiinae and Acraeinae, suggest that relatively recent speciation from a single common ancestor, but in isolation from the other groups as would occur in islands of habitat, has occurred. The close evolutionary ties between butterflies and their host plants (which were undergoing the same "islandizing" and subsequent range expansions) also explains some of butterfly species diversity. (We will consider this "coevolution" of plants and butterflies in Chapter 4.)

Another example of the effects of rainforest refuge islands can be seen in the parallel radiations and remarkable concurrent mimicry patterns of the genus *Heliconius*. The two species *H. erato* and *H. melpomene* look almost identical—you need to be an expert to be able to tell them apart—and occur together in more than a dozen regions (see the illustration on page 98). Their bold color patterns change dramatically, but always together, from region to region: within any given part of their range, the two species look more alike than do the same species from two adjacent regions. There is almost perfect geographic concordance in the regionality of their patterns, *and* there can be up to a half-dozen or more species of *Heliconius*—plus up to a dozen or two species from entirely different families or subfamilies—all sharing almost exactly the same color pattern.

Parallel races of two species of *Heliconius* mimic each other throughout the neotropics, sharing the same patterns in the same area. This is the small postman, *H. erato* (Nymphalidae) from Costa Rica.

As unbelievable as this might sound, it gets even more astounding: there may be up to four or five different color patterns, each with its own complement of species, in the same region! See the photo on page 99 for an example.

So, here we have some ideas about how and where butterfly species diversity arose, but it is worth remembering that diversity is area-specific; in other words, there has to be a defining context. Diversity information can be presented as number of species per hundred or thousand square miles (259 to 2590 square kilometers), by region, or by encounter time (e.g., so many butterflies per hour in the habitat). For example, in Britain, butterfly diversity varies from fewer than 10 to more than 40 butterfly species per 39 square miles (100 kilometers square). Compare this with a

39-square-mile portion of the Rondonia region of southwestern Brazil and neighboring Bolivia—one of the postulated rainforest refugia during the ice ages—that has more than 1,400 species.

Another way of looking at diversity is to consider the rate at which new species are encountered. In the area above that is now known as the Rondonia Rain Forest Reserve, approximately 840 species were encountered by a small team of investigators during the first month. About 220 more species were added by more than two dozen investigators during the subsequent two months, but adding a further 360 species took many subsequent visits over the following two or three years. This declining encounter rate is typical because some species are common; that is, they are more numerous, so they are encountered more often. Rare species, because they are less numerous, are encountered, less often. This brings up the next question: What factors determine the abundance of individual species?

The other half of the paired parallel races of Heliconius, in Costa Rica, is the postman, *H. melpomene* (Nymphalidae). The length of the yellow ray in the hindwing can be used to differentiate the two species: it does not reach the edge of the wing in *H. melpomene*.

The classic example of Müllerian mimicry is the parallel race formation between co-occurring members of the postman and the small postman, *Heliconius melpomene* and *H. erato* (Nymphalidae), respectively, throughout South and much of Central America. Wherever they occur together, they mimic each other and other species—Heliconiines and members of other families and subfamilies—mimic them. After Turner, 1975.

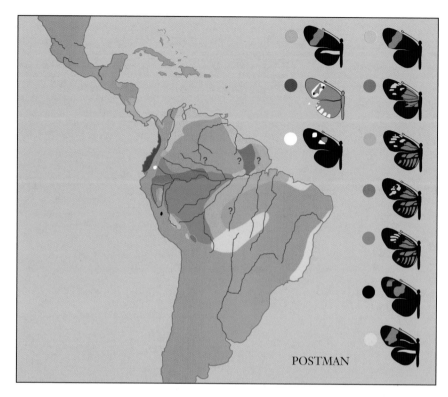

POSTMAN

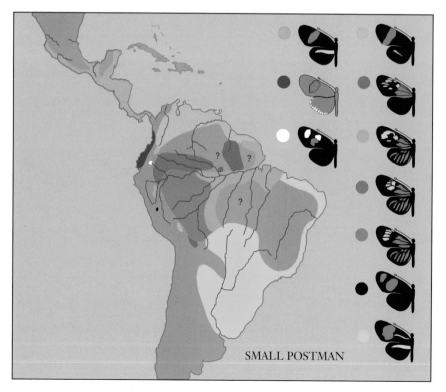

SMALL POSTMAN

98

Various members of six different color/pattern mimicry systems found near Sirena, Costa Rica. Note that the top "butterfly" in each of the complexes is actually a day-flying pericopine moth (Arctiidae; Pericopinae). FAR LEFT, TOP TO BOTTOM: moth, *Archonias eurytele* (Pieridae; Pierinae), *Dismorphia eunoe* (Pieridae; Dismorphiinae), *Napeogenes peredia* (Nymphalidae; Ithomiinae), *Eresia coela* (Nymphalidae; Nymphalinae), *Heliconius hecale* (Nymphalidae; Heliconiinae). CENTER LEFT: moth, *Dismorphia amphiona* (Pieridae; Dismorphiinae), *Melinaea ethra* (Nymphalidae; Nymphalinae), *Heliconius ismenius* (Nymphalidae; Heliconiinae), *Hypothyris euclea* (Nymphalidae; Ithomiinae), *Eresia mechanitis* (Nymphalidae; Nymphalinae). CENTER RIGHT: moth (*Dysschemia jansonius*, female), *Archonias tereas* (Pieridae; Pierinae), *Parides arcas* (Papilionidae; Papilioninae), *Eurytides euryleon* (Papilionidae; Papilioninae), moth. *Actinote anteas* (Nymphalidae; Acraeinae). FAR RIGHT: moth (*Dysschemia jansonius*, male), *Dismorphia theucharila* (Pieridae; Dismorphiinae), *Oleria paula* (Nymphalidae; Ithomiinae), moth, *Heliconius hewitsoni* (Nymphalidae; Heliconiinae), *Heliconius pachinius* (Nymphalidae; Heliconiinae).

Population Biology

Ecology is the study of the distribution and abundance of organisms. Distribution, of course, requires an area or region—some geographic context—but, then, so does abundance. Raw abundance may be just a number of individuals, but it's pretty useless information without some context. What good does it do to say "There are 200 butterflies" if the statement doesn't provide some limits? Is that 200 butterflies in your backyard? in your county? in your country? in the world? As you can see, a geographic context is pretty important. Our problem here is that "population size" should depend less on the word "size" and more on the word "population."

A good working definition of a population is any group of individuals of a single species that is separated in space or time from other groups of individuals of the same species. In fact, a species *is* a population, but it's far more useful to consider smaller units. The simple act of labeling a group of butterflies of the same species a "population" doesn't mean that they're completely isolated. How we define the context of a population matters less than that we do so! If we were to say, "There are 200 butterflies in this field" or "There are 17 caterpillars on this plant," then we've placed some limits on the population. However, a better way to think about abundance is to consider a population's density—that is, the number of butterflies or caterpillars per some definable unit of area (or time).

This division between space and time is reflected in the two major aspects of population biology: studies of population structure and studies of population dynamics. The former is the study of populations in space, while the latter looks at changes in populations over time. Of course, we can't really examine one without the other, because by the time we've determined what the spatial structure of a population is, it has probably already changed to some degree. Similarly, we must have some idea of what the spatial structure is before we can understand a population's dynamics.

Factors that are normally considered in investigations of population structure of butterflies include the distribution of host plant and adult food resources, environmental parameters, potential sources of mortality, and flight ability and dispersal tendencies. Aspects of population dynamics that are frequently considered in population studies include changes in abundance, density and sex ratio. The processes that affect these three parameters, including how long individuals remain in populations, mating patterns, flight and activity schedules and how these processes relate to population growth or decline, are also important considerations.

POPULATION STRUCTURE

The butterfly population in one field is (or the caterpillars on one plant are) quite likely a part of a larger local population, and that local population is probably part of a larger regional population, and so on. We could consider each population as an island and, just as in island biogeography, the distance between the populations and the relative size (in both distribution and abundance) of the populations will affect how many individuals move between the populations. A large "regional population" that is composed of many local sub or satellite populations like our field of butterflies, which may intermittently exchange individuals, is called a "metapopulation." The population structure of many butterfly species can be characterized as metapopulations.

The metapopulation structure of the Glanville fritillary, *Melitaea cinxia* (Nymphalidae), has made it the most studied butterfly species in the world, at least in terms of numbers of satellite populations.

Metapopulations are frequently characterized by so-called source/sink dynamics. A source population is a subpopulation that produces more individuals than it supports with the result that the surplus individuals emigrate from the subpopulation. A subpopulation that remains viable only if individuals immigrate into the population is considered a population "sink." A metapopulation will include satellite populations that become extirpated (go locally extinct) for short periods, but individuals from other subpopulations frequently recolonize the vacant satellites. The gist of all of this is that, contrary to the worry of early conservationists, some local populations go extinct on a regular basis. The real concern should be that there is always a

source of colonists—a large nearby "island"—to repopulate these sometimes-vacant habitats. From a conservation viewpoint, the absolute size of a population may be secondary to the connectedness of adjacent populations.

It is difficult to generalize about differences in populations because butterflies use such a wide variety of habitats in so many places. Some species, like the small or cabbage white (*Pieris rapae*, Pieridae), which use many varieties of mustards (Cruciferae) as host plants, are found from early spring through late autumn in many regions and in many habitats around the globe. Others such as the West Virginia white (*Pieris virginiensis*, Pieridae) are found only in the spring in the moist, rich north temperate woods of eastern North America that contain populations of toothwort (*Dentaria diphylla* or *D. laciniata*, Cruciferae), its larval host plants. The only safe generalization that can be made about butterfly populations is that they *may* be found where all environmental conditions meet the requirements of that species.

The most important abiotic or environmental factors (as opposed to biotic or biological factors) for most butterflies are temperature and precipitation. The location (latitude, longitude and altitude) of any given butterfly population influences the prevailing environmental conditions and how those conditions might change. A tropical population does not have to contend with winter but may be greatly affected by predictable changes in environmental conditions such as wet and dry seasons. Similarly, a tropical population may be subject to large unpredictable perturbations like hurricanes or monsoons that may have a smaller effect on more temperate populations, while temperate populations must contend with greater daily and seasonal fluctuations in temperature. Populations of the same species may face drastically different conditions in different parts of the species range.

Of course, just because the conditions are right doesn't mean that a butterfly will occur where you expect it! I regularly visited a bog in central Ontario that had a population of shrubby cinquefoil, *Potentilla fruticosa* (Rosaceae), the larval host plant of the Dorcas copper, *Lycaena dorcas* (Lycaenidae), over three consecutive flight seasons, but I never found the butterfly. I was well within the known range, all of the environmental parameters seemed suitable and the obligate larval host plant was present, but the butterfly did not occur there. This "island" was either too small or too far away from a source of colonists (or perhaps it was a "momentarily" vacant satellite of a metapopulation).

COMMONNESS AND RARITY

It is, perhaps, axiomatic to say that some species are common and that others are rare. But why should this be so? What factors determine abundance? If you were to count the number of individuals of just about any group (or even all) of the species in any defined area, you would find the same pattern or trend. Why? In part, it has to do with inherent properties of the organism itself, but ultimately it comes down to two major factors: the distribution of, and competition for, resources and the relative numbers and kinds of predators. Some species are better at using whatever resources might be available while others have fairly specific requirements. Similarly, some species are better at avoiding predators than others.

Common or rare? Small or cabbage whites, *Pieris rapae* (Pieridae), like this mating pair, are quite common almost everywhere.

103

Butterflies are usually more common at the center of the species range than they are near the edges. Populations at the limits of a species' range are utilizing more marginal habitat that does not meet the optimum criteria of the species (which is why it is the limit of the species range). The host plant may be less common or less suitable in some way, or at the limits of its own range, or the species may not be able to contend with seasonal phenomena of the region. Essentially, populations at the limits of their range are less stable and are subject to more of the stress of living under suboptimal conditions. Populations that are stressed are more vulnerable to stochastic, or random, events such as unseasonable freezes, hurricanes and droughts. Small populations under stress are more likely to go locally extinct.

One intriguing point to keep in mind is that "rare" can mean several different things. For example, a species that is encountered infrequently (e.g., the local population density is low so the organism is not seen very often) is rare. However, "rare" also describes a species that is limited to a relatively small area (e.g., the species has a defined geographic range, say, the piney woods of the southeastern United States), or a species has specific habitat requirements (e.g., habitat specificity). If you use Geographic Range (large or small), Habitat Specificity (wide or narrow) and Population Size (large or small) as criteria, then only one combination of these three (large range, wide habitat preference and large populations) describes an organism that is common. All of the other seven categories describe different forms of "rare."

In a "classic" rare species—one in which individuals have small restricted distributions or geographic range and narrow habitat specificity—the limits of their spatial distribution are frequently dispersal limits, but may also include current habitat availability and other factors such as competition and predation. So why are some species rare? There are too many definitions of "rare" to answer this question definitively. It's better to ask "Why is a particular species rare?" In a few cases we've observed the changes from abundant to rare, so we know "why" (e.g., the bay checkerspot, *Euphydryas editha bayensis*, Nymphalidae, has declined as a result of habitat fragmentation, and some named varieties and subspecies of

OPPOSITE: **Common or rare? A close "sister" to the cabbage white, this mating pair of veined or mustard whites, *Pieris napi* (Pieridae), may be common in specific habitats but are far less common over wide areas.**

the Apollo, *Parnassius apollo*, Papilionidae, may have suffered from overcollection). Some species persist at "rare" levels for extended periods, particularly those with a metapopulation structure, as a mosaic of strong and weak populations. A good example of such a classic rare species is the Karner blue (*Lycaeides melissa samuelis*, Lycaenidae) of the northeastern United States and southeastern Canada.

POPULATION DYNAMICS

Populations, regardless of their structure, change over time. As individual butterflies eclose (emerge), die, immigrate into, or leave a population, the structure of the population is affected. If, for instance, the replacement rate is less than one—that is, more individuals leave the population (there are more deaths and emigrants) than are recruited into the population (through natality and immigration)—then the population level will decline. Ecologists want to know how and why the replacement rate changes in a population, so they ask questions: Why is this population declining while another one is increasing? What factors are responsible for the growth of a population? Why do some populations reach outbreak proportions in one generation and become quite rare in others?

Changes in the size of a population are often the result of an organism's response to some change in the availability of needed resources. If resources (e.g., host plants) become more plentiful, then it may be possible for more eggs to be laid, more caterpillars to survive through to pupation, and more pupae to eclose and thus increase the number of butterflies. The problem is that butterflies are also resources to their predators and parasitoids: if an increase in the availability of host-plant resources translates into more butterflies, then it is quite likely that an increase in the availability of butterflies will also translate into more butterfly predators. Under such a scenario, predators may then reduce the size of the butterfly population. This leads to what is called "predator–prey tracking," where predator population sizes depend on prey population sizes, and they cycle together through time, waxing and waning, one after the other.

Butterflies must deal with a wide variety of predators, but they can also be considered as predators themselves: they eat plants. Even if the number of butterfly predators does not increase following an increase in butterfly population size, it is almost certain that an increase in the number of butterflies will yield an increase in the number of eggs laid and the numbers of caterpillars preying on the host plant. With more plant tissue being consumed by caterpillars, the plants will grow more slowly, and some of the caterpillars will not complete their development. Thus there may be fewer butterflies in the subsequent generation. The lesson here is that the size of the butterfly population affects the other organisms around it, both prey and predators, which in turn affect the population size of the butterfly.

Every so often, the regulation mechanisms break down and a population grows so fast that it outstrips its own resources. A wonderful example of such an outbreak occurs relatively frequently in the snout butterfly, *Libytheana bachmanii* (Nymphalidae), in Texas. This species overwinters in south Texas and is often reasonably common in the spring but has a larger second brood in the fall. Outbreak populations usually occur in the fall, and the explosive growth of the population is due to the combination of the breaking of a drought and the decline of natural predators and parasitoids during the drought period. The flush of new growth on the host plant after a significant rain, together with a lack of significant numbers of predators and parasites, yields a situation whereby almost every caterpillar survives to become an adult. The end result is a mass dispersal.

In the fall of 1998, I had occasion to witness one of these outbreaks and was astounded at the numbers of butterflies involved. I estimated, conservatively (by repeatedly counting the numbers of butterflies that flew past me in one minute), that as many as 500 to 600 butterflies per hour were passing me, all flying in a northeasterly direction, over the course of seven or eight consecutive days. If that continued for eight hours per day over eight days, more than 32,000 butterflies may have passed by. On one unforgettable afternoon, I estimated, by counting the number of butterflies on one clump of flowers and then multiplying by the number of clumps, that I was sharing a 5-acre (2-ha) meadow with more than 5,000 butterflies! On that particular afternoon, I watched in amusement as the snouts moved northeast, and about 50 to 60 monarchs (Danaus plexippus, Nymphalidae) per hour simultaneously migrated southwest.

There may be large differences in the abundance of some butterfly species between distinct generations or subsequent broods. Many temperate species that overwinter in immature stages face extreme environmental hazards that result in fewer butterflies in the spring brood than in later generations. Other species may have overlapping generations in which population levels gradually increase during the flight season. Some species produce only a single brood per year; still others may produce a brood only every two or three years, usually because of host plant and length of season limitations.

There may also be significant variation in the abundance of butterflies from year to year. Some species, like the falcate orangetip (*Anthocharis midea*, Pieridae) or the checkered white (*Pontia protodice*, Pieridae), may be very common one year and quite rare in the next. These fluctuations are often due to mortality differences between years, brought on by environmental (weather) or biotic (predation, parasitism) factors. Still others, such as many arctics (*Oeneis* sp., Nymphalidae), take two years to complete their life cycle, so are found only in alternate years. Interestingly, some of these species have populations that are out of phase with each other; that is, one or more populations fly in even-numbered years while others fly only in odd-numbered years.

For example, Canada's Macoun's arctic (*Oeneis macounii*) is found east of the Manitoba–Ontario boundary (approximately) in even-numbered years and west of it in odd-numbered years. In another example, Uhler's arctic (*Oeneis uhleri*) is far more common in odd-numbered years in western Canada, but it is found every year. In both cases, it is possible that the populations may have been concurrent at some time in the past, but a short, harsh season may have forced one or the other to diapause for two years instead of the usual one. It is equally possible that a longer-than-usual summer and the occurrence of a few relatively rare mutants that were able to

Periodic outbreaks of snouts or beaks, *Libythea bachmanii* (Nymphalidae), in south Texas are responsible for their sometimes massive migrations. This particular butterfly was photographed at Point Pelee National Park in Ontario, Canada, in 1988.

Uhler's arctic, *Oeneis uhleri* (Nymphalidae), is an example of a butterfly with a biennial life history that has population consequences. In western Canada this species is far more common in odd-numbered years.

complete their life cycle without an obligatory diapause allowed one to skip a year.

TO STAY OR TO GO: DIAPAUSE, DISPERSAL AND MIGRATION

When environmental conditions vary outside of the acceptable range of a population, then the individuals that make up that population must decide what to do: go or stay? The strategy that most butterflies employ is usually species specific and depends on how the conditions have changed. Some butterfly species choose to stay where they are regardless of the conditions, and have developed life-history adaptations, such as diapause, hibernation or aestivation, that allow them to avoid environmental perturbations. Others are habitual dispersers; they rarely stay in any one place for long but are constantly on the move. Still others are migrating species: they stay in one place for a while until conditions become untenable, then they move to another place, where the environment lets them survive.

Hibernation and aestivation are both forms of dormancy generally employed by adults. Dormancy is a period in which the processes that sustain life are minimized; "hibernation" is the term used to describe cold-period or winter dormancy, while "aestivation" refers to summer dormancy. They are essentially identical except that the cues that induce or break the dormancy may differ. Relatively few species use dormancy strategies to avoid suboptimal conditions. In the north temperate region, some Nymphalids overwinter as adults. A good example of this is the Camberwell beauty or mourning cloak, *Nymphalis antiopa*, which can often be found flying in the late winter while there is still snow on the ground.

I recall one glorious winter day in mid-March in central Ontario, Canada, when I came upon a small sunlit, wind-protected clearing in a treed hedgerow that was full of butterflies. The snow had been melting for three or four days but was still very much in evidence on the road beside the hedgerow. Inside the glade, however, spring was in full swing! Much to my delight, there were five species of relatively large Nymphalids sunning themselves, gliding about, or visiting the sap exuding from one of the surrounding trees. The species included mourning cloaks (*N. antiopa*), red admirals (*Vanessa atalanta*), American painted ladies (*V. virginiensis*), and two or three small (Milbert's) and large (Compton's) tortoiseshells (*N. milberti* and *N. vaualbum*). What a way for a frustrated lepidopterist to break his own winter-enforced dormancy.

Diapause is usually used by immature stages, although not exclusively, as we shall learn, and involves not just a slowing of life processes, but also an interruption of development, growth or metamorphosis. It is a common strategy used by the majority of temperate butterfly species. The stage at which diapause occurs varies between species but is usually synoptic or species-specific. The cues that induce or break diapause include changes in host plants, temperature, photoperiod (day length) and population density. It's fairly easy to see why decreasing temperature and/or declining photoperiod would induce diapause, or why increases in either of these would break diapause, since these are harbingers of winter and spring, respectively.

In most species, diapause is obligate, meaning that, when the conditions are right, the caterpillars or pupa has no choice in the matter: diapause is an

Outbreak "migrants," like the extremely large numbers of these African migrants, *Catopsilia florella* (Pieridae), assembled beside a cattle pond in Botswana in 1991, are often a relatively common species that seem to be predisposed to "disperse."

automatic response to changing conditions. Many checkerspot butterflies (*Euphydryas* sp., Nymphalidae) have an obligate larval diapause. We know that it is obligate because diapause can be induced, or broken, artificially, and all individuals react in the same way. Some species, however, can "choose" whether or not to enter diapause; in other words, for them diapause is facultative. In some cases, such as the viceroy, *Limenitis archippus* (Nymphalidae), northern populations enter diapause while southern populations do not. In other species, like the black swallowtail (*Papilio polyxenes*, Papilionidae), some of a fall brood may complete development while most enter diapause as pupae.

The alternative to waiting for conditions to change is to leave. The problem is that some species of butterflies don't wait for conditions to change; they leave anyway. Some species of butterflies, like the small or cabbage white, *Pieris rapae* (Pieridae), can be characterized as "continuous dispersers." They, like many Pierids, never stay in one place for very long but often strike out in seemingly straight-line flight without any apparent destination. The question, of course, is why would a butterfly ever choose to go? If it has successfully matured in the habitat, then it is its own incontrovertible evidence that the habitat is suitable. It appears that, much like people, some butterfly species are "travelers" while others are "stay-at-homes."

Some continuously dispersing species, such as the painted lady or cosmopolitan butterfly, *Vanessa cardui* (Nymphalidae), and the monarch, *Danaus plexippus* (Nymphalidae), have carried dispersal to extremes. During outbreak conditions, the snout also fits the description of a continuous disperser. However, some of these species are also known to migrate. The painted lady, and the monarch especially, are famous migratory butterflies. So the question we have to ask here is how dispersal differs from migration. The difference is that migration is a directed, long-distance, seasonal movement of individuals, whereas dispersal does not necessarily require long distances or need to be seasonal. In reality, species like the monarch combine continuous dispersal in their northward journey with a true migration in their journey south.

Migration is another of the possible responses that some organisms choose in response to environmental perturbations that are predictable, for example, winter in the north temperate region. The monarchs of eastern North America conduct the longest, certainly the best-known, migration of any butterfly. Those that eclose in the early autumn enter reproductive diapause, that is, they emerge without fully developed reproductive organs, and may make an astounding southward migration of up to 2,500 miles (4,000 km) over a period of up to three months. It is thought that reproductive diapause is what allows this generation of monarchs to live up to six to eight months when the previous non-migratory generation had an average lifespan of about a month. The butterflies feed on the abundant fall wildflowers and stockpile the energy from the nectar in a fat body in their abdomen. The fat body is metabolized to provide energy for the southward flight but also provides stores of energy to permit their extended lifespan.

Why a butterfly should choose to make such a long migration that is fraught with hazard over an overwintering diapause by immatures is unknown, but it is likely, in the monarch's case, that it is really a tropical species that colonized the temperate zone gradually. As the glaciers retreated, their host plants expanded their range northward, and the butterflies followed them. Eventually, summer conditions in the south became too hot and dry for the host plants to survive, so the butterflies were limited to the northern limit of the host plant's range. Their long migration may have been much shorter at some time in the past.

HABITAT PREFERENCE

Early lepidopterists often wondered why butterflies that use very common host plants were not more abundant. The consensus was that, because the "world is green," species that depend on plants should never be rare. Yet some were and others were not. If host-plant resources were not limiting the butterfly population, then what was? In fact, it turns out that how we perceive the availability of host-plant resources matters much less than how butterflies perceive them. It's not unusual, in conducting population studies of butterflies, to find that some plants are clearly preferred over others that are not visibly different and are located right beside the chosen ones. The differences may be in the sensory capability of individual butterflies, or in

The larval host plant of the frosted elfin, *Incisalia irus* (Lycaenidae), is far more common than one would expect from the relative rarity of the butterfly. Note that this individual is "stealing" nectar through a hole in the side of a blueberry flower (*Vaccinium* sp. Ericaceae).

perceived qualities of the preferred/avoided plants (e.g., plant size, location, leaf shape, flowering status, or tissue maturity or chemistry), or even be related to other components of the surrounding community (e.g., the presence of ants, predators, or other eggs or larvae).

The lesson that can be learned from this is pretty straightforward: mobile organisms such as butterflies have control over where, and even

114

when, they live; that is, they show habitat preference. The strategies that are used to avoid suboptimal conditions—dispersal, dormancy, diapause and migration—are really aspects of habitat preference. Similarly, a female's host-plant choices, or a male's favorite perch, or where either sex chooses to fly or obtain nourishment, is an aspect of habitat preference. Populations occur where many individuals make the same choices. Of course, the variation in preferences among individuals is what makes populations dynamic.

One interesting facet of habitat preference is that males and females of the same species often make markedly different choices. This is due, at least in part, to differences in the resources needed by the two sexes. For example, females need to mate only once (although many species do mate more than once) and they spend the bulk of their time looking for host plants, feeding on nectar or other energy sources, and resting in proximity to these two resources. In contrast, males are looking for a slightly different mix of nutrient, energy and pheromone resources, and usually choose to "rest" where they might encounter freshly eclosed, virgin or unmated females. Obviously, the chosen habitats of males and females must sometimes coincide or there wouldn't be any reproduction at all.

Habitat preference might be engendered by something as simple as the angle of sunshine in the morning, the presence of fallen leaves on the forest floor, or the availability of perches or other landscape features. However, the main features of habitats chosen by butterflies are often the same from species to species: the ready availability of host plants and nectar sources, suitable temperature and moisture regimes, and the presence of other members of the same species. Regardless of how or why butterflies choose habitats, the end result is the same: butterflies, like all other organisms, do not live in a vacuum. They live and participate in communities of organisms, and we would do well to remember this one fact when contemplating conservation plans.

A Butterfly's World

If you were a butterfly, what challenges would you face in your day-to-day life? You are familiar with the pressures that assail a relatively large (albeit intelligent) mammal, but what about the challenges that beset a relatively large insect? Size might be an obvious place to start. "Walk a mile in my shoes" takes on a whole new meaning for a caterpillar. How many more "steps" would be required to cover the same distance if you had the stride length of a caterpillar?

What about other challenges? Let's consider a few possibilities from the point of view of a young female butterfly that has recently mated and is ready to lay eggs. First, you need to be able to fly, as flight is essential in order for you to find plants on which to lay your eggs. So you also need a source of energy, nectar from flowers, to fuel the flight "machinery." During the search for host plants, you must also avoid predators, navigate over terrain that you have never seen before, be able to locate likely host-plant candidates (then be able to discriminate among the best ones) and, finally, lay an egg. This process must then be repeated as many times as you are able. Some females will also re-mate, and must be able to fly to find another mate. Conversely, you may need to fly to avoid harassment by overly amorous males if you don't want to mate.

An egg is totally dependent on its mother's host-plant choice for concealment from predators and parasites and for the environmental conditions necessary for survival. A young caterpillar must successfully hatch out of the egg, then quickly find its first meal, again dependent on the host chosen by its mother, and manage to avoid desiccation, predators, parasites and other hazards during its search. On your way to adulthood, your sole task is to eat and grow, but to accomplish these ends you must avoid a wide array of hazards (predators and parasitoids chief among them), molt successfully four or more times, and ensure that you have an adequate food supply. Finally, you must find a place to pupate to begin your transformation into a butterfly.

As a chrysalis, you are totally dependent on the location you chose as a caterpillar and on your ability to blend in with your surroundings. Assuming that you survive the hazards of the environment, you must successfully eclose from your pupal prison, expand and dry your wings, and take flight in order to find the nutrients and energy sources necessary to maintain yourself so that you can successfully reproduce. If you become a male, your task is to find a female, but, before you do, you must ensure that you have the necessary nuptial gift and pheromones to entice her into mating with you. This may involve feeding for a number of days, including finding alternative food sources, such as mineral salts, amino acids and specific chemical compounds, before you attempt to court a female. Of course, the female may exert choice of her own and reject your courtship.

Sound complicated? It is, but gaining some understanding of the day-to-day life of a butterfly will give you a healthy respect for what a butterfly goes through in order to survive and successfully replace itself in the next generation. And you will have a far better understanding of why knowing the biological needs of butterflies is an essential step in formulating a plan for their conservation.

Being a Good Egg

Eggs come in a variety of shapes and sizes. They are also laid in a variety of ways, and in places and positions on or near a seemingly bewildering array of potential hosts. In the typical situation, eggs are placed on specific host plants that the caterpillars feed on. Some species, such as the harvester

A wolf in sheep's clothing: the caterpillars of the aptly named harvester, *Feniseca tarquinius* (Lycaenidae), eat wooly aphids, using the "wool" of their prey to disguise themselves.

(*Feniseca tarquinius*; Lycaenidae) of North America, however, have caterpillars that are carnivorous and feed on wooly aphids instead of plants. The female harvester must find an aphid colony and then lay her eggs nearby so that the young larvae have a good chance to find their prey. Other species, such as Europe's large blue (*Maculinea arion*; Lycaenidae), begin feeding on a particular kind of plant (thyme, *Thymus* sp.; Labiatae), but then drop off the plant and depend on being picked up and carried into the nests of particular species of ants (*Myrmica* sp.; Formicidae), where they feed on ant larvae. So the female must find the proper host plant *and* ensure that there are ants of the correct species nearby.

Some species lay their eggs in batches or clumps; others lay them one at a time. Eggs in batches, because they are laid all at once, often hatch simultaneously, and the subsequent sibling caterpillars feed in groups, develop at the same rate, pupate at the same time and eclose as butterflies en masse. Populations of batch-laying butterflies often have very discrete generations, or abundance peaks, with little overlap, whereas eggs that are laid singly, often over a number of days, result in steady succession of butterflies being added to the population.

Eggs have no control over their world and are completely dependent on the choices made by their mother. If the female makes a mistake and lays an egg on the wrong plant or too far away from a food source, then the caterpillar won't survive. If the egg is laid in an exposed position where it can overheat or dry up, or where it is vulnerable to the many kinds of egg predators, parasites and parasitoids (parasites live off their host but do not kill them; parasitoids do), then it will also not survive. So what makes a "good egg"?

Eggs are fertilized as they are laid, and their shape makes them pretty efficient. As the zygote develops, it consumes the nourishment around it (inside of the egg) until, finally, it has become a caterpillar and eats through the outer shell to hatch. There are a few common ways that things can go

wrong before the hatch. Since butterfly eggs are so small, are packed with nutrients and energy, and are usually laid on plants, fungi and disease pathogens are real concerns. Being exposed to the wind, sun and rain that can overheat, desiccate, wash off or drown an egg can also be deadly. Since eggs are packed with energy and nutrients, they are considered a very good food choice for small predators (i.e., ants, beetles) and many small parasitic flies and wasps. Sometimes the larva that develops is the caterpillar of the butterfly and sometimes it is that of a parasite.

So, a "good egg" makes use of protective devices such as camouflage, position and chemical defenses provided by the female. Most eggs are white or a pale cream when they are laid, but some eggs are pale green or yellow, to match the substrate where they are laid. Many butterflies lay eggs

Some species are "batch" layers like this female Gillette checkerspot, *Euphydryas gilletti* (Nymphalidae), photographed next to her egg clutch in Yellowstone National Park.

119

ABOVE: **Most butterfly species lay their eggs singly. Here an apollo, *Parnassius apollo* (Papilionidae) oviposits on a stonecrop, *Sedum* sp. (Crassulacceae), in Bavaria.**

RIGHT: **Butterfly eggs are nutritious to a variety of small predators including ants. Here an ant attacks an egg of the variegated fritillary, *Euptoieta claudia* (Nymphalidae), on its Jamaican host plant, *Viola patrinii* (Violaceae).**

120

LEFT: **A plant mite takes opportunistic advantage of the presence of an egg of the old world swallowtail, *Papilio machaon* (Papilionidae).**

BELOW: **Eggs change color with age, as seen here in these eggs of the Mexican fritillary, *Euptoieta hegesia* (Nymphalidae). The darker, redder eggs are older than the lighter, cream-colored eggs as a consequence of the growth of the caterpillar within them. Captive females laid these eggs; normally there would not be as many eggs on a single leaf!**

beside veins or in surface depressions of leaves to help hide them or protect them from environmental extremes, although this strategy may also leave them vulnerable to fungi and pathogens. Other eggs are brightly colored or boldly patterned (see color plate 1 on pp. 31) as a warning that they contain nasty chemicals and that they would not be a very good meal. However, some eggs don't have these chemicals and imitate those that do (more on this mimicry strategy, which can be found in all life-history stages of butterflies, later).

All eggs change color as they age. Most become darker as a caterpillar develops. Just before the egg hatches, the caterpillar will have eaten most of the interior of the egg, so the eggshell becomes almost transparent and the dark head capsule of the larva is easily visible. Eggs that have been parasitized also commonly become darker with age as the parasites develop inside what used to be a butterfly egg. Eggs may also appear dark due to the presence of abdominal hairs lost, or deposited as camouflage, by the laying female.

Other eggs, like those of many Pierids, turn bright red or orange as they age. Art Shapiro, a researcher at the University of California at

RIGHT: **A female Olympia marblewing,** *Euchloe olympia* **(Pieridae), oviposits on a host plant** *Arabis lyrata* **(Cruciferae)—that already contains a half-dozen or more eggs—in Ontario, Canada.**

Davis, calls this the "red-egg syndrome" and suggests that, because the host plants of many Pierids are small and can only support a single caterpillar, females examine prospective host plants for the presence of other eggs. In theory, the bright color makes them easier to see, so fewer oviposition "mistakes" are made. However, I've found as many as a dozen eggs, at various stages of development (from white through to bright orange), including first-instar caterpillars, of the Olympia marblewing (*Euchloe olympia*; Pieridae) on a single host plant. It's possible that a scarcity of acceptable host plants may override the female's distaste for using a host that is already occupied.

While a female can, and often does, assess particular oviposition sites—including host identity, situation, location, and the presence or absence of other organisms—a "good egg" is also a lucky egg. How lucky an egg has to be depends on the prevailing environmental conditions: egg development time is largely determined by temperature, humidity and sometimes by day length. A drop of only a few degrees in temperature may add days to the development time, thus increasing the chance that the egg will be found by a predator or parasitoid. Under optimal conditions (which, of course, vary from species to species and place to place), the eggs of most species develop in three to ten days; however, some temperate species overwinter as eggs, that may last up to ten months. Still, despite a female butterfly's precautions, whether a predator or parasite finds an egg is often a matter of chance.

Growing Up Big and Strong

Caterpillars are eating machines. Matt Douglas, author of *The Lives of Butterflies*, points out that they eat "as if each day were their last." The best description I can give of a caterpillar is that it is an open-ended tube with a mouth at one end, an anus at the other, and a stomach in between. What goes in one end of a caterpillar comes out the other with very little change because caterpillars are extremely efficient at removing the necessary nutrients, energy and other compounds from what they eat, and most of

Caterpillars are capable of almost doubling their size in any given period of time. This photo shows the difference in size of the first through fourth instars of the Texas subspecies of the Mexican fritillary, *Euptoieta hegesia hoffmanni* (Nymphalidae). The stages shown represent the equivalent of about eight days of growth.

the plant tissue that they eat is indigestible. They grow incredibly fast, almost exponentially—meaning that they can almost double in size for each unit of time. Evidence that they're very good at what they do is easy to find since caterpillars, by the time they are ready to pupate, can be more than 3,000 or 4,000 times larger (both in volume and in mass) than they were at hatching!

Freshly hatched caterpillars are, of course, not much bigger than the egg that they came from, and often find their first meal by turning around and finishing off the rest of the egg shell. This habit accomplishes two things: it "destroys the evidence" that a young and mostly defenseless caterpillar has just entered the world at this location, and it provides the young larva with its last "free" meal, full of all of the vital nutrients it needs. One problem with this strategy is that nearby eggs may also be considered a "free meal," which leads to a certain predilection for cannibalism.

Inevitably, however, the young caterpillar has to come to grips with its new world. It's now mobile, but, let's face it, freshly hatched caterpillars move slowly enough to easily become some enterprising predator's favorite food. Not much of a choice here: move and be eaten, or stay put and starve. And it gets worse: as the larva gets larger, it becomes even easier to find *and*, because it contains more food energy, it becomes far more valuable to a predator. So it should come as no surprise that caterpillars have developed a wide array of predator-avoidance strategies.

The first act of most freshly hatched caterpillars is to eat the remainder of their egg as seen in this Japanese larva of the yellow swallowtail, *Papilio xuthus* (Papilionidae).

In theory at least, finding food shouldn't be too hard since, in the vast majority of species, the egg was laid on a plant that was "acceptable" to its mother. But, there are degrees of "acceptableness," and a variety of other obstacles may compound the problem. If the plant was not the preferred host (but merely acceptable), then the caterpillar feeding rate will be affected, possibly leading to a slower subsequent growth rate (since assimilating the required nutrients from the poorer host may be more difficult or require more food to be eaten). Even if it is the preferred host, the egg may have been laid on a stem or an older leaf that is tough, waxy and not nearly as nourishing or easy to eat as younger tissue. Anything that slows growth and development is potentially dangerous since it increases the chance that the larva will succumb to disease or be found by parasitoids and predators. So the young larva must seek the best-quality food, even on a preferred host.

The caterpillar must also deal with competition for the available food, especially if the choice tissue is in short supply. If environmental conditions have not been favorable, then the plant may be growing slowly, if at all, and more nutritious younger growth may be in short supply. The caterpillar may be alone on the plant but chances are that it has siblings nearby (if the laying female has been forced by the available number of preferred hosts to, or simply chooses to, repeatedly lay eggs on the same plant). This is especially common for gregarious larvae (where the female lays a batch of eggs on the same plant at the same time). Chances are, too, that, if it is a

Batch layers should oviposit on large plants or on very common ones. Here a great southern white, *Ascia monuste* (Pieridae), is laying a clutch on a very small Jamaican host plant that will not be able to support the growth of the caterpillars.

"good" plant, other females will lay eggs on it as well. In any case, the end result is often multiple larvae on single plants.

This illustrates another potential problem: Is the host plant large enough to support the complete development of the caterpillar? If the caterpillar is only one of many that are trying to use the same host plant, then this issue becomes especially important. Host plants provide the caterpillar equivalent of both luxury accommodations and fine dining, and gives the idea of "eating yourself out of house and home" a whole new meaning. One way around this problem is to lay eggs on small but extremely, or locally, common plants, so that, even if the caterpillar

OPPOSITE: Family groups of caterpillars, like these *Heliconius hewitsoni* (Nymphalidae), that hatch, feed, pupate and eclose in synchrony, are a consequence of eggs laid in batches.

defoliates a plant, it can easily find another. This is the case for many grass-eating species such as many Satyrids (Nymphalidae) and skippers (Hesperidae), but it is also true of the variegated fritillary (*Euptoieta claudia*; Nymphalidae) in the Blue Mountains of Jamaica. There, the caterpillars feed on a locally abundant violet, and it is common to find them wandering around on the ground, searching for another host. The violets are small, but there are so many of them that a caterpillar can be reasonably sure of finding another acceptable host regardless of which direction it happens to wander.

ABOVE: A variegated fritillary, *Euptoieta claudia* (Nymphalidae), oviposits on a blade of grass beside a Jamaican host plant, *Viola patrinii* (Violaceae), possibly as a response to ant predation. The host is very small but so common that a caterpillar is bound to find one in just about any direction that it wanders.

Caterpillars are, more or less, mobile (at least they're far more mobile than they were as eggs, or will be as pupae). Many predators cue in on movement, so simply walking on the surface of a leaf may be life-threatening. Other predators, and most parasitoids, cue in on contrast, that is, something that "sticks out" or doesn't fit into the usual background. So,

RIGHT: Many parasitoids attack caterpillars, depositing their eggs on them, as seen with this Tachinid fly egg (Diptera; Tachinidae) on the head of an American painted lady caterpillar, *Vanessa virginiensis* (Nymphalidae).

while movement makes a caterpillar more conspicuous than an egg, not moving can be just as dangerous because some predators and parasites search for prey that is associated with a specific kind of plant. In fact, eating may also help predators and parasites, which may cue in on the presence of feeding damage or frass (a fancy name for caterpillar excrement), to find a caterpillar.

Predators and parasitoids may cue on the kind of host plant or the host-plant location to find their prey. In my butterfly garden, I grow a few varieties of passion vines (*Passiflora* sp.; Passifloraceae). Many of them are host plants that are used by the gulf fritillary, *Agraulis vanillae* (Nymphalidae) and they can frequently defoliate the vines. I hear complaints from other passion-vine growers about their defoliated plants that rarely get the chance to flower (never mind set fruit), but I never have this problem (or, at least, I have it to a lesser extent). The reason is that I've adopted a "live and let live" attitude for

The feeding damage left behind on leaves can be used as a location cue by predators and parasitoids of the caterpillars. Here a family group of tawny emperor larvae, *Asterocampa clyton* (Nymphalidae) feed together on a leaf of their larval host plant, a hackberry tree (*Celtis* sp.; Ulmaceae).

all of the insects and other animals that live in and around the house, including the yellowjackets and paper wasps (*Vespula* and *Polistes* sp.; Hymenoptera) that construct their nests under the eaves. The hornets and wasps have learned that, if they patrol up and down the stems of the vines in the garden, they can find caterpillars. The friendly green anole (*Anolis carolinensis*; Iguanidae) that lives around the front porch also seems to know this, and I frequently find it climbing the vines, or jumping from leaf to leaf, searching for dinner.

So, caterpillars use a variety of strategies to make themselves less conspicuous, including modifying their time or position of feeding. Many young larvae feed on the underside of leaves, where they are less visible. Many of the violet-feeding Argynnines (e.g., *Speyeria cybele*; Nymphalidae)

Despite feeding on plants of the Passifloraceae (passion vines) that contain cyanide, the caterpillar of the gulf fritillary, *Agraulis vanillae* (Nymphalidae), is the target of a number of predators. Here, it is the prey of an assassin bug, *Zelus longipes* (Hemiptera; Reduviidae).

do most or all of their feeding at night, when presumably they are less visible, and there are fewer predators and parasites about. Another defense, although not strictly a way to blend in to one's surroundings, is to keep a "lifeline" available. All caterpillars have the ability to manufacture silk (this ability becomes vitally important just before pupation), and many use it to lay down trails on the host so that they may find their way around more easily. This is similar to tying a string around a tree so that you can find your way back out of the woods that you're exploring. This lifeline can also be used, and is used by some species, to simply drop off of the leaf whenever they're disturbed (see photo on page 132). They hang in the air and climb back up when the disturbance is gone.

Another conspicuousness-reducing strategy involves the use of color, shape and pattern. It's easy to see that a green caterpillar would be less visible on a green leaf than, say, a bright orange one would be. The little "chameleon" lizard (green anole) that prowls my passion vines seems to

Some parasitioids, once they have completed their development inside the caterpillar, form pupae on the exoskeleton, like these on a *Pyrrhogyra* (likely *P. neaerea*; Nymphalidae) caterpillar from Costa Rica.

One way of minimizing exposure to predators and parasites is to construct a leaf shelter as done here by the caterpillar of a silver-spotted skipper, *Epargyreus clarus* (Hesperiidae).

already know this, because it often changes color to match whatever it's prowling on: green on the vines and leaves, or brown on the trunks and stems. This ability is partly responsible for its success as a predator. Caterpillars can also change their color and pattern, although they can do so only during a molt.

First instar larvae of the orange tip (*Anthocharis cardamines*; Pieridae) are bright orange but become pale green and white, countershaded (a strategy where animals are darker on the top than they are on the bottom to reduce shadow contrast) and thus more cryptic in later stages. The bright orange caterpillars are probably too small to interest many visually hunting predators, but are useful cues to an ovipositing female that this plant is already occupied. It's likely that the first instar coloration is a continuation of the strategy employed in the "red-egg syndrome." This example shows that the usefulness of colors and patterns may change as the caterpillar increases in size; however, it's important to realize that the kinds

ABOVE: **Small caterpillars that are disturbed by predators often seem to simply drop off of their host plant, but using a silken thread as a lifeline, they remain tethered to the plant and crawl back up once the disturbance is ended. Here, a second instar larva of the Mexican fritillary, *Euptoieta hegesia hoffmanni* (Nymphalidae), has avoided predaceous ants that were patrolling the host plant.**

The larva of the giant swallowtail, *Papilio cresphontes* (Papilionidae), does a passable imitation of a very large bird dropping.

OPPOSITE BOTTOM: While not as dramatic as the following, the Jamaican larvae of the Mexican fritillary, *Euptoieta hegesia* (Nymphalidae), change their appearance between the second and third instar. The later instar (top) has developed longitudinal white lines. The black dots adjacent to the lines will merge in subsequent instars until the white lines are edged with black. The brick-red color of the younger instar (bottom) will eventually give way to a blood red, almost maroon, color that reinforces the lines.

of predators a caterpillar must deal with also change with caterpillar size. Small larvae are more commonly the prey of other invertebrates, such as beetles, spiders, wasps and small parasitoids. Small larvae may not be worth the effort of larger predators, such as birds, lizards and mammals, but large larvae become choice, worthwhile food items.

A mostly tubular caterpillar may also augment any color-reduced visibility by resting on an appropriate background: on a stem rather than on a flat leaf surface. And if there should happen to be a pattern on the caterpillar's body that imitates the appearance of the stem, then so much the better. Regardless of its current appearance, one of the few advantages that a caterpillar has is the ability to change its appearance at each molt. At

133

Caterpillars may change their appearance dramatically between molts. Here a larva of the spicebush swallowtail, *Papilio troilus* (Papilionidae), has just "stepped out of its skin" and, in the process, goes from looking like a bird dropping to resembling a snake.

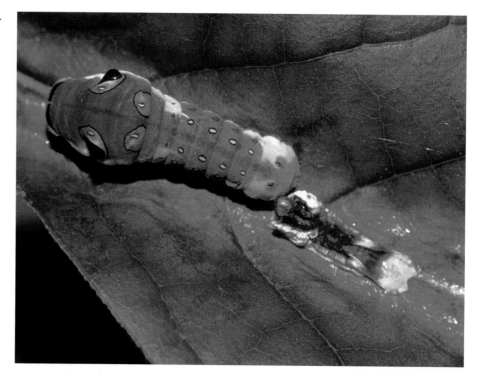

its most extreme, this can involve wonderful camouflage: many anglewings (*Polygonia* sp.; Nymphalidae) resemble bird droppings as caterpillars, and this resemblance becomes more pronounced with each succeeding molt. Such species combine their appearance with appropriate behavior and rest in full view on the tops of leaves, where one would *expect* to encounter a bird dropping.

Some species become progressively more warningly colored, or aposematic, in later stages. For example, the caterpillar of the spicebush swallowtail, *Papilio troilus* (Papilionidae), goes from looking like a bird dropping to imitating a rather fierce-looking snake! Many swallowtails, in addition to being cryptic or brilliantly colored and patterned, or chemically defended, also defend themselves with a retractable fleshy tubercle called an "osmeterium." The osmeteria, which are normally hidden but can be extended or everted if the caterpillar is disturbed sufficiently, are usually bright orange or red and release an unpleasant odor. Even without the odor, their appearance, not unlike the forked tongue of a snake, can be quite startling (and, in the case of the spicebush swallowtail, reinforces

134

LEFT: The resemblance of the spicebush swallowtail caterpillar, *Papilio troilus* (Papilionidae), to a snake increases as it gets larger.

BELOW: Swallowtail larvae have an additional defense mechanism: an osmeterium. Here we see it in action in the pipevine swallowtail, *Battus philenor* (Papilionidae). The larva, feeding on a flower of *Aristolochia erecta* (Aristolochiaceae), responds to a predator by everting the brightly colored Y-shaped osmeteria behind its head. It "rears," then angles its head towards the predator to ensure that the predator gets a good strong sniff of the foul osmeterial secretion.

their similarity to the head of a snake).

Another strategy used by caterpillars to protect themselves from those that would use them as food is to group together in clumps of larvae. This strategy relies on the assumption that "there's strength in numbers" and is species dependent, usually, on the egg-laying pattern of the female. This means that gregariousness is not so much a strategy as it is a species trait; still, it can be quite effective. Individual caterpillars may be cryptic, but together they become quite conspicuous. If the species is one that

Gregarious larvae, like these bordered patch caterpillars, *Chlosyne lacinia* (Nymphalidae), present a "unified defense." Note the variation, a polymorphism where there are three identifiable morphs, in the caterpillars of this species. The combination of black, orange, and black and orange caterpillars is a strong warning signal to predators.

Some gregarious larvae, like these caterpillars of the Baltimore, *Euphydryas phaeton* (Nymphalidae), live in a silken web that also acts to deter potential predators and parasites.

incorporates defensive chemical compounds in their bodies, then any predator that attacks an individual caterpillar soon learns to leave the group of caterpillars alone. Such groups also gain the advantage of being able to present a group response to intruders. Many caterpillars will "twitch" in response to disturbance, likely an attempt to startle the intruder, but when a single individual of a group is disturbed, *all* of the caterpillars twitch. It can be, and often is, a very effective display that discourages many predacious birds.

The caterpillars of many Lycaneids depend on ants to protect them from harm. This symbiotic relationship benefits both parties since the larvae provide the ants with a nutritious "nectar" from pore cupola organs on their abdomens. Here, a group of ants, *Oecophylla* sp. (Hymenoptera; Formicinae), tend a centaur oak blue larva (*Arhopala pseudocentaurus*; Lycaenidae).

Some caterpillars do not fare so well with ants. Here a "sugar ant" that normally visits the extra-floral nectaries of *Turnera ulmifolia* (Turneraceae), the host plant of the Mexican fritillary, *Euptoieta hegesia* (Nymphalidae), in Jamaica, attacks an early instar larva.

Gregarious species such as many *Euphydryas* sp. (Nymphalidae) also tend to live in webs. Originally, the web may have been a simple consequence of many larvae, all laying down silk trails, living together in close proximity. It is likely that, by augmenting the number of silk threads and then living within the resulting "tent," the group gains protection against a wide variety of invertebrate predators and parasitoids.

Another defense, used by up to one-third of all butterflies, is to attract—and subvert—a group of predators into protecting the caterpillars. Ants are ubiquitous, so it should come as no surprise that they can be quite voracious predators of caterpillars. Because of their social lifestyle, ants work in concert to effect specific goals, and the gathering of food is one of those common activities. Food, for many ant species, includes the nectar of plants and flowers, and the larvae of Lycaenids and Riodinines have evolved to make use of this preference. The caterpillars of many species in these families have specialized organs, generally on the upper side of their abdomen, that provide sugary secretions, and even have other organs that produce sounds that are attractive to ants. The ants, in essence, "farm" the caterpillars for their nectar (which often contains compounds that the ants cannot obtain from plants) and in so doing protect them against parasitoids and predators.

Of course, plants have also recruited ants to defend themselves against insect herbivores such as butterfly caterpillars. The relationship between ants and plants, called myrmecophily, is very old and is thought to underlie the evolution of plant traits such as extra-floral nectaries (nectar-producing glands that are not in flowers). The caterpillars cuckold the plant by making the ants both traitors (they're eating the plant tissues that the ants are supposed to be defending) and sentinels (the ants protect the caterpillars against other predators and parasites that would also be, inadvertently, protecting the plant). Phil DeVries, author of *The Butterflies*

A caterpillar of a Costa Rican Riodinid butterfly, *Juditha molpe* (Lycaenidae), visits an extrafloral nectary of its passion-vine host plant, *Passiflora auriculata* (Passifloraceae), while being tended by *Delichodeus* sp. ants that are also visiting the nectaries. By interposing itself in the mutualistic relationship between the ant and the plant—and offering a reward to the ants—the butterfly has ready access to a host that is vigorously defended against competing herbivores, as well as gaining a large contingent of pugnacious bodyguards that will protect it from predators and parasitoids.

of Costa Rica, calls this subversion—the caterpillar invasion of an ant-plant mutualism—"adding insult to herbivory."

Of course, none of these factors can (or should) be taken in isolation: a caterpillar must deal with all of these problems simultaneously. All things being equal (which they never are), the caterpillar that has the most nutritious food will grow and develop fastest. This is important because every day that a caterpillar spends on a plant is another day that it could be found by something that wants to eat it. But even here, the trade-offs between growth and potential benefits are rather murky. If a caterpillar can successfully evade the many predators and parasitoids that it encounters (or that encounter it), and can find a nutritious food supply that allows it to grow up big and strong, then it may finally reach the point where another change of life must be undertaken: the final molt into the pupa or chrysalid.

Gregarious larvae often give rise to gregarious pupae. Here a family group of black-veined whites, *Aporia crataegi* (Pieridae), have pupated together on a branch of their host plant, bird cherry, *Padus avium* (Rosaceae), a small tree.

Most chrysalids are solitary, although clumps often form in favored locations. The gulf fritillary pupa, *Agraulis vanillae* (Nymphalidae), shown here is nearing eclosion (the cuticle of the chrysalis has become transparent and the wings are visible).

The Big Sleep

The caterpillar, often after a short resting period, wanders away from its host plant in search of a place to begin the transformation into a butterfly. Some species pupate directly on the host plant, but most undergo a

Sexual characters of the developing butterflies become apparent for the first time with the pupae, although the differences are not usually as pronounced as those seen here in a comparison of the male (top) and female (bottom) pupae of the orange tip, *Anthocharis cardamines* (Pieridae).

wandering period before finally settling down to their final molt. This is when the spinnerets and silk glands finally come into their own. The majority of species spin a loose, but firmly attached, silk pad on the substrate of their chosen pupation site and then fix themselves to it with their cremaster, a small anal hook. The position of the chrysalis is characteristic in most families (see plate 3, page 33), with most Papilionids, Pierids and many Lycaenids being upright or horizontal and spinning a U-shaped girdle, kind of like an electrical worker's safety harness, around their thorax to hold them in position. Most others hang, head down, although a few species pupate in loose soil, under leaf litter or in a loosely spun, crude cocoon.

In some ways (and certainly in ecological terms), the pupal stage is similar to the egg stage because both are immobile and dependent on position and any inherent characteristics for their protection from the elements, disease, parasites and predators. Even in developmental terms, the similarity is striking, because both the egg and the pupa are "assembly" stages; that is, both proceed from "raw" materials to a more complex stage. Throughout the life history of moths and butterflies, each stage is progressively more complex than the last. The penultimate pupal stage is both more complex than a caterpillar and less complex than the adult butterfly, since it involves the dissolution of the larval body and the simultaneous manufacture of the imaginal one.

People always seem to be surprised when I tell them that, by the time a caterpillar has shed its final exoskeleton and taken on the appearance of a chrysalis, it is already well on its way to becoming a butterfly. Metamorphosis begins long before the last larval instar but accelerates during the resting period before the caterpillar finds a final pupation site.

During this period, called the prepupal stadium, the chemical building blocks that compose the body of the caterpillar begin to be recycled as the body is slowly taken apart. At the same time, the imaginal disks, regions of previously undifferentiated cells that act as organizing centers for the adult tissues, begin directing the assembly of the butterfly body from the released building blocks. Generally, as the larval tissues are disassembled, adult tissues take their place, but how this occurs is still pretty much a mystery.

One major ecological difference between an egg and a pupa is that a pupa is much bigger than an egg and therefore is a considerably larger "prize" to a foraging predator. Researcher Richard White once lamented that "the problem with butterflies" was that too few biologists were studying the immature life-history stages of their subjects, and that we should give more attention, especially, to the pupal stage. His reasoning was that, because the process of metamorphosis involves the simultaneous disassembly and reassembly of the body, a pupa is really just a sac of freely available, predigested chemical building blocks that would be very attractive to predators. It's probably also true that pupae are the prey of larger predators than those that go looking for eggs. Still, the situations are similar enough that many of the same ecological pressures apply.

Variation in pupal color can hide or reveal a chrysalis to predators. The color of the pupae of the black swallowtail, *Papilio polyxenes* (Papilionidae), can range from brown to green. The green chrysalid on the branch at right would probably be at a disadvantage in the wild. The pupa in the center is not a different color morph but has cleared, revealing the butterfly preparing to emerge.

Neither larval nor pupal color can protect the immature butterfly from parasitoids. Here a short-tailed Ichneumon wasp (Hymenoptera; Ichneumonidae), has emerged from the chrysalid of a black swallowtail, *Papilio polyxenes* (Papilionidae).

A pupa's primary defense against predation is its immobility and camouflage: the closer to the appearance of "lifelessness," the better. Some species, like the viceroy (*Limenitis archippus*; Nymphalidae), hide within rolled or folded leaves, while others, such as a variety of skippers (*Thymelicus* sp., *Hesperia* sp.; Hesperiidae), construct a loose nest or tent of silk. The grayling (*Hipparchia semele*; Nymphalidae) and the spring azure (*Celastrina* sp.; Lycaenidae) hide in loose soil or under rocks and dead leaves. Other Lycaenids, such as *Jalmenus evagorus* from Australia, pupate within the nests of their ant prey. Here they are completely defended against predators and parasites because they have taken on the "odor" of the colony and are considered "one of the family." Once they eclose, they lose their pheromonal protection, however, and are, at the most vulnerable moment of their adult lives, in danger of being attacked by the ants that they've been successfully cuckolding. Intriguingly, such species sometimes have superfluous, easily removed scales. Suggestions have been advanced that the scales may aid the freshly eclosed butterfly by giving the ants something inconsequential to bite, or that they help prevent more serious scale loss while climbing up to the surface through the narrow nest entrance before expanding their wings.

Pupal crypsis or camouflage may involve resembling some natural part of the environment such as a dead leaf, the general background of the pupation site, or background matching in both color and structure. Many Papilionids and Pierids are capable of modifying their cuticle color to match the substrate on which they pupate; however, mistakes—for example, being green against a brown background—are usually fatal. Some pupae, such as those of *Mechanitis* sp. (Nymphalidae), are so brilliantly

Chrysalids like that of this Ithomiid, *Mechanitis* sp. (Nymphalidae), that are brightly shiny or reflective would appear to be prime candidates for predation, but the mirror-like reflection allows them to take on the appearance of their surroundings and makes them well camouflaged.

Even at this late stage, molting and eclosure errors can be hazardous to a butterfly's life. This painted lady, *Vanessa cardui* (Nymphalidae), photographed near Goshen in New York State, has a large piece of its pupal case still attached to its abdomen. Such errors are so disastrous that they are rarely seen in nature.

shiny and mirror-like that at first glance they appear to be anything but cryptic. But being silver or metallic is extremely useful because, from only a moderate distance away, the reflective surface takes on the appearance of whatever site the pupa has found itself in.

Pupae are also subject to very similar environmental mortality sources as eggs, due to seasonal mistiming of prevailing weather conditions and the length of time that they remain pupae. Development rate during the pupal stage—and thus the length of the stage, like that of the egg stage and the growth of the caterpillar—is dependent on temperature, humidity and day length. Too much of a good thing, that is, overexposure to sun or wind, can also be dangerous. On average, most species spend from four to fourteen days as a chrysalis, but pupation can take as long as two years in some arctic species.

Pupae have access to one defense that eggs do not: limited movement. I don't mean that pupae can move from place to place, but, like caterpillars,

OPPOSITE: A gulf fritillary, *Agraulis vanillae* (Nymphalidae), hangs from its pupal case near Oracabessa, Jamaica. It has successfully expanded its wings and is waiting for them to dry. If you look carefully you can see a drop of meconium on the abdomen.

147

Some Heliconiines, like this zebra longwing, *Heliconius charithonia* (Nymphalidae), are pupal maters—males actually insert their abdomen into the female pupa before, or just as, it ecloses. The only description that does this habit justice, certainly from the female point of view, is "rape."

they are capable of anti-predator or anti-parasite "jerking." Pupae often twitch or jerk in response to a disturbance; however, this in itself can be dangerous since it may dislodge the pupa. If the pupa falls to the ground, the chances are that it will either break open (pupae, like caterpillars, are hydrostatically pressurized) or become the prey of roving terrestrial predators.

When metamorphosis is complete, the butterfly ecloses: wet, crumpled wings not yet expanded—and vulnerable. This is a dangerous time, since the butterfly is unable to fly away and is not really built for walking any distance. They don't even have the option of dropping to the ground, because most must assume a hanging position in order to pump up and dry the wings so that they stay flat. To make matters worse, freshly eclosed females are actively sought by males, because, as you will shortly learn, virgin females are a limited resource for males.

Given the chance, males will mate with a female long before she has any choice in the matter. Some species, such as the zebra longwing (*Heliconius charithonia*; Heliconiidae) have gone so far as to not even bother to wait for the female to eclose; instead, they insert their abdomen into the pupa and mate with the female up to a day *before* she emerges. It's not unusual to find an active group of males swarming over a female pupa.

In many butterfly species females are larger than males. This has as much to do with increased weight due to the eggs that she carries as it does with the earlier pupation of males so that they emerge before the females. Here, the male (below, wings closed) of a mating pair of white peacocks, *Anartia jatrophe* (Nymphalidae), is only about half of the size of the female.

149

The head of a butterfly, a little glasswing skipper, *Pompeius verna* (Hesperiidae), has pairs of large eyes, elongated antennae and a proboscis. Together with the advent of wings and long articulated legs (note also the tibial spur on the leg), they presage a total change of lifestyle.

Changes in Lifestyle

Butterflies are reproduction engines. As caterpillars are to growth, butterflies are to reproduction. Author and researcher Matt Douglas once described butterflies as nothing more than "flying sex organs and dispersal agents." All of the things that we admire about butterflies—their colorful wings, their ability to fly and their close association with flowers—are superb adaptations to accomplish a relatively simple goal: ensure that there is another generation of butterflies. But that is far more problematic than it sounds.

To this point in our perusal of the ecology of eggs, caterpillars and pupae, we haven't considered sex at all—neither as a factor inherent to the biology of the stages nor as a characteristic that explains differences

150

between individuals. The reason is that there's really no such thing as a male or a female caterpillar or egg; they simply don't have any gross sexual characteristics upon which we can hang a name. Of course, all eggs and caterpillars will eventually become either male or female, but, for the most part, during those stages what they *will be* does not affect what they *are*. One exception is that females of many species are larger than males. To become larger, they must feed more, or feed longer, as caterpillars, and generally they take the latter option. This means that they may be vulnerable to predators and parasites for a longer period than caterpillars that will become males. Pupae, on the other hand, do have sexual characteristics, that is, the sexes can be distinguished, but this doesn't have a great bearing on their relationship to their environment.

One look at the most apparent body features of a butterfly should immediately tell you something about their biology and ecology. The head is dominated by three structures that were almost invisible during the caterpillar stage: a pair of huge compound eyes, two elongate and noticeably clubbed antennae, and the coiled proboscis. All of a sudden, they have wings where there were none before, and even the long, articulated legs have become very different from the short, stubby ones of the larva. From these clues, it is easy to surmise that the senses, such as sight, smell and even aspects of touch, are far more important to a butterfly than they were to a caterpillar. And the development of wings and the change in visible mouth parts presage a complete shift in how they get around and what kinds of food they eat.

Butterflies have excellent sensory capabilities. They're able to see color

The proboscis (haustellum) is composed of two galae or lobes that must be fused together soon after eclosure. The hollow center is used, like a straw, to suck up liquid nourishment, like the tree sap being fed on here by a tawny emperor, *Asterocampa clyton* (Nymphalidae).

151

and can, in fact, see "colors" that we can't. Butterflies have the widest visual spectrum of any animal and are able to see from the red end of the spectrum all the way to the near ultraviolet. (In comparison, we can see red but not ultraviolet, and bees can see ultraviolet but not red.) A butterfly's eyes are compound; that is, they're composed of many individual facets (ommatidia). While they do not have the visual acuity or sharpness that many animals do, they are very good at sensing the slightest movement. The antennae are used to sense vibration (including sound and air movement that can be interpreted as flight direction and attitude) as well as chemical signals (what we would call odors). They're also used in tactile (touching) encounters between sexes. The feet (tarsi) have chemical receptors that allow them to "taste" whatever they land on, useful both for finding food and for assessing potential host plants. There are additional "food receptors" on the end of the proboscis that tells them when to begin feeding.

While the freshly eclosed, teneral butterfly's wings are drying, the butterfly must accomplish three very important tasks before it can begin its new life: It must dispose of the waste products, called "meconium," from its last larval meal and the transfiguration process. The meconium, a bright red, almost blood-colored fluid, must be voided before the butterfly can fly. The new butterfly must also join together the two halves of its new tubular proboscis so that the enclosed channel between them can serve as the drinking straw that it's intended to be. Without a working proboscis, the butterfly won't be able to acquire the necessary energy to fuel the flight machinery. Finally, it must clean any remaining dead cells and old shed skin off of its new antennae so that the sensilla (sensory organs) are unencumbered and ready to do their work.

Sex, Survival and the Single Butterfly

Butterflies are, by their very nature, the most active—and thus the most conspicuous—stage of the life history. The addition of wings has made them appear to be much larger than they are, even though the average

OPPOSITE BOTTOM: The caterpillar stage of the butterfly life cycle—due to their relatively poor escape abilities and the length of time that they remain at this stage—is the most dangerous. Here a fifth instar larva of the Mexican fritillary, *Euptoieta hegesia hoffmanni* (Nymphalidae), has succumbed to, and then been swarmed by, predaceous fire ants, *Solenopsis invicta* (Hymenoptera; Formicidae).

LEFT: The hazards of butterfly life are plentiful. Here a gulf fritillary, *Agraulis vanillae* (Nymphalidae), has just been caught in a spider web. Intriguingly, research has shown that the majority of butterflies that get caught like this are males.

153

RIGHT: **Orb weavers like this yellow garden spider,** *Argiope aurantia* **(Araneidae), wrap up large prey, an unknown butterfly in this case, to immobilize them.**

BELOW: **The behavior of "mate-carrying," where one butterfly carries the other while still copulating, can be doubly dangerous. A pair of Satyrines, the gatekeeper,** *Pyronia tithonus* **(Nymphalidae), is caught here—still conjoined.**

154

butterfly weighs only about one-third of what it did as a caterpillar. Regardless, the activities that they undertake—flying, feeding, mate locating and egg laying—ensure that we, as well as prospective predators, take note of them. There's little doubt that most butterflies are more conspicuous and easily seen than caterpillars, and, unless you're actively looking for them, we rarely (if ever) see pupae or eggs. But there are fewer butterflies than there were pupae, many fewer pupae than there were caterpillars, and far fewer larvae than there were eggs; butterflies are the rarest stage of the life history.

In many species, only one or two out of every hundred eggs will survive to become a butterfly. Mortality rates vary with life-history stage—from 10 to 60 percent for eggs to 45 to 90 percent for pupae—but the most dangerous and vulnerable stage of the life cycle is the caterpillar. In any case, the potential for mortality—from inherent complexity (each molt is a complex sequence of events during which any single thing that goes wrong can be disastrous), environmental uncertainty, fungi and pathogens, parasites and parasitoids, and from predators—looms large in the immature stages. And, as you will see, it doesn't really get any easier for the reproductively mature, adult stage.

In some ways, butterflies face the same kinds of ecological pressures as caterpillars do. They must avoid predators when they're active as well as when they're inactive, and they must do so while they undertake other business (eating and growing as caterpillars versus locating mates and reproducing as butterflies). To do this, they adopt a number of similar strategies, including camouflage or crypsis (look—and act—like the background), and warning coloration or aposematism (advertise the presence of chemical defenses or substances that make you taste bad), but also add a few new strategies to their defensive arsenal. The big problem is how to balance mate attraction and reproduction with predator avoidance and survival. A butterfly can't do one without the other. Whether the butterfly does not survive to mate, or mates, but then does not survive to successfully reproduce, is moot: the end result is the same—they won't get their genes into the next generation of butterflies.

OPPOSITE: **Even carnivorous plants can catch butterflies, as seen in this unique photo of a grayling, *Hipparchia semele* (Nymphalidae), caught by a sundew, *Drosera rotundifolia* (Drosaceae), in the Netherlands.**

Life and Death: Games Butterflies Play

The variety of potential predators of butterflies is staggering: birds, mammals, lizards, amphibians, dragonflies, spiders, assassin bugs and more. Some of these, such as web-spinning or crab spiders and ambush bugs, are typical "sit and wait" predators. This strategy can be, and is, very successful (which is why there are so many kinds of sit-and-wait predators), and it's not unusual to find butterflies trapped by them. Even some plants, such as the carnivorous sundews or the intricately "clawed" flowers of milkweeds, act as sit-and-wait predators of butterflies. But, such predators are relatively "casual"—they're sitting and waiting, but they don't really care what comes by; they'll catch anything within range of their mandibles, claws, sticky hairs, complex flowers or whatever. There's little that a

Crab spiders, like this goldenrod spider, *Misumena vatia* (Thomisidae) with its inornate ringlet prey, *Coenonympha inornata* (Nymphalidae; Satyrinae), are effective predators of butterflies. This particular species of crab spider may be white or yellow depending on the flower it waits within.

156

RIGHT: Flowers also have their dangers. Here a small or cabbage white, *Pieris rapae* (Pieridae), has been caught by its proboscis in a groove of the gynostegium (central column) of a common milkweed, *Asclepias syriaca* (Asclepiadaceae). Note the pollinia (pollen sacs) on the leg and the palps of the butterfly.

BELOW: Visiting some flowers is a dangerous proposition if a sit-and-wait predator is lingering to nab an unsuspecting visitor. In this photo an ambush bug, *Phymata* sp. (Hemiptera; Phymatidae), holds its prey, a small or cabbage white, *Pieris rapae* (Pieridae).

OPPOSITE: An unsuspecting Japanese skipper, *Parnara guttata* (Hesperiidae), has become the prey of a Chinese mantid, *Tenodera aridifolia* (Orthoptera; Mantidae). Note the removed forewing in the flower.

Not strictly a sit-and-wait predator, jumping spiders (Salticidae) like this one feeding on a European skipper, *Thymelicus lineola* (Hesperiidae), also forage for their prey.

The crab spider with spread forelegs that resemble the front claws of a crab, waits to nab any insect that visits this *Turnera ulmifolia* flower (Turneraceae). Here an ant means double jeopardy to an unsuspecting flower visitor. Butterflies that do not "look before they leap" are best known by their other name: prey.

A variety of active predators prey on butterflies including this skimmer dragonfly, *Libellula* sp. (Odonata; Libellulidae), that has captured a tawny emperor, *Asterocampa clyton* (Nymphalidae).

ABOVE: **Caterpillars are more liable to succumb to a predator than are adults. Here a paper wasp, *Polistes metricus* (Hymenoptera; Vespidae), looking to provision a cell in her nest, attacks a black swallowtail larva, *Papilio polyxenes* (Papilionidae). Note the everted osmeteria of the caterpillar in response to this attack.**

LEFT: **This gulf fritillary,** *Agraulis vanillae* **(Nymphalidae), has become the prey of a robber fly,** *Promachus hinei* **(Diptera, Asilidae).**

OPPOSITE BOTTOM: **Birds are common predators of butterflies as evidenced by the relative commonness of "beak-marked" adults. Here a rufous-tailed Jacamar,** *Galbula ruficauda* **(Galbulidae), eats a blue Morpho,** *Morpho peleides* **(Nymphalidae) in Costa Rica.**

Lizards like this anole, *Anolis* sp. (Squamata; Iguanidae) eating a moth in the Dominican Republic, on the Caribbean island of Hispaniola, are frequent and important predators of butterflies (and moths) in tropical and subtropical regions.

butterfly can do to avoid these kinds of predators save being alert and watchful: avoid "funny-looking" flowers, don't land on anything without checking it first, and so on.

The other kinds of predators, active predators that specifically seek out butterflies, regardless of whether they're birds, lizards, dragonflies or whatever, are united by one trait: they hunt by sight. Butterflies can, and have, developed defenses against visually hunting predators. The trade-off comes in balancing color and size, which are useful in attracting mates, with regulating heat and their ability to fly (a process known as "thermoregulation") and the details of wing pattern. Butterfly sight is not sharp enough to discern the finer points of another butterfly's wing pattern, but the eyes of visually hunting predators are. So the wing patterns of

164

To avoid predators, butterflies have elevated camouflage or crypsis to a fine art. Here a cracker, *Hamadryas amphycloe* (Nymphalidae), perches in a typical pose on the trunk of a tree. Their finely detailed markings echo the color and pattern of the bark perfectly.

Besides finely detailed markings, another component of crypsis is to break up a recognizable outline with a complex wing shape. This is typical of many anglewing butterflies, like this question mark, *Polygonia interrogationis* (Nymphalidae), feeding on animal "residue." The silver marks on the underside of the hindwing are the "question mark" of its common name.

The opposite of "blending in to your background" is to stand out from it. Warning coloration, illustrated by this isabella heliconian, *Euides isabella* (Nymphalidae), sends a message of "I'm not good to eat" to a prospective predator.

butterflies have become incredibly detailed, not because of their own eyes, but because they can use this detail to fool the animals that would hunt them down. I call them "talking wings" because butterflies use their wings for more than just flight.

HIDE AND SEEK . . .

Like caterpillars, butterflies have become adept at imitating parts of their environment. Some butterflies, such as the Indian leaf butterfly, *Kallima inachus* (Nymphalidae), look so much like dead leaves, right down to imperfections such as fungus spots and torn edges, that it boggles the mind. Others, such as *Hamadryas* sp. (Nymphalidae), have such finely detailed patterns that they blend in perfectly with the bark of the trees that they rest on, or, like *Polygonia* sp. (Nymphalidae), have such complex wing shapes that they are virtually undetectable resting among the dry leaves on the forest floor. The trick is to both look and act like the background. The message is "I'm not here!" If they don't move, and they don't look like food, then the chances are that they will be invisible to predators. The problem is

166

that butterflies can't spend all of their time imitating the background: they have to go out looking for food, mates or host plants sometime. Movement advertises presence and negates the "I'm not here!" message. So, an alternative to camouflage is its exact opposite: bright colors and bold patterns that cannot fail to be noticed and can upset the eye, or (assuming they have the chemical protection to back it up) the stomach, of a potential predator.

Warning colors and patterns take a variety of forms, and the strategies employed, and the messages conveyed, also vary from "I'm not good to eat" to "I'm not what you thought I was." Many butterflies are cryptic, or camouflaged, on the underside of the wings, and aposematic, or warningly colored, on the upper side. The Mexican fritillary, *Euptoieta hegesia* (Nymphalidae), with its bright orange and black upper side and cryptic brown-patterned underside, is a fine example. Having access to these alternatives is useful because the butterfly has two options to protect itself: close its wings and blend in with the background, or hold its wings open and advertise that it may not be good to eat. Butterflies that are behaving cryptically, resting or perching with their wings closed, but are discovered by a predator such as a bird or a lizard, will often flick open their wings and "flash" their warning colors. When they immediately close their wings up, concealing the warning colors, they leave the startled predator—that now has a search image of a brightly colored prey—wondering why the food has disappeared.

Many butterflies hedge their bets by combining underside crypsis with dorsal warning coloration, but because forewings are longer than hindwings, the tips that stick out are often cryptic like the rest of the underside. Some butterflies have developed a "flash" and "conceal" strategy that takes advantage of this. The painted lady, *Vanessa cardui* (Nymphalidae), shown here is able to be cryptic ("conceal," left) but can "flash" bold colors to disorient a predator by simply flicking its forewings forward (right).

Another strategy to avoid predation is to direct the attack of a predator to a less vulnerable part of the body: set up a "false head." The champions of this strategy are Lycaenids and the combination of converging lines and an "eyespot" at the anal angle, as seen in this *Arawacus sito* (Lycaenidae; Riodininae), works to deceive.

This "flash and conceal" strategy is employed by a large number of species and has been progressively fine-tuned by some until all that's necessary is to flick the forewings forward from behind the hindwings. If you look closely, the undersides of the forewing tips, just the area near the apex of the wing, of species such as the red admiral or the painted ladies (*Vanessa* sp.; Nymphalidae) are cryptically patterned just like the underside of the hindwing. The reason is simply that the forewings are longer than the hindwings, so the tips always stick out. But just behind those cryptic forewing tips is a bold stripe of bright pink or red. The butterfly doesn't even have to open its wings, just flick the forewings forward until the color shows, startling the predator, then hide the color and "disappear" into the background.

TRUTH OR DARE . . .

Other butterflies use a combination of cryptic coloration and misdirection to protect their most sensitive body parts. While flash-and-conceal techniques work to fool a predator's eye for a fraction of a second—and are usually a "last ditch" defense—the various misdirection elements attempt to prolong and intensify the protection. Butterflies employ an arsenal of potentially misleading elements to "lie" to predators. The elements of this defense include lines of pattern that can lead the eye of a predator, elements that disrupt the recognizable outline of the wings, a few large or many small eyespot-pattern elements on wing edges, and the presence of "tails" on the anal angle of the hindwings. When combined with a battery of strategic behaviors, these elements present a remarkably believable and unified message: "Bite me here!" A wonderful example of this is found in the neotropical hairstreaks of the genus *Arawacus*.

Eyespots on the wings are so common within some subfamilies of the Nymphalidae (Brassolinae, Satyrinae, Morphinae, Charaxinae, etc.) that the common names of the groups frequently refer to this characteristic. Some eyespots are so incredibly detailed (e.g., most any *Caligo* sp.,

The "proof is in the pudding!" Here we see two different adults of the neotropical mosaic, *Colobura dirce* (Nymphalidae), perched in typical head-down fashion on the trunks of trees. The damage to the anal angle of the butterfly on the right is symmetrical, meaning it affects both hindwings and is probably the result of a single predator attack, and beautifully illustrates the effectiveness of the "false head."

169

Eyespots are common in butterflies and are thought to be anti-predator devices. That they work is wonderfully shown by this photo of an owl butterfly, *Caligo atreus* (Nymphalidae), taken in Costa Rica. The beak-shaped tear centered on the hindwing eyespot is the result of a failed attack by a bird.

OPPOSITE BOTTOM: Even without a defined eyespot, the location of the bright contrasting color marks, the pronounced tails and the wing markings that converge on those two features attract a predator's attention away from the real head of this Canadian tiger swallowtail, *Papilio canadensis* (Papilionidae).

Brassolinae) that you'd swear they *were* eyes, while others are rudimentary but usually colorful contrasts with other pattern elements on the wings (e.g., many swallowtails; Papilionidae). The function of eyespots is simple: direct the attack of a predator away from life-threatening sensitive body parts to the relatively insensitive wings. It works because most vertebrate predators have learned that the eyes of their prey are sensitive to attacks. It's not unusual to find butterflies with evidence (beak or jaw marks of a predator—imprinted on the wings—visible as missing scales or missing areas of the wing that formerly included an eyespot) of the attack-attracting

LEFT: Lycaenids combine the appearance of a "false head" with movement to attract a predator's attention. After alighting, these butterflies appear to "rub" their hindwings together, causing the "antennae" to move like this Jamaican St. Christopher's hairstreak, *Chlorostrymon simaethis* (Lycaenidae).

power of eyespots. It's much better to lose an insignificant part of the trailing edge of a wing, which doesn't even put a severe crimp in your flight ability, than to risk damage to any part of the body.

Some species (actually whole families and evolutionary lineages) do not have, or are unable to develop, detailed eyespot elements on their wings. For these species, the best alternative is to combine a poor "eyespot" (more often than not, simply an area of contrasting color that often does not occur elsewhere on the wing, surrounded by one or a few concentric pattern bands) with other elements that "lead the predator's eye" away from the head. In essence, the elements combine to produce a "false head" that the predator mistakes for the most sensitive part of its prey. Converging

Butterflies such as this gray hairstreak, *Strymon melinus* (Lycaenidae), move their hindwings to reveal that the upper side of the hindwing also has a rudimentary eyespot.

lines of pattern can "lead" the eye to the convergence point where a small or rudimentary eyespot will be most noticed. The convergence point is usually at the anal angle of the hindwings (not insignificantly the farthest point from the real head!), which is where hindwing tails can be found. The tails give the impression of antennae or horns to strengthen the illusion.

The tiger swallowtail, *Papilio glaucus* (Papilionidae), with its black and yellow tiger stripe pattern that converges on the anal angle where the wing tails and the bright blue eyespot are, is a reasonable example, but the masters of this falsehood are members of the Lycaenidae. These little butterflies combine all of the pattern elements (anal eyespot, converging lines and anal tails) with behaviors that reinforce the appearance of a false head: they simply "rub" their closed wings together. By alternately moving their left and right hindwings, they make it appear that the "antennae" are

172

Despite the bright black and yellow warning colors, and almost indolent flight style, even zebra longwings, *Heliconius charithonia* (Nymphalidae), are not immune to attacks from predators. This individual has escaped the attack of a bird or two.

moving! An interesting additional note is that part of the upper side of the anal angle of the hindwing is revealed when they rub their wings past each other. It too has an "eyespot."

TO BOLDLY GO . . .

Still other species have chosen, as researcher Deane Bowers once wrote, the "lifestyles of the warningly colored and unpalatable." They advertise their distastefulness at all times, even going so far as to adopt slow, almost "I dare you to attack me" flight styles. The message here is "I taste bad." A perfect example is the zebra longwing, *Heliconius charithonia* (Nymphalidae). The bright black and yellow stripes of this butterfly are an almost perfect advertisement that any predator that attacks them is going to be sorry. They have adopted a flight style that matches their audacious appearance. They fly in plain view, slowly, gently fluttering along with such an obvious confidence that you know that no self-respecting predator is going to think about attacking them. Color patterns that are associated

173

ABOVE: **A female polydamas swallowtail,** *Battus polydamas* **(Papilionidae), carefully places an egg on a fresh young shoot of a pipevine (***Aristolochia*** sp.; Aristolochiaceae).**

with warning coloration include orange on black; combinations of orange, red or yellow and black; and pure white or pure yellow (sometimes with black edges).

The basis of this strategy, of course, is a warning. Butterflies are very precise in their choice of host plants, more often than not limiting themselves to one or a few species of a single genus in a single family. This specialization on relatively few host taxa was the source of lepidopterist Paul Ehrlich and botanist Peter Raven's "coevolution" observations. At its core, they surmised, were differences in the constituent chemical compounds of the various groups of plants used by butterflies as hosts. Briefly, they suggested that plants defended themselves against herbivores by evolving a variety of noxious or deterrent chemical compounds that butterflies (and many other plant-eating insects) have, over time, been able to circumvent. This "arms race" continued to escalate, with plants alternately escaping from herbivores through the development of novel compounds or falling prey to herbivores that have adapted to the compounds. Some butterfly lineages

LEFT: The larvae of Heliconiines, like this gulf fritillary, *Agraulis vanillae* (Nymphalidae), on *Passiflora suberosa* (Passifloraceae) in Jamaica, feed on host plants containing compounds that release hydrogen cyanide. Some Heliconiine species manufacture their own cyanogenic compounds while others are now known to obtain them from their host plants.

OPPOSITE: Warning coloration, or, when combined with a chemical defense, aposematic coloration, is used by caterpillars as well as adults. The bold black and white stripes, with their contrasting yellow marks, of this queen butterfly larva, *Danaus gilippus* (Nymphalidae), warn predators that they contain noxious substances.

have gone so far as to accumulate the defensive chemistry of plants in their own tissues for their own defense, and this is the ultimate basis of aposematism, or warning coloration.

For example, pipevine swallowtail butterflies (*Battus* sp.; Papilionidae) lay their eggs only on plants in the family Aristolochiaceae, the pipevines. These plants contain compounds (aristolochic acids) that the caterpillars incorporate into their bodies as a very effective defense. Other species, such as the monarch, *Danaus plexippus* (Nymphalidae), feed on plants in the Apocynaceae or Asclepiadaceae, the milkweed family, and sequester

cardenolides or cardiac glycosides (compounds that act much like digitalis, itself a plant product from the foxglove, *Digitalis pupurea*, Scrophulariaceae) for their own defense. *Heliconius* butterflies feed on a variety of passion vines, *Passiflora* sp. (Passifloraceae), which contain compounds that release hydrogen cyanide. Specialization has reached extremes in this group because some *Heliconius* species will use only a single species of *Passiflora* as a host, and others have gone so far as to manufacture their own cyanogenic compounds instead of sequestering it from their hosts.

Not all sequestration of plant compounds is completely effective. The buckeye caterpillar, *Junonia coenia* (Nymphalidae), feeds on a wide variety of plant species and families that are similar only in their chemistry. The host plants of this butterfly contain compounds known as iridoid glycosides that protect the caterpillars, but the compounds are metabolized during the pupal stage and the last vestiges of the defense are excreted with the meconium. Thus, these compounds defend the larvae and pupae, but not the adult butterflies. Note, however, that the buckeye is cryptic on the underside and relies on the large eyespots on the upper sides of its wings, and the underside of the forewing tip, for its defense: it's a member of the "flash and conceal" club. I think that a similar phenomenon, a poor (or maybe lacking) adult defense with well-protected caterpillars, also occurs in the Mexican fritillary: this species is likewise cryptic on the underside and boldly patterned in orange and black on the upper side. Intriguingly, the compounds that defend the caterpillars of the Mexican fritillary are the same cyanogenic glycosides used by the brilliantly aposematic *Heliconius* butterflies.

LEFT: The viceroy, *Limenitis archippus* (Nymphalidae), has long been thought to be a superb mimic of the monarch, *Danaus plexippus* (Nymphalidae). Recent research has suggested that the viceroy may be just as unpalatable as its model, so the mimicry may be less one-sided than was once thought.

OPPOSITE: These two buckeye caterpillars, *Junonia coenia* (Nymphalidae), feeding here on Texas paintbrush, *Castilleja indivisia* (Scrophulariaceae), are protected by the chemistry of their host plants, but the chemicals are metabolized during pupation. As a consequence, buckeye butterflies are somewhat cryptic, using camouflage and large eyespots to deceive predators.

The monarch, *Danaus plexippus* (Nymphalidae), shown here nectaring at one of its milkweed host plants (*Asclepias* sp.; Asclepiadaceae), gains protection from predators by advertising that it contains unpalatable host-plant chemicals. Note that the easiest way to tell the viceroy and monarch apart is to examine the hindwing for the presence of a black line that parallels the hindwing margin: monarchs lack this line.

IMITATION IS MORE THAN JUST FLATTERY

In the introduction to this book, I wrote about the marvelous diversity of wing patterns in butterflies, mentioning that the upper and under surfaces usually had completely different but mostly unique patterns. The vast majority of species can be identified by sight, but some butterflies are almost impossible to discern on sight. They are the liars and cheaters of the butterfly world, and they survive largely by raising imitation to new heights of outrageous flattery. The phenomenon is called "mimicry" and it relies on a relatively simple concept: if predators learn to avoid warningly colored butterflies because of their unpalatable chemistry, then any butterfly that imitates the look of the protected species also gains protection. It's a simple idea but it gets a lot more complicated—and far more interesting—than that.

The most famous example of mimicry is probably that of the viceroy, *Limenitis archippus*, for the monarch, *Danaus plexippus*, both in the Nymphalidae. As researcher Lincoln Brower discovered in a well-known series of experiments, the chemically protected monarch elicits an emetic

response in naïve birds that try to eat it (emetic is a fancy term for "make something throw up"). After this experience, the birds quickly learn that monarchs are to be avoided. It was assumed (this should be your first clue that something is not quite right here) that the remarkable resemblance of the viceroy and the monarch was a case of what has become known as "Batesian mimicry" (after author and South American explorer Henry Bates). In this form of mimicry, a palatable mimic (the viceroy, in this case) closely resembles an unpalatable model (the monarch) in order to gain protection from predators.

In south Florida, where monarchs (*Danaus plexippus*; Nymphalidae) are less plentiful, the viceroy, *Limenitis archippus* (Nymphalidae), is much darker and takes on the appearance of the queen, *Danaus gilippus* (Nymphalidae).

179

The evolutionary basis of Batesian mimicry is that a mutation or variant of the mimic species happens to look more like some model species than it does others of its own species. It doesn't really matter how close the resemblance is, just that the variant gains some advantage, however small, by the difference in its appearance. Any further variance in the appearance of the mimic species such that it more closely resembles the model is advantageous, so it, potentially at least, leaves more progeny in the following generation(s). Think of it as an "umbrella" of protection: once the mimic is "under the umbrella," the closer it gets to the center of the umbrella, the better protected it is. After a period of time, the resemblance can be uncanny, as it is between the viceroy and the monarch. The hardest part is getting "under the umbrella" in the first place.

Now, this is all fine and good only as long as one of the models is attacked before a predator meets a palatable mimic. Alternatively, what if the mimics are so much more numerous than the models that a naïve predator is more liable to meet a palatable butterfly first? The answer, such as it is, is that even a little protection is better than none at all. Let's suppose that a mimic outnumbers a model four to one. Chances are that a predator that has never eaten a butterfly that looks quite like our model/mimic pair will, on average, encounter a palatable mimic before it

All over the world, members of the Danainae (Nymphalidae) are models for mimics. In this unique photo, a plain tiger or African wanderer, *Danaus chrysippus* (left) is found nectaring at a Lantana bush (*Lantana camera*; Verbenaceae) alongside a female mimic, *Hypolimnas misippus* (Nymphalidae), in India. Mimicry in action!

An extensive sylvaniform mimicry system from South America. As you might imagine, identifying the species in such large assemblages of similar-appearing taxa requires that they be captured and examined closely. FAR LEFT, TOP TO BOTTOM: *Melinaeae imitata* (Nymphalidae; Ithomiinae), *Eresia philyra* (Nymphalidae; Nymphalinae), *Ceratinia diona* (Nymphalidae; Ithomiinae), unknown. CENTER LEFT (PARTIAL COLUMN): *Mylothria malenka* (Pieridae; Pierinae), *Protogonius cecrops* (Nymphalidae; Nymphalinae). CENTER RIGHT: *Heliconius telchinia* (Nymphalidae; Heliconiinae), *Dismorphia praxinoe* (Pieridae; Dismorphinae), *Ceratinia fenestella* (Nymphalidae; Ithomiinae), unknown. FAR RIGHT: Lycorea atergatis (Nymphalidae; Danainae), *Euides zorcaon* (Nymphalidae; Heliconiinae), *Tithorea hippothous* (Nymphalidae; Ithomiinae), *Mechanitis doryssus* (Nymphalidae; Ithomiinae).

meets a model (actually it's probability of encountering one or the other is always 50 percent since there are only two morphs; however, since there are four times as many of the mimics, they will be encountered more frequently). The crux of the matter is that the very first mimic that is encountered *after* the first encounter with a model, regardless of how many mimics have already been attacked, will be "under the umbrella." A little bit of protection *is* better than nothing!

The problem with the monarch–viceroy system was, as Dr. Brower's former student David Ritland was to discover, that the viceroy was not always as palatable as was assumed. Viceroys from Florida—which more

One of the most interesting mimicry systems—because the participant species vary considerably in how they mimic the models—is based on the pipevine swallowtail, *Battus philenor* (Papilionidae), found in southern North America. The aristolochic acids sequestered from its pipevine host plants, *Aristolochia* sp. (Aristolochiaceae), provide protection from predators.

closely resemble the queen, *Danaus gilippus*, than they do the monarch—were found to be just as protected as their putative model. This mimicry system becomes still more complex when we learn that there is variation for the amount and quality of cardenolides among the milkweed host plants of the monarch. In other words, some monarchs are as unprotected and palatable as their putative mimics, a phenomenon called "automimicry" (wherein a species "mimics" other protected members of its own species).

With the addition of the queen, *Danaus gilippus*, and the soldier, *Danaus eresimus*, the monarch–viceroy mimicry system more closely resembles Müllerian mimicry (named for the Müller brothers, who, like Bates, were South American explorers) already made famous by *Heliconius* and its neighbors (see below). Each species in a Müllerian mimicry system acts as both model and mimic. The Müllerian mimicry system differs from the Batesian system because it broadens "the umbrella": as a new species join the ring, the reinforcement of a shared pattern better educates the local predators. Of course, as the viceroy–monarch system demonstrates, the Batesian and Müllerian mimicry systems are really just the opposite ends of a continuous spectrum of mimicry types.

In Chapter 3, I mentioned the remarkable concordance in the ranges of various species and forms of the boldly aposematic and chemically defended *Heliconius* butterflies in South America (and promised to return to the subject). Long ago, Heliconiids stumbled upon a variant of the Batesian mimicry system: two distasteful models that share the same aposematic pattern can educate their predators faster and gain protection from each other. As more and more distasteful co-models are added to such a system, the benefits to all of the participating species expands, because the pattern becomes more common and the predators have to learn only one "keep away" warning scheme.

Above and beyond the geographic component of the variation between patterns, the *Heliconius* model rings also include: (1) the co-occurrence of multiple Müllerian model rings (e.g., as many as five or six well-differentiated mimicry rings coexisting in the same place and time), (2) the presence of other co-models (Ithominae, Acraeinae) that have a completely different chemical basis for their protection, and (3) true Batesian mimics of entirely different families (Pieridae, some day-flying moths) that are completely palatable. The rings are marvelously (and sometimes bewilderingly) complex, contain many species from a variety of evolutionary lines and, most important, they work!

The black swallowtail, *Papilio polyxenes* (Papilionidae), is a Müllerian mimic, or co-model, of the pipevine swallowtail *Battus philenor* (Papilionidae). It feeds on members of the carrot family (Umbelliferae) that contain noxious furanocoumarins.

MIMICRY IN THE PIPEVINE SWALLOWTAIL MODEL SYSTEM

My favorite mimicry ring is one that includes a variety of taxa in eastern North America. The ring is based primarily on the pipevine swallowtail, *Battus philenor* (Papilionidae) but includes both co-models and mimics plus some rather interesting variations on these themes. The various taxa involved include:

TAXA	HOST	PALATABILITY (CHEMISTRY)	STATUS
Papilionidae			
Pipevine Swallowtail *Battus philenor*	pipevine (Aristolochiaceae)	unpalatable (aristolochic acid)	model
Black Swallowtail *Papilio polyxenes*	parsley/carrot (Umbelliferae)	unpalatable (furanocoumarin)	co-model
Spicebush Swallowtail *Papilio troilus*	spicebush (Lauraceae)	unpalatable (benzoic acid)	co-model
Androgeus Swallowtail *Papilio androgeus*	citrus trees (Rutaceae)	palatable	mimic
Tiger Swallowtail *Papilio glaucus*	tulip tree (Magnoliaceae)	palatable	sex-limited, geographic mimic
Nymphalidae			
Diana Fritillary *Speyeria diana*	violets (Violaceae)	palatable(?)	sex-limited mimic
Red-spotted Purple *Limenitis arthemis*	poplar/aspen/oak (Betulaceae/Ulmaceae)	palatable	geographic mimic

This system includes some interesting variations on the standard model/co-model/mimic theme like sex-limited mimicry in the diana fritillary, geographically limited mimicry in the red-spotted purple, and the combination of both sex-limited and geography-dependent mimicry in the tiger swallowtail. The tiger swallowtail is normally black and yellow striped (hence the common name) and males are always thus, however, the females may be "male-like" in color or mimic the pipevine swallowtail. They have two distinctive appearances (phenotypes or morphs). Intriguingly, northern

Like the black swallowtail, *Papilio polyxenes*, the spicebush swallowtail, *Papilio troilus*, (Papilionidae), is a co-model of the pipevine swallowtail, *Battus philenor*, due to the benzoic acids found within its spicebush (Lauraceae) host plants.

females, beyond the range of the pipevine swallowtail are almost always male-like but the frequency of the mimetic morph increases southward.

The diana fritillary also exhibits sex-limited mimicry but without the morphism in the female: females always resemble the model but the males

The tiger swallowtail, *Papilio glaucus* (Papilionidae), like the male shown here, does not resemble the spicebush swallowtail, *papilio troilus*, at all.

are always brown/black and orange and strikingly different. The red-spotted purple does not show sex-limited mimicry, males and females always look alike, but does display geographically-limited mimicry. This species has two startlingly different morphs, the southern mimetic morph or subspecies is the red-spotted purple, *Limenitis arthemis astyanax*, while

Female tiger swallowtails, *Papilio glaucus* (Papilionidae), however, can either resemble the male, like the female at the top, or mimic the pipevine swallowtail, *Battus philenor*, like the female at the bottom. Sex-limited mimicry, in which only one sex, usually the female, is a member of a mimicry ring, is relatively common. The black mimetic morph is almost nonexistent in the north of the range where the pipevine swallowtail is rare.

Mimics of the pipevine/black/spicebush swallowtail(s) are not limited to the Papilionids. The diana, *Speyeria diana* (Nymphalidae), is a fritillary that, like the tiger swallowtail, has sex-limited mimicry. Again, the male, (top), shown here nectaring at butterflyweed, *Asclepias tuberosa* (Asclepiadaceae), does not resemble the model swallowtails at all but has the orange and brown/black coloring of the fritillaries. The resemblance of the female diana (bottom), *Speyeria diana* (Nymphalidae), to the model swallowtails, however, is pronounced. This female is nectaring at a blazing star, *Liatris* sp. (Compositae). Unlike the tiger swallowtail, the diana's distribution is limited to the south where one or more of the models is nearly always present.

The geographic component of the mimicry of the pipevine/black/spicebush swallowtail(s) by the tiger swallowtail is expanded upon by the red-spotted purple/white admiral complex, *Limenitis arthemis* (Nymphalidae). The southern subspecies, the red-spotted purple, *L. a. astyanax*, is a superb mimic of the model swallowtails.

the northern morph, the white admiral, *Limenitis arthemis arthemis*, is non-mimetic, having broad white bands across both the upper and undersides of both the forewing and the hindwing. These two true subspecies intergrade where the ranges meet producing, amongst others, the banded purple, or "proserpina" form.

The northern subspecies of the complex *Limenitis arthemis* (Nymphalidae), the white admiral, *L. a. arthemis*, does not mimic the pipevine/black/spicebush swallowtail(s) at all because they do not commonly occur in the same region at the same time.

Staying Ahead of the Game

Butterflies, like caterpillars, must also deal with the vagaries of unpredictable weather that limit their activities. A succession of cool or rainy days can prevent a butterfly from flying. Imagine being trapped wherever you happen to be, with no food and no way to carry on with your daily routine—for days on end. Remember that the average lifespan of a butterfly is measured in days. The amount of time that a female butterfly can spend flying to lay her eggs has been shown to be one of the single most important factors in the population dynamics of some butterflies. Flight time also has major effects on survival, since butterflies that cannot fly to find the high-energy nectar they need for flight will perish. Their dependence on flight in order to find food illustrates one of the more obvious differences between butterflies and caterpillars: food is no longer

Butterfly flight is an important aspect of their biology. Among other reasons, flight allows them to locate and visit flowers for their energy-rich nectar. Here a pair of long dash skippers, *Polites mystic* (Hesperiidae), line up to visit, then almost disappear within, the deep corolla of a hedge bindweed bloom, *Convolvulus sepium* (Convolvulaceae).

189

RIGHT: Some butterflies, like these long dash skippers, *Polites mystic* (Hesperiidae), may also act as "nectar theives" of flowers: when they cannot access a flower's nectar in the usual way, and thus achieve the flower's pollination, they find ways to "steal" what they need.

OPPOSITE: When people think of butterflies, they associate them with flowers. Here a Russian black-veined white, *Aporia crataegi* (Pieridae), visits a scarlet lychnis, *Lychnis chalcedonica* (Caryophyllaceae).

immediately at hand for a butterfly, so one of its major activities is acquiring food.

Butterflies seem to spend 50 percent or more of their time looking for food (of course, they also seem to spend 50 percent of their time resting). Many species have characteristic feeding times, search strategies and food types (including specific kinds of flowers), but other factors that affect food choice include the sex or age of the individual butterfly, the prevailing weather conditions, and the type and abundance of locally available flowers or other food resources.

Butterflies are intimately associated with flowers. They need the "high

Butterfly flowers usually include a "landing pad," like this king devil hawkweed, *Hieracium pratense* (Compositae), being visited by an inornate ringlet, *Coenonympha inornata* (Nymphalidae).

OPPOSITE BOTTOM: Butterflies also eat a variety of alternative foods including sap, the sugary secretion of trees. Here a Japanese constable, *Dichorragia nesimachus* (Nymphalidae), shares a meal with a pair of scarab beetles (Coleoptera; Scarabaeidae).

energy" of flower nectar, composed mostly of sugar, to sustain their flight muscles: flight uses lots of energy. "Butterfly flowers" have relatively deep corollas that suit the length of an uncoiled proboscis, produce nectar that is composed of 20 to 25 percent sugars, and are often flattened to present a horizontal or vertical "landing pad." Favorite flowers include the milkweeds (Asclepiadaceae), asters or daisies and many other Compositae, the mustards (Cruciferae), mints (Labiatae), peas (Leguminosae) and vervains (Verbenaceae).

While it's true that the nectar from flowers makes up the bulk of the diet of the majority of species, many other kinds of food are available, and butterflies are supreme opportunists. Their need for other compounds—nitrogen, salts, amino acids (another source of nitrogen as well as building blocks for other compounds) and precursors for pheromones—drives their need to seek out alternative food sources. These include tree sap, wet soil, flower pollen and such unappealing foodstuffs as rotting fruit or vegetables,

192

ABOVE: Fallen, rotting or fermenting fruit is a favorite food for a wide variety of butterflies. Here a two-tailed pasha, *Charaxes jasius* (Nymphalidae), feeds on some fallen watermelon in southern France.

193

Less appetizing to us, but quite appealing to many butterflies, are the juices of dead animals. Here a water ringlet, *Erebia pronoe* (Nymphalidae), feeds on a dead shrew.

Other alternative butterfly foods include the excretions of many kinds of animals. A poplar admiral, *Limenitis populi* (Nymphalidae), left, shares a piece of fox dung with a scarce fritillary, *Euphydryas maturna* (Nymphalidae).

Bird droppings are very attractive to many insects. Here a tropical skipper (Hesperiidae) shares a bird dropping with a fruit fly (Diptera; Drosophilidae), a spider and other visitors.

Even owl pellets, the regurgitated remains of the small mammals that owls eat, are attractive alternative foods for butterflies. Here a Compton's tortoiseshell, *Nymphalis vaualbum* (Nymphalidae), feeds on an old owl pellet in Ontario, Canada.

carrion, dung, urine, bird droppings and sweat. Many of these items are definitely not what springs to mind when we think of "butterfly food," yet they are common alternatives to flower nectar.

The problem lies, not in the food of butterflies, but in the food of caterpillars. Plant tissues have almost none of the salts that all animals need for survival, so butterflies, like deer and other large mammals that eat plants exclusively, must seek out salt. Similarly, plants are often limited by the amounts of "free" nitrogen available to them. Consider, for example, the fertilizers that you use to keep your plants healthy: The "N," "P" and "K" on the label stand for nitrogen, phosphorus and potassium, respectively. You give your plants nitrogen because it is in relatively short supply in their environment. This deficiency in nature translates into limited amounts of nitrogen available for the plants and any caterpillars that feed on them, so the "nitrogen deficit" is passed on to the butterfly. Interestingly, the two sexes deal with these deficits in salts and nitrogen differently.

Many kinds of animals have developed mate-feeding or nuptial gifts: male birds offer food items to females or build elaborate nests or other structures to show that they can be good providers, and primates (we humans are an excellent example) offer gifts to enhance our reputation as "good providers." Male butterflies, too, give females a "gift" during copulation—a package of nutrients, salts and sperm called a "spermatophore." These are not small gifts—a spermatophore can weigh up to one-half as much as a male butterfly—and females depend on it to provision their eggs. It also greatly reduces the amount of time that the female must spend foraging for these compounds and enables her to concentrate on laying eggs. This has led to drastic differences in feeding behavior between males and females.

Since females can depend on receiving a "care package"—and, in fact, some species choose a mate on the basis of the male's ability to provide a large nuptial gift—they do not have to spend as much time searching for these compounds. This means that the female can concentrate her efforts on maintaining her flight machinery and on finding host plants on which to lay eggs. Males, on the other hand, have to seek out these compounds, so

Many butterflies are opportunistic feeders, such as this gold-banded forester, *Euphaedra neophron* (Nymphalidae), at a slug trail in Kenya.

RIGHT: **Mushrooms and fungi can be irresistible to some butterflies, like these European commas, *Polygonia c-album* (Nymphalidae), clustered on a rotting stinkhorn mushroom (Gastromycetes).**

they spend much of their time foraging in different ways and in different places to females. Males will often visit specific kinds of flowers or plants (that females show no apparent attraction to) for specific compounds that are found in the nectar or other secretions. Many male Danaines, including the monarch (*Danaus plexippus*; Nymphalidae) visit specific kinds of plants, often being attracted in large numbers to seemingly dead plants, to obtain compounds (pyrrolizidine alkaloids) that are precursors for the pheromones they use to entice females to mate with them. Females can actually assess the ability of males to provide a large nuptial gift based on their odor!

LEFT: **Male queens,**
Danaus gilippus
(Nymphalidae), compete for
access to the dry flower head
of a flossflower, *Eupatorium*
***greggii* (Compositae). The**
males obtain pyrrolizidine
alkaloids from the dead tissue
to manufacture their sex
pheromones.

OPPOSITE BOTTOM:
A mating pair of titania
fritillaries, *Boloria titania*
(Nymphalidae), from
Switzerland share a floral
perch with a hover fly
(Diptera; Syrphidae). The
smaller male (below) will pass
a nuptial gift, in the form of a
spermatophore, to the female
during copulation.

SOCIAL BUTTERFLIES

The salts that are missing from larval meals are usually acquired from natural mineral salts dissolved in or near damp ground. These areas, often around puddles or beside streams, are natural butterfly "salt licks," and butterflies will congregate, sometimes in incredible numbers (thousands or tens of thousands), in these "puddle clubs." The butterfly aggregation may be all individuals of the same species, or may be composed of individuals of multiple species. Such aggregations have come to be known as "puddles,"

199

Butterflies sometimes congregate in incredible numbers at damp ground as seen in this beautiful photo of black-veined whites, *Aporia crataegi* (Pieridae), clustered along the banks of a stream near Novosibirsk in western Siberia, Russia.

A mixed species group of "puddlers" in Argentina includes apricot sulphurs, *Phoebis argante*, straight-line sulphurs, *Rhabdodryas trite*, and one androgeus swallowtail, *Papilio androgeus* (Papilionidae).

and the activity is called "puddling" because of the stereotypical behavior of the individual butterflies.

The vast majority of the butterflies found in these puddles, usually more than 95 percent, are males. How the first butterfly finds the best spot is something of a mystery—it's probably just trial-and-error probing of areas

A group of pearl crescentspots, *Phyciodes tharos* (Nymphalidae), "puddling" in a dry streambed near Peterborough, Ontario, Canada. "Puddle clubs" form when butterflies congregate around the margins of puddles, ponds and rivers looking for mineral salts. Most are males because females receive the salts from males as a nuptial "gift" when mating.

Sucking up massive quantities of water to obtain the dissolved salts leaves the butterflies with a problem: how to get rid of the excess liquid. Some butterflies regurgitate it back out the proboscis while others dispose of it anally, although relatively few eject it explosively like this five-bar swallowtail, *Graphium antiphates* (Papilionidae), from Sulawesi.

ABOVE: **A close-up view of a European skipper,** *Thymelicus lineola* **(Hesperiidae), on wet ground in Ontario, Canada, using its proboscis to probe the mud. Like other animals that feed on plants, mineral salts that are required but not available in their food must be obtained from other sources—puddle margins and streamsides are the "salt licks" of butterflies.**

of damp ground—but there's little doubt that other butterflies cue in on the fact that there's a butterfly already there. Of course, once two butterflies are there, the congregation becomes seemingly irresistible to a third, and so on. Gradually their numbers increase, as the attractiveness of the congregation grows, although the number of butterflies is limited by their abundance in the general population. Puddle clubs in the tropics tend to be larger and attended by multiple species more often than those in temperate regions.

The butterflies alight on the soil and probe the dirt with their proboscis. If the soil is dry, they will regurgitate a small drop of fluid to dissolve some surface minerals and then suck the drop back up. If the soil is wet (which probably makes the activity easier or makes the salts easier to detect), then the butterflies will take in excess water with the salts. Sometimes the water will be regurgitated back out the proboscis, but some species forcibly eject the water out of the anus.

From a prospective predator's point of view, a puddle club of inactive butterflies appears to be an easy meal, and for some it is. I once watched a leopard frog (*Rana pipiens*; Ranidae) prey on a puddle of pearl crescents (*Phyciodes tharos*; Nymphalidae) in Ontario. I found the frog sitting in the middle of about a hundred butterflies. It waited for a butterfly to land within reach of its tongue and suddenly it was gone. The fun, and completely unexpected, part was watching what the frog did next: it jumped out of the puddle and then hopped right back in again! In doing so, of course, it disturbed the butterflies, which erupted into the air, flew madly about for a few seconds, and then began to settle back down on the soil. Apparently the chances that one would land within reach of its tongue were higher than if it just sat there and waited for an opportunity.

LEFT: The nitrogenous waste of many mammals, more commonly known as urine, is very attractive to a wide variety of butterflies. Here a tight group of aphrodite fritillaries, *Speyeria aphrodite* (Nymphalidae), visit leaves that have been coated in moose urine, while a white admiral, *Limenitis arthemis arthemis* (Nymphalidae), can be seen on the ground below.

OPPOSITE BOTTOM: The activity around a "mud puddle club," even among common small or cabbage white butterflies, *Pieris rapae* (Pieridae), can be fun to watch but maddening to a potential predator. If disturbed, these butterflies fly up—looking like summer snowflakes—in a dazzling but dizzying display that confuses the predator and provides protection for the participants.

For most predators, however, puddles of butterflies are not easy prey. A typical sequence of events would have a predator rushing in to catch a butterfly, any butterfly, and the butterflies reacting by boiling up from the ground in a cloud of activity. If the predator fails to catch one of them on the ground, the chances of it catching anything at all drop to near zero. Such "confusion displays," a mass response that makes it almost impossible

203

for a predator to concentrate on any individual in the swarm, are common among animals (e.g., flocks of birds, schools of fish). Having played the part of the "disturbing predator" at more puddle congregations than I can remember, I can attest to the remarkable efficiency of the display.

Finally, urine-soaked ground—as unpleasant as it may sound to us—offers many butterflies, especially many Nymphalids, with the best of all possible worlds. First, there's a detectable odor, which makes it much easier to find. Second, urine is primarily composed of nitrogenous waste, waste amino acids, excreted sugars and other carbohydrates—and salt! To an unmated male butterfly, this may be the closest thing to Nirvana. The same goes—double—for feces, and triple for carrion.

PAJAMA PARTIES

Some butterflies congregate in colonies, or roosts. The best-known examples are the overwintering colonies of monarchs (*Danaus plexippus*; Nymphalidae) in Mexico or California or other places, but a surprising number of species aggregate for a wide variety of reasons. Roosts are often formed for diapause or dormancy reasons. It is thought that the purposes of these roosts are primarily protective because they most often occur in distasteful or warningly colored species.

However, some evidence argues against this: monarchs are regularly preyed upon at their overwintering roosts in Mexico by two species of birds that have become quite adept at avoiding the noxious nature of their prey. Similarly, the roosts of the monarch's close relative, *Anetia briarea* (Nymphalidae), on the island of Hispaniola often fall prey to rats that decimate the entire colony. Such seasonal or diapause-driven roosts are more likely a result of the suitability of the location and conditions rather than of the unpalatability of the participants. Rather than presenting a group advertisement of their unpalatability, Larry Gilbert, a researcher at

Monarch butterflies, *Danaus plexippus* (Nymphalidae), form transitory overnight roosts on their migration south. This one was photographed in a live oak (*Quercus* sp.; Fagaceae) in Camp Wood Canyon, Real Co., Texas.

204

Overnight roosts of zebra longwings, *Heliconius charithonia* (Nymphalidae), are more permanent than those of migratory monarchs, *Danaus plexippus* (Nymphalidae). The long-lived adults of the zebra longwing return to the same roost each night and new recruits to the roost soon learn the "daily routine."

the University of Texas at Austin, suggests that overnight roosts of long-lived species such as *Heliconius* sp. (Nymphalidae) really do serve a social function: information sharing. Gilbert asserts that, because of their long lifespan, pollen feeding, the relative scarcity of unpredictable flowers (in both time and space) and the ability of Heliconiines to remember the locations of food sources and capitalize on them by "trap-lining," roosts serve the essential purpose of educating new recruits. A freshly eclosed butterfly will follow an older butterfly or two, potentially its great-great-grandparents, to learn the locations of flowers, other nectar sources and even female pupae.

Roost fidelity, that is, returning again and again to the same roosting colony, is pronounced in *Heliconius*, but some species aggregate in overnight groups for no obvious or apparent reason, and the next night may see all of the previous group's individuals alone. Others, such as the great southern white, *Ascias monuste* (Pieridae), whose displays at times reach densities so great that they cover foliage like snow, are obviously density-dependent phenomena. In general, most butterflies, whether they roost together or not, choose their overnight sleeping quarters with great care: being in the wrong place, unprotected, when a storm breaks in the middle of the night can mean death. Alternatively, being in the right place when the sun comes up can mean the difference between being the first butterfly to a flower full of nectar, or second to an empty one. Early risers also have the best chances of finding freshly eclosed females. Rising early, however, means being the first to fly, and that, in turn, means being able to fly at all after a cool night of inactivity.

The great southern white, *Ascia monuste* (Pieridae), of the Florida Everglades is so common at times that it appears to cover trees and shrubs like snow.

HEATING THINGS UP
Butterflies, like all insects, are ectothermic (or poikilothermic), meaning that their internal body temperature depends on the ambient temperature

of their environment. We mammals are, in contrast, endothermic (or homeothermic) because we manufacture our own body heat and try to maintain this temperature regardless of the temperature of the environment. Body temperature is important because all biological processes have optimum temperatures at which they are most efficient. For us this temperature is 98.6°F (37°C), give or take a degree or two.

Butterflies and other insects, however, cannot generate their own body heat and so must depend on, or capitalize on, aspects of their environment to regulate their body temperature. How well they can or cannot do this affects many facets of their lives, including their lifespan, daily activity regimes, flight ability and timing, and reproductive success. For example, a butterfly that is unable to fly because its flight muscles are too cold may be unable to avoid predators, find nectar sources or mates, or locate suitable host plants for oviposition.

Insects used to be considered "cold-blooded," but this is not really true. Anyone who has watched butterflies frolicking over a sun-drenched meadow will know that "cold-blooded" is definitely not an appropriate term. Butterflies are exceptionally good at regulating their internal temperature, and this process—avoiding overheating, on the one hand, and increasing their heat differential over the environment, on the other—is called, appropriately enough, "thermoregulation." Butterflies, as I often tell people, are consummate sunbathers, and for most some kind of basking is second nature. They have developed very sophisticated behaviors that allow them to regulate their temperatures with uncanny control. They also possess a physiological mechanism to raise their flight-muscle temperature that many people who live in the cold climates of far-northern or far-southern latitudes can identify with—namely, shivering, or muscular thermogenesis.

Most butterflies need thoracic temperatures (keeping in mind that the thorax houses the flight muscles) of between 77 and 111°F (25 and 44°C) in order to fly well. Not too surprisingly, the optimum temperature is not very

Overwintering mourning cloaks, or Camberwell beauties, *Nymphalis antiopa* (Nymphalidae), are consummate sunbathers. Contrary to popular belief, they are not warming their wings in the sun but using the sun and their dark wings to warm the air trapped between the wings and the ground—circulation of the trapped air transfers heat to their bodies. Note also the structural coloration of the spots on the hindwings that change with the angle of the light.

different from the maintained body temperature of most mammals. For some temperate species, such as the mourning cloak, *Nymphalis antiopa* (Nymphalidae), which overwinter as adult butterflies, this becomes an important component of the success of their spring broods. They can often be found flying on relatively warm days, whenever the temperature reaches 50°F (10°C) or so, in midwinter. This means that the difference between their minimum flight temperature and the ambient temperature may be as much as 27 to 36°F (15 to 20°C). How do they manage to acquire so much heat on a midwinter's day?

They begin by "shivering." Butterflies have two opposing sets of thoracic muscles that are both used to lift and then lower the wings. In flight, the two sets of muscles are contracted and relaxed, respectively, and then the sequence is reversed. However, if the two sets of muscles are contracted synchronously rather than alternately, the wings do not move. Some butterflies, like our mourning cloak, have learned to use this as a means of exercising the wing muscles to generate heat in the thorax. This muscular thermogenesis begins with very slight contractions that increase

Small tortoiseshells, *Aglais urticae* (Nymphalidae), sharing a warm spot after a night of inactivity. In this position, dorsal basking, they are using the direct rays of the sun on their bodies to raise their body temperatures.

Butterflies that normally rest with their wings closed over their body, like this inornate ringlet, *Coenonympha inornata* (Nymphalidae), bask by resting perpendicular to the sun and then leaning away from it to expose the lateral side of the body to the direct rays.

in amplitude as the muscles begin to heat up, eventually culminating in the ability to move the wings. Think of it as being something like the stiffness that you feel when you've been in the same position for too long: working the muscles helps them to move easier. Once a butterfly has worked up enough heat to get the wings going, it can move to a site where it can acquire heat from its environment. In other words, it finds a place to sunbathe or bask.

This postman, *Heliconius melpomene* (Nymphalidae), is body-basking by exposing as much of its thorax and abodmen as possible to the warming rays of the sun.

Different species bask in different ways, and there are four reasonably distinct kinds of basking: dorsal, lateral, body and reflectance basking. Dorsal-basking species typically rest with their wings outspread in the direct sun, often with the wing tips touching the substrate. In contrast, lateral-basking species rest with their wings closed over the body and orient themselves so that they are broadside to the direction of the sun, and then lean or tilt over to present as much of the side of the body to the sun as is possible. Body- and reflectance-basking species both hold the wings

Pierids, like this West Virginia white, *Pieris virginiensis* (Pieridae), are able to use their partially open, highly reflective white wings to concentrate or direct the sun's rays toward their bodies. This modified body basking is called reflectance basking.

partially open, usually at angles between 60 and 120 degrees, and orient their bodies so that the open portion of the wings faces the sun.

The difference between these last two strategies lies in the color and pattern of the wings: reflectance-basking species, such as many Pierids, have largely unpatterned wings that are highly reflective on the upper side, while body-basking species have patterned wings that are darker at the base. Reflectance-basking species depend on the heat of the sun being concentrated by reflection off of the wing pairs down onto the body, while body-basking species utilize the direct rays of the sun to warm the top of

In especially cold climates butterflies like this lesser spotted fritillary, *Melitaea trivia* (Nymphalidae), may use the reflected heat off rocks or other surfaces together with sunshine to heat both sides of the body simultaneously. The wings are pressed to the rock face to trap air between the warm surface and the body, a behavior sometimes called contact thermoregulation.

the body. This means that body-basking species must be more careful with their orientation toward the sun than reflectance-basking species, whose margin for error may be larger because of the reflective nature of their wings.

Our overwintering example, the mourning cloak, is a dorsal basker. It will move to find a sun-drenched pool of warmer temperatures on a branch or the ground, alight, and press its body to the substrate. On a branch, it will wrap its wings as far forward as it can to expose as much of its body as possible to the warming rays of the sun. On the ground, the dark-brown wings serve as heat collectors that warm, not the very slow and almost insignificant amount of haemolymph that circulates through the wing veins, but the air sandwiched between the wing and the ground. With the wingtips pressed to the ground, the air circulates close to the body, transferring the heat indirectly.

Butterfly size has a pronounced effect on their ability to thermoregulate. The reason is found in physics: the volume of an object affects how fast the object will gain or lose heat—the greater the volume, the lower the heat loss, but the longer it takes to heat. This means that butterflies with very small bodies, such as many Lycaenids, both acquire and lose body heat much quicker than do large-bodied butterflies such as Nymphalids. The biological effect of this is that large-bodied butterflies may be prone to overheating, while small-bodied butterflies have great difficulty maintaining their body heat. A secondary factor that mitigates heat gain is, unexpectedly, flight.

Forward flight, even at the relatively slow flight speeds of butterflies, sets up a breeze that can carry heat away from a small body. The spring azure (*Celastrina ladon*; Lycaenidae) can be found flying in woodlots in Ontario on relatively warm days in March. At this time, they are fast, erratic fliers that never fly very far, probably averaging no more than 30 to 50 feet (10 to 15 m) on any one flight, but always land in a spot of sunshine on the forest floor. They rotate until their body is broadside to the direction of the sun, and then tilt themselves over, with their wingtips pointing away from the sun. They'll rest like this for a few minutes, and then they'll be off again on another short flight. They lose heat in flight faster than they acquire it on the ground, so are limited to short flights.

The furriness of the body helps to trap warm air near the body by preventing it from being whisked away on the slightest breeze. Not too surprisingly, smaller butterflies, like this provence hairstreak, *Tomarus ballus* (Lycaenidae), which lose heat quickly, are often quite "hairy."

Arctic and alpine butterflies are not large in order to retain heat but are medium-sized so as to balance heat loss with heat gain. Here a pair of arctic graylings, *Hipparchia autonoe* (Nymphalidae), mate on a warm rock in their arid western Siberian habitat in Russia.

Many arctic species are under similar but more extensive constraints. The flat, treeless tundra offers few windbreaks, so butterflies have learned to stay relatively close to the ground, where the winds cannot strip them of heat. One might expect that, because of the coolness of the arctic climate, even in midsummer, arctic butterflies would be large or have large bodies, but in fact they tend to be medium-sized. If you think about this for a second, it does make sense. Given the nearly constant sunlight of midsummer, even with the cooling and drying winds of the tundra, a large body would be thermally overbalanced; that is, it would pick up and retain too much heat.

At the opposite end of the spectrum, the butterflies of the tropics are more variable in size but also have access to a far more diverse selection of habitats. It can be surprisingly cool in the darkness under the canopy of a tropical rainforest, but ambient temperatures are much closer to flight-muscle "operating" temperature, and temperature extremes are greatly reduced everywhere. The problem in tropical environments is more likely to be the dissipation of excess body heat. The presence of scales and hairs on the wings that trap heat, especially next to the body, near the bases of

the wings, can reduce heat loss by up to 20 percent. As you might expect, there are a variety of clearwing butterflies in the tropics, but few in the Arctic. Do you think there's a relationship between body hairiness and location?

Mating Rituals

As I write, there is a goatweed butterfly, *Anaea andria* (Nymphalidae), perched on the power line right outside my window. It attacks anything that moves nearby, especially anything red or orange. It attacked me when I went out to check for mail, although I should say that I am not wearing anything orange, and it's already attacked a nectaring female gulf fritillary, *Agraulis vanillae* (Nymphalidae), twice and will likely take another run at her shortly. What is it looking for? It just flew out to investigate a falling oak leaf. I haven't seen it visit the flowers that the *Agraulis* is visiting. Why does it hang there on the wire, and then fly out at passing objects? It hangs upside down more often than not, but also alternates between sunning itself by laterally basking, body broadside to the sun, and perching so that its wings are edge-on to the sun, seeming to hide in its own shadow.

On another occasion, late in the spring, while driving through the relatively flat countryside near our home, I noticed the seeming dearth of butterflies: there was remarkably little on the wing. But as I approached the end of a short hill, I saw a black swallowtail, *Papilio polyxenes* (Papilionidae),

OPPOSITE: **Clearwing butterflies, which have no scales on their wings, are far more common in the tropics than in temperate regions. This is *Cithaerias menander* (Nymphalidae), a satyrine that rarely leaves the deep forest floor. This habit and its clear wings combine to protect it from predators since it mimics other distasteful clearwing butterflies. It is transparent enough to be difficult to see in the dark forest understory, and, as researcher James Marden once pointed out, birds cannot dive for it without crashing into the ground.**

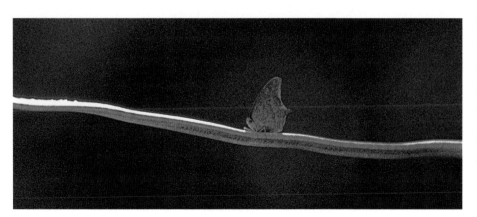

LEFT: **An electrical cable outside the station house at the Stengl "Lost Pines" Biological Station in central Texas is a preferred perch for this goatweed butterfly, *Anaea andria* (Nymphalidae).**

Features of the landscape such as hilltops become sites of aggregation for male butterflies that are seeking mates. The black swallowtail, *Papilio polyxenes* (Papilionidae), is a well-known "hilltopper" and the resting posture of this female explains the penchant for males to investigate any basking butterfly.

fly by, heading uphill. When I reached the crest of the short hill, the road being at the northwest end of the northwest–southeast running hill, I saw them: dozens of black swallowtails, all flying the length of the hill, obviously seeking something. What were they looking for? They'd frequently check

A mixed aggregation of males of a half-dozen species of Coliadines (*Phoebis* sp.; *Colias cesonia*; *Eurema mexicana*; *Anteos* sp.; all Pieridae) may soon go from congregation to confrontation as the behavior of the males changes from the acquisition of one resource (mineral salts) to the acquistion of another (unmated females).

216

each other out, spiraling around each other and up a dozen or more feet before breaking apart and heading back the way they'd been going before they got sidetracked. They'd stop to nectar infrequently, and sometimes just stop to sun themselves, wings spread to catch the afternoon rays. Of course, every time one of them stopped to bask, another one would come along, and they'd be off again, chasing and swooping. Why were they all here, when there was all of the surrounding countryside to explore?

Welcome to the wonderful world of male mate-location behavior and territoriality. Having acquired the necessary components of a nuptial gift and/or the precursors for the pheromones that may be needed to entice a female to mate (or encourage other males to keep their distance), the male must search out a female. One of the most fascinating aspects of butterfly habits to me is that, once the required compounds are in their possession, male butterflies change behavior completely. They go from aggregating and congregating with other males to the monastic life of the single, bachelor butterfly—seemingly overnight. One day they're puddling with a bunch of other males, and the next they're not only actively avoiding other males, but becoming quite single-minded about maintaining a "male-free space" around themselves, and some even go so far as to become quite territorial and overtly antagonistic toward other males! Where they once shared a common goal, with relatively abundant resources, they now are in direct competition with each other for a limited resource: females.

Males have two ways in which they can search for and locate potential mates. They can adopt a wait-and-see attitude, taking up a perch in a position or situation likely to attract a female, like the *Anaea* outside my window, or use a go-and-seek strategy to actively find a female. Both of

BELOW: Competition for mates can be fierce. In this sequence a mated pair of southern hairstreaks, *Fixsenia favonius* (Lycaenidae), is approached by one male who tries to "horn in on the action," then another male is attracted to the fray. In the end the two extraneous males both try to grasp the female and dislodge the mating male, without success.

A female goatweed butterfly, *Anaea andria* (Nymphalidae), rests between bouts of egg-laying under a leaf of a host plant, wooly croton (*Croton capitatus*; Euphorbiaceae). This female was a fixture around the station house at the Stengl "Lost Pines" Biological Station in central Texas a little over a week after the male took up his perch on the electrical cable.

these mate-location strategies, called "perching" and "patrolling," respectively, can be quite successful. There are a number of species that use both, but, more often than not, the strategy used by a particular species is a species-specific trait. Some species are inveterate patrollers, while others always perch. Both strategies may include the establishment and

maintenance of a territory from which they try to exclude other males. The problem that the males have is that, as you'll recall, females have been exploiting different habitats from those the males have been using. So where should the eminently attractive bachelor set up housekeeping when he has courtship on his mind?

Both the wire-perching goatweed butterfly and the congregation of black swallowtails on a hilltop should provide a clue: the male should set up somewhere where one could expect a female to go—often some unique or strategic feature of the landscape, such as a hilltop, a sunlit clearing in the woods, or a sunny trail that butterflies use as flyways. It's obvious that females can be found at these locations, otherwise there would be no swallowtails on the hilltop in the next generation, and the female *Anaea* that is busily laying eggs on the wooly croton (*Croton capitatus*; Euphorbiaceae) in my front yard wouldn't be! Visibility is the key. Even in the relatively dark rainforest understory, reflectively colored butterflies

A male purple emperor, *Apatura irus* (Nymphalidae), perches at a "landmark" (in this case a tree branch within his territory), waiting for anything that resembles a female to pass by.

219

The brilliant metallic blue of the upper side of a Morpho, *Morpho cypris* (Nymphalidae), reflects the smallest amount of light. In flight they appear to flash on and off, or appear and disappear with every wingbeat—a signal that can be seen over surprising distances.

such as the blue morphos (*Morpho* sp.; Nymphalidae) signal prospective mates from significant distances with alternating flashes of brilliant color like a lighthouse in the fog.

Perch sites, or patrolling corridors or landmarks, are used repeatedly. Over the past few months I have seen the *Anaea*, an emperor (*Asterocampa* sp., Nymphalidae), a question mark (*Polygonia interrogationis*; Nymphalidae) and a variety of Lycaenids, including a gray hairstreak, *Strymon melinus*, all perch on the same wire. It is a strategic location: the southeast corner of the house, out from under the trees, so it gets bright light all day long; the house and the trees opposite force butterflies to fly in particular directions,

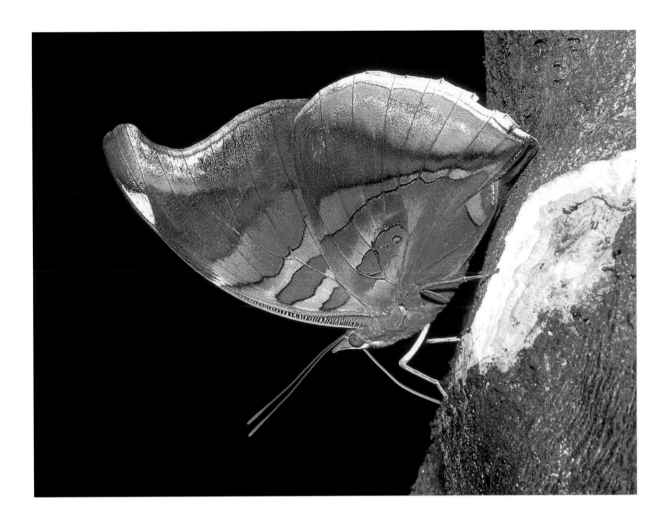

and it's directly over a butterfly garden with a multitude of nectar plants. Males can regulate their body temperature to sustain flight readiness while they watch for prospective mates to pass by. What more could an amorous male need? Right—he needs a female, but before we get to that let's consider why a male butterfly sets up, and defends, a territory.

NOT IN MY BACKYARD

A male needs to be able to correctly identify a female of his own species. Sounds obvious (and easy), but it's not. Males depend on and use predominately visual cues—color and pattern—to assess the butterflies that they encounter. The problem for many species is that both sexes look exactly the same. Picture this: a male butterfly perched in a prominent

Favorite perches of butterflies are used again and again, often by successive generations of butterflies or by a variety of species. This orion, *Historis odius* (Nymphalidae), photographed in Grenada, feeds on tree sap and reveals a typical resting posture.

221

Males are not always discriminating in their choice of females to court. Here a male little yellow, *Eurema lisa* (Pieridae), is smitten by—and harasses—a female cloudless sulphur, *Phoebis sennae* (Pieridae), despite (or maybe because of) it being more than three or four times his own size. The male chased the female until she was forced to reject him but, seemingly unable to take "no" for an answer, the male actually lands on the female's wing before being shaken off. When she left he continued "the chase."

location spots a butterfly that is about the same size, shape and color, with a similar flight style, so he flies out to see if it's the right species and if it's a female. What if it is the right species but it's an intruding male? What if the interloper decides to claim the perch? Preferred perches (or forest clearings for a patrolling species) are usually rare; thus, they are a limited resource.

Butterflies are surprisingly territorial and can be quite pugnacious about it. I had no idea how pugnacious until one day when I was walking along a path that traverses a narrow stretch of wood between two fields. I was just about to enter the area where the path widens out into the next field when, suddenly, something was flapping in my face—I mean directly in front of my nose! I was so startled that I stopped and stepped back, which seemed to do the trick, since whatever it was disappeared. I moved forward again and, out of the corner of my eye, I saw it: a medium-sized butterfly had been perched, face downward, on the trunk of a small tree to the right of the path. As I completed my step, there it was, in my face again—a crazed butterfly on a suicide mission. I had just had an encounter with a northern pearly eye (*Enodia anthedon*; Nymphalidae). When I stepped back, it returned to its perch, but every time I stepped forward it attacked me! Not exactly what you'd expect from a butterfly.

Why would a butterfly, a softly fluttering symbol of gentleness, have the temerity to set up a territory, never mind try to defend it? The idea of a butterfly defending anything seems a little far-fetched! To be truthful, territorial defense in butterflies is probably nothing like you imagine. It's more like a game of blind man's bluff than a contest of champions. I don't

want to downplay this—there are reports of butterflies buffeting each other with their wings so strongly that it's audible and it has been suggested that the loss of scales or damage to their wing margins resulting from such encounters might affect their flight ability, thermoregulatory capability, survival or reproductive success. Still, the normal interplay between "contesting" males at a territorial site is more a matter of possession: Who was here first?

Butterfly territories may be a particular rock or twig of a shrub, a spot along a wooded path where the sun reaches the forest floor, a tree trunk

A *ménage à trois* of giant swallowtails, *Papilio cresphontes* (Papilionidae), leaves the observer wondering, "Who's courting whom?" This appears to be a male chasing a male chasing a female (note the relative sizes of the abdomens).

A pearly eye, *Enodia anthedon* (Nymphalidae), very similar to the pugnacious individual that once "attacked" me, perches on a tree within his territory.

Territories are usually set up where a male can expect to meet a receptive female. Here a male empress leilia (as strange as "male empress" may sound), *Asterocampa leilia* (Nymphalidae), basks on a perch in his territory.

along a forest opening, or a tree-fall clearing or other corridor or right-of-way. However, the best territories, that is, the locations where a male has the best chance of meeting females, are in short supply. This means that the male population, depending on their abundance at any particular time, can be categorized into two groups: territory holders and "floaters" that either do not have a territory or hold an inferior territory. Any butterfly that enters a territory and resembles, even vaguely, the territory owner's species is investigated and pursued. How the pursuit ends depends on whether the intruder is a congeneric female, a congeneric male, or something else. If it's not a female, then it is, by definition, a waste of the territorial male's time and energy. A butterfly that is not congeneric is virtually ignored, and the resident will quickly return to his perch or patrol. A congeneric male, however, is an intruder and is perceived as being in direct competition for two resources: the territory and the opportunity to meet females.

The optimal strategy would be to quickly chase the interloper off, and

224

this would be easiest if the interloper knew how to respond to being the intruder. This is, in fact, exactly the case. Studies show that the resident or owner always wins in these encounters, and the intruder is "driven" off. Of course, an intruder is relatively easy to chase off once it has learned that a territory is occupied; however, it pays a "floater" to test territories periodically to determine if an owner is resident. Experiments in which the territory owner is removed generally show that the first floater to enter an unoccupied territory will assume ownership. If it is allowed to hold the territory for any length of time, it will defend the territory against the original owner when it is released—and it will win. Possession *is* nine-tenths of the law.

COURTSHIP DANCES

Finding prospective mates is, of course, only half the battle. The male must correctly assess the species, sex, condition and willingness to mate, while the female, assuming she is willing to mate, chooses males through a combination of size, color and brightness, scent, and courtship "etiquette" and tenacity. Together these characteristics allow the female to assess the male's age, general level of health, ability to survive local predators and potential ability to provide needed egg-provisioning nutrients in the nuptial gift, the spermatophore. The number of descendent progeny in the next generation is the measure of reproductive success, but how this is achieved is different for each sex: male success is ultimately measured in the number of females mated, while female success is measured in the number of eggs produced. Females in many species will mate only once, so the correct choice is crucial. Males prefer larger females but are far less discriminating than females.

Both sexes identify themselves visually; however, the final arbiter of identity is often a unique mix of pheromones, a species "signature" scent, coupled with a specific—and correct—sequence of signals and responses in a courtship ritual. This sequence of courtship behaviors, called a "signal-response chain" by behavioral biologists, requires that the courting male send a signal, which may be visual, olfactory (a pheromone or chemical odor or scent) or both, to which the female responds. Her response is a

NEXT PAGE: **A male small postman, *Heliconius erato* (Nymphalidae), sits on a pupa waiting for the female to emerge. Females in some species have no choice in their initial mate although, at least in the case of some *Heliconius* sp., females do live long enough to remate.**

225

signal that the male responds to in turn, and so on. Any break in the "chain" of behavioral signals and responses—for example, an incorrect, missing or unexpected response—will terminate the encounter.

Females are enticed into mating, it is thought, by the use of aphrodisiac-like pheromones produced by special androconial, or scent scales on the wings or dedicated androconial organs in males, but these compounds may simply identify the male to the female. Regardless, a female must receive the "message" in the pheromones, so the male adopts one of two strategies to ensure that the scent is wafted her way. The courtship behaviors of remarkably few butterflies have been examined in any detail, but those that have generally proceed along similar lines. Perching males always encounter females while in flight, but patrolling males may find females in flight or resting; thus, there are two general classes of courtship sequence. If a female is encountered on the wing, then the male attempts to fly under her and up in front of her so that the pheromones are carried back to the female's antennae by their forward motion. The female may choose to

While butterflies rely heavily on vision, they are also extremely reliant on pheromones and chemical communication. Here an Ithomiine butterfly (Nymphalidae) has raised the pheromone disseminating fringe of the leading edge of the hindwing. The pheromones are attractive to females and to other males, who add their scent to the "call," thus increasing the distance over which they can communicate.

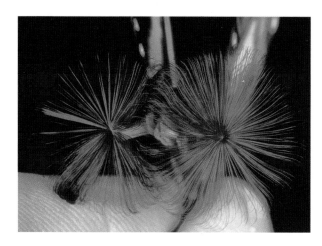

Danaines have retractable/eversible abdominal organs called hairpencils for releasing their sex pheromones. These are the hairpencils of a tiger mimic queen, *Lycorea cleobaea* (Nymphalidae).

continue flying, thereby rejecting the male's advance, or alight on the ground or vegetation. If the female continues flight, then the male will resend the signal in an attempt to obtain the expected response.

Once the female is stopped, then both strategies continue along the same general pattern: the male hovers, fluttering, over the female, touching her with his wings, legs and/or antennae. The female may be resting with her wings closed or open, but the activity of the male usually causes her to either flutter her wings slowly in response or open/close them partially and hold them steady. If the female does not reject the male's advances at this stage, then he will land beside her. There may be some species-specific orientation behaviors involving wing flicks,

A male buckeye, *Junonia coenia* (Nymphalidae), harasses a female that appears to be far more intent on a meal than on courtship.

palpation of antennae or posturing while facing each other, but eventually they end up facing in the same direction and the male attempts to curl his abdomen around to grasp hers. A receptive female will extend and offer her abdomen for coupling, but an unreceptive female may reject the male by adopting a "rejection posture," holding her abdomen up vertically between her partially closed wings so that it makes it impossible for the male to grasp her.

Once a courting pair has landed, the male extends his abdomen in an attempt to couple, as seen in the pair of queen of Spain fritillaries, *Issoria lathonia* (Nymphalidae).

The male grayling, *Hipparchia semele* (Nymphalidae), once alighted, orients to face the female and "bows" to her. By elevating his hindlegs, the male tilts forward far enough that "flicks" of his wings close over the female's antennae, bringing them into direct contact with the androconial scales on his forewings. The female either flutters her own wings and lifts her abdomen in a rejection posture, or acquiesces by elevating her wings and allowing the male to grasp her abdomen. Similar behavior has been

RIGHT: **If a female does not want to mate she assumes a rejection posture, like this Berger's clouded yellow,** *Colias australis* **(Pieridae). With her abdomen elevated between her hindwings it is all but impossible for a male to clasp the end of her abdomen.**

OPPOSITE: **Some butterflies have a ritualized sequence of movements or postures that are necessary components of courtship. The "wing wave," where a male uncouples his forewings and uses them to "salute" a potential mate, as seen here in the black-veined white,** *Aporia crataegi* **(Pieridae), is one such posture used by some Pierids.**

noted in various small sulfurs, *Eurema* sp. (Pieridae), where the male's uncoupled forewings are used to palpate the female's antennae in what has been described as a "wing wave," and in the bowing of the silver-washed fritillary, *Argynnis paphia* (Nymphalidae), after the pair have alighted. The bowing of the silver-washed fritillary, however, is preceded by a courtship flight characterized by straight-line flight of the female and a sawtooth-shaped flight of the male as he continually flies up in front of the female from behind and under her. This flight sequence ensures that the male's pheromonal scent is carried to the female's antennae.

In the queen, *Danaus gilippus* (Nymphalidae), the male pursues the female in the air, overtaking her and fluttering in front of her, with the

A male queen, *Danaus gilippus* (Nymphalidae), hovers above a female that has stopped to nectar at *Eupatorium greggii* (Compositae). Whether she stopped because she was hungry or because she was being courted is immaterial to this male.

distinctive androconial organ of the Danaids, the hairpencil (an extrudable abdominal organ containing pheromones), everted. A receptive female will alight, and the male will continue to hover above her with his hairpencil extended. It is thought that the pheromone exuded by the hairpencils operates to arrest the female's flight and prevent her from leaving once she has alighted. The abdominal response (extension for coupling) of receptive females of the small sulfur, *Eurema lisa* (Pieridae), has been shown to be a direct response to pheromonal contact. At this stage of the courtship, a female's status may lead her to reject the male's advances by assuming the rejection posture or allow copulation to occur. The combination of an aerial component and a terrestrial component of courtship is common among most of the species that have been investigated, even for those species such as *Colias* sp. (Pieridae), that rely heavily on visual cues.

On one occasion, during the height of a migration of snouts, *Libytheana*

The successful culmination of courtship is mating as seen in this pair of queens, *Danaus gilippus* (Nymphalidae). The butterfly on top is the male in this case (note the presence of androconial patches on the hindwings).

233

A male pale clouded yellow, *Colias erate* (Pieridae), hovers above a female with the intent to woo.

A sequence showing courtship by the American snout, *Libythea bachmanii* (Nymphalidae), during one of their periodic outbreaks in Texas in 1998. The female, above, is not amenable and rejects the male's advances throughout.

bachmanii (Nymphalidae), I witnessed and photographed the unsuccessful courtship of a female on a branch of Yankee weed (*Eupatorium compositifolium*; Compositae). The female maintained a classic rejection posture, abdomen elevated between partially closed wings, while the male faced her and alternately flicked his wings shut with almost audible force, then slowly opened them again. The forceful snapping shut of the wings was likely "driving air," laden with pheromones, toward the female. He repeated this a number of times before finally giving up and leaving. I still wonder whether the rejection of the female was due to a migratory reproductive diapause or whether she had already mated. The population of snouts around the house the following spring leads me to favor the latter explanation. It was, nonetheless, fascinating to watch, and I later learned, when my slides came back from processing, that the entire sequence had been mirrored by a second pair of butterflies in the background!

During the course of writing this book, I had occasion to visit south Texas during the peak of an empress leilia, *Asterocampa leilia*

234

(Nymphalidae), population. A track through dry
scrub habitat surrounded by their hackberry host
plants (*Celtis* sp.; Ulmaceae) was occupied by an
abundance of perching males. As we progressed
down the track, we disturbed male after male,
each flying in a circle around us to the limits of
its territory, up and down the track, intercepted
on both sides by the males that held the adjacent
territories. At one point, a receptive female flew
down the track, eliciting a veritable flurry of

activity (although most of it was directed at each other and territorial
squabbles) that culminated in a courtship and copulation with a successful
male. The male fluttered above the female in the air and she alighted in
three or four places—on the ground, a cactus, a large-leaved shrub—before
finally alighting on a hackberry branch. At each landing, she fluttered her
wings slowly, abdomen level, seeming to investigate the suitability of each
site. When she finally alighted on a host plant, the male landed in front of
her, facing her, for a few seconds, both with their wings beating slowly but
with evident force, before turning around, bending his abdomen around
and coupling.

MALE–MALE INTERACTIONS

When a female rejects a territorial male, whether by avoidance flight or a
rejection-posture encounter, the female generally continues on her way and
the male returns to his territory. Encounters in species that are sexually
dimorphic generally terminate easily because the visual cues are explicit;

however, species in which males and females are not visually differentiated become problematic if the male is unable to discern the difference between a congeneric male and a congeneric female. While it is not common, it is not too unusual to find a pair of coupled males in the field despite the sometimes elaborate courtship rituals that are supposed to prevent this from happening. A male–male coupling is, evolutionarily speaking, similar to an interspecific coupling: it is largely a waste of time for both parties since no progeny can issue from it. The territorial behavior of males is one strategy by which such useless encounters can be avoided, yet these couplings do occur.

Interactions between sexes in most species yield an immediate recognition, possibly due to visual cues or to the pheromonal scent emanating from a female, but in others the male begins every encounter by sending the signal that he would send to a prospective female. If he receives the appropriate response that lets him know that he's found a female, then he responds in kind by sending the next signal in the chain. However, if he doesn't receive the proper response, as if a female were playing "coy," then

Courtship in sexually dimorphic species, like this non-mating pair of common blues, *Polyommatus icarus* (Lycaenidae), has some benefits. Males are less likely to approach other males, resulting in fewer male-male interactions, because their "search image" is based on a different visual cue.

he resends the signal. What happens if there is another male on the receiving end of this signal? At the least, the sending male will not, or cannot, receive the appropriate response to his behavioral signal because the receiving butterfly is not a conspecific female. It is far more likely that the second male will initiate his own courtship sequence by sending a signal identical to the one that the first male is sending.

The first male has left a territorial perch, or was patrolling a territory, so has encountered the second male, the "unrecognized" potential female, in flight. Remember that males attempt to fly under and up in front of a prospective female in order to ensure that the female receives a pheromonal signal in addition to a visual one. When the intruding second male sees the first male, an "unrecognized" potential female, fly up in front, it also attempts to fly under and up in front of the defending male. The

There is little doubt, especially when one sees interactions like this one between two male monarchs, *Danaus plexippus* (Nymphalidae), that most male-male interactions are based on sexual misidentification. Males, too, it seems, know how to give a rejection posture.

result of this horizontal circling of each other, combined with the upward component of the flight, is the so-called spiral flights that are often put forward as "evidence" of territoriality. Eventually, one of the participants realizes that the expected female response will not be forthcoming and they break off, the resident returning to his perch or patrol, and the intruder continuing on his way. There is little doubt that butterflies are territorial, but male–male interactions of this type are not sufficient evidence, in my opinion, to suggest that a species is territorial.

IT TAKES TWO TO TANGO
Once a male and female are joined in copulation, abdomen to abdomen, they may stay joined for as little as thirty minutes or as long as twenty-four or more hours. During copulation, the spermatophore is passed from the male to the female. Copulation times, like eclosure times, are often predictable: most Nymphalids and Lycaenids conduct these activities in the mornings, although not exclusively, while Papilionids, Pierids and Satyrines (Nymphalidae) prefer the afternoons. This coincidence probably has more to do with availability of freshly eclosed virgin females during normal eclosure times than it does to any propensity for mating at particular times. The co-occurrence of these two activities is reinforced in species where males patrol near host plants, searching for female pupae. In some species, females are often mated as soon as they eclose by one of a cadre of waiting males. Some *Heliconius* sp. (Nymphalidae) carry this to extremes by actually mating female pupae before they eclose. Since the females have no choice in the matter, this can be considered the butterfly equivalent of "rape."

In the majority of species, however, copulation is the result of a successful courtship. Copulation may occur horizontally on the ground or vegetation, or it may occur vertically with one of the pair grasping vegetation while the other one hangs free. If the pair are disturbed while *in copula*, they will take to the air, one of the pair "carrying" the other, while still coupled. Interestingly, the sex that carries the other is usually species-specific: in most species, the female is the larger of the pair and will carry the male. Mate-carrying behavior, while often necessary to escape some disturbance, may also be used by females to attempt to dislodge a male after

An attempted copulation by a male alcon blue, *Maculinea alcon* (Lycaenidae), shows the extension of the abdomen and the open claspers ready to take hold of the female's abdomen.

the spermatophore has been transferred. At this point, copulation is complete and the male becomes a liability that the female can ill afford.

The spermatophore contains not only the sperm necessary to fertilize the female's eggs, but also male-contributed nutrients in the form of fats, salts, nitrogen and chemical compounds that are used to provision eggs and help to maintain the female. In some species, females will solicit multiple matings from different males for the nutrient value of the spermatophore. The problem with this, from a male's point of view, is sperm precedence, that is, that the sperm of the last male mated is generally the sperm that is used to fertilize the eggs. A male that has foraged long and diligently for

Intermorph matings, between two geographic forms of the postman, *Heliconius melpomene* (Nymphalidae), occur in hybrid zones but are relatively uncommon. This captive pair was photographed at Butterfly World in Florida.

OPPOSITE: Males of many Nymphalid species will repeatedly visit conspecific pupae seeking otherwise elusive virgin females. Many species of Heliconiines, such as this *Heliconius hecalasia* (Nymphalidae), take this habit to extremes and will stand guard on a female pupa and mate with her just before or as she ecloses.

the necessary nutrients to form a substantial nuptial gift may have wasted his time and effort if his sperm is not used to fertilize the eggs. So it should come as no surprise that males have developed ways to ensure a female's chastity.

The most common is the contribution of an "anti-aphrodisiac" that leaves a female with a lingering pheromone, or scent, that is actively

This photo from Dr. Larry Gilbert's experiments on post-mating odors of butterflies shows four male small postmen, *Heliconius erato* (Nymphalidae), perched on a female pupa waiting for her to emerge. When an unmated female that has eclosed in isolation is brought near the males there is no reaction, however, when a mated female is brought near the males, the group will quickly disperse, even though the virgin female has not yet emerged from the pupa.

OPPOSITE: **Male swallowtails "protect" females from further matings, thus ensuring their paternity. They excrete a sphragis to physically prevent copulation with another male. This female Eversman's Parnassian, *Parnassius eversmanni* (Papilionidae), is "protected" so well it's doubtful that she will be able to oviposit until the sphragis wears off.**

avoided by other males. The existence of such compounds has been shown by manually introducing a female to a group of *Heliconius* butterflies that are clustered on a female pupa. The males immediately disperse if the female has been mated, but do not if the female is unmated. The anti-aphrodisiacs last for a week or more, which ensures that the male will fertilize at least some of a female's eggs. A second strategy is to mechanically block the female's bursa copulatrix so that a following male cannot insert his adeagus, or penis. In some Papilionids, such as *Parnassius* sp., this takes the form of a "sphragis" that hardens over the female's abdomen and effectively prevents the female from re-mating until the sphragis becomes brittle and falls off. This strategy may backfire if the sphragis also prevents the female from laying eggs.

Completing the Cycle

After mating, a female must seek out host plants on which to oviposit or lay eggs. Often there is a delay between mating and the onset of oviposition as the female processes the spermatophore. Females eclose, depending on species, with varying numbers of oocytes (egg nuclei that develop into eggs) and mature eggs, but even the mature eggs must wait until the female is ready to fertilize them. For example, Edith's checkerspot, *Euphydryas editha* (Nymphalidae), has about 1,100 oocytes, 200 of which are mature at eclosure, while *Heliconius ethilla* (Nymphalidae) has about 160 oocytes, but

LEFT: A Jamaican clearwing, *Greta diaphana* (Nymphalidae), lays a clutch of eggs on the leaf of *Cestrum coelophlebium* (Solanaceae), a larval host plant. This is the subspecies from the Dominican Republic.

OPPOSITE: Long-lived Heliconians obtain the necessary nutrition to provision eggs from their unusual ability to feed directly on flower pollen. Here, a postman, *Heliconius melpomene* (Nymphalidae), has coated its proboscis with pollen and, while resting, it will process this "pollen load" by dissolving the pollen with regurgitated liquids.

245

none of them is mature at eclosure. Both of these species may have quite similar lifetime reproductive success or fecundity—they may each lay 600 eggs in their lifetime—but Edith's checkerspot may lay 100 eggs per day over six days, while *H. ethilla* lays an average of six eggs per day over 100 days.

The difference between them is that Edith's checkerspot uses larval resources to produce eggs, while *H. ethilla* utilizes adult-acquired resources for egg provisioning. The long lifespan of the tropical butterfly *H. ethilla* is facilitated by the ability of various *Heliconius* sp. to feed directly on pollen, thus acquiring a reasonably continuous source of nitrogen throughout their lives. This dependence on adult nutrition is reflected in their overall ovarian capacity, number of mature oocytes at eclosure, and oviposition rate. The temperate North American Edith's checkerspot, however, has an average lifespan of only a couple of weeks and must deal with nectar resources that are less predictable in time and space. Thus, her ovarian capacity is quite large, as is the number of mature oocytes at eclosure and the potential oviposition rate.

The process of oviposition is complicated. Females must be able to discern the differences between all of the available plants in any given location and select only specific species, often using only particular plants that meet species-specific criteria. If you think about it, butterflies are actually remarkably good botanists. Once a female has discovered a potential host plant, she must assess its condition and chemistry; the suitability of its location; and the presence of other eggs, larvae, predators or parasitoids, before deciding whether or not to lay an egg. The specific suitability of any given host plant may be due to the presence or absence of specific chemical compounds, the presence of fresh new growth or leaves, or the presence of other organisms. For example, the presence of a caterpillar on a reasonably large, robust plant may be considered evidence that there are few predators or parasitoids in the vicinity and the female may be more likely to lay an egg on an occupied plant. Regardless, once the egg is laid, it is committed, and its future cannot be changed.

OPPOSITE: **An unusual habit of clutch layers is the construction of "egg towers" where each individual egg is placed one on top of the other. Here a European map butterfly, *Araschnia levana* (Nymphalidae), carefully places another egg on a tower.**

A World for Butterflies?

THE WORLD IS CHANGING. OF COURSE, IT WOULD CHANGE ON ITS own, but we are causing changes that would not have occurred naturally and are accelerating other changes to unnatural rates. We change landscapes and habitats to suit ourselves, put farmer's fields where there were once forests, divert rivers, level mountains, manufacture lakes, and build cities and towns. By doing so, we fracture, fragment, degrade, damage and otherwise change the habitats of the plants and animals around us. Inadvertently, under the guise of the inexorable march of technological progress, we introduce man-made chemicals to the environment and intentionally spray pesticides and herbicides to protect our crops. We cause acid rain, deplete ozone levels, increase carbon-dioxide levels, and are accelerating the rate of climate change across the entire world. Many biologists believe that our actions are precipitating an extinction crisis. To think that all of our activities have no effect on the creatures with which we share this planet—including butterflies and other insects—is denying reality: it's ill-informed and dangerous.

We *have* made tremendous strides in the past thirty years. Slowly, but surely, we are becoming informed of the problems that we create and continue to cause, realizing how our everyday lives contribute to them, and we are finding ways to mitigate the effects of our actions or, better, not cause the problems in the first place. Mindsets and preconceived notions are changing. Where we once professed to have "dominion" over all creatures, we are now acknowledging and accepting our stewardship role.

248

Some butterflies, like these European skippers, *Thymelicus lineola* (Hesperiidae), are very common. But, in northeastern North America, where this photo was taken, this species is an alien invader that may be responsible for declines in the abundance of the native species that it competes with.

We *are* saving increasing numbers of species from certain extinction, but we cannot relax, stop or rest on our successes. We are largely failing to stop the rampaging juggernaut that is habitat loss, especially in the forests of the tropics (where much of butterfly diversity is found) and we still have an incredibly long way to go. There is so much still to be done, old problems that are not being addressed, new problems that are escalating in seriousness, and many species continuing to decline and go extinct at accelerating rates. The vast majority of these species are unknown insects.

Think about this: the human population of the world has just surpassed 6 billion, and our population is expected to pass 8 billion within the next twenty-five years. The consequences of this unprecedented growth continue to be worrisome. Our need to feed our increasing population fuels our inclination to clear more land for more crops, manufacture more and better pesticides and herbicides to protect them, build more pollutant-emitting vehicles to transport them and, despite our best intentions, the cycle of habitat loss, damage and species extinctions continues. What will happen in the next twenty-five years depends on how we act now. Will the plants, animals and insects that we know now still be around for our children to see? Will there still be new species for them to discover? For

Populations of the Canadian tiger swallowtail, *Papilio canadensis* (Papilionidae), declined dramatically in Ontario, Canada, in the year after efforts were made to control the alien gypsy moth (*Lymantria dispar*; Lymantriidae). It happened because the control agent used was not specific to the target insect and the swallowtail caterpillars were feeding on their host plants at the same time as the larvae of the gypsy moths.

them to know the joy of seeing what no one else has seen? Can we share this planet with the other life around us? Is there a world for butterflies?

Causes of Butterfly Endangerment

After reading to this point in the book you should have a reasonably thorough understanding of the scope of butterfly diversity, important factors in butterfly population biology, their habitat requirements and the strategies that they use to cope with day-to-day life. I hope that you have been impressed by the complexity of their seemingly simple lives and that you now can appreciate that butterfly endangerment from a wide variety of natural and unnatural causes is a real threat. Natural threats include the direct effects of weather, fire, flood or other animals (and indirect effects that these may have on butterfly host plants and habitat) and the occurrence of competing organisms (flora and fauna), or organisms that affect the balance between butterflies and their host plants, predators, parasitoids and diseases. Unnatural causes include deliberate burning or flooding of habitats; the intentional or inadvertent introduction of exotic species, pesticides and pollutants into habitats; possible overcollecting; as well as the multitude of habitat changes, direct and indirect, that result from the encroachment of people on natural areas.

For example, I conducted a three-year study to document the diversity of butterflies in Peterborough County in central Ontario, Canada. During the first summer, near an area called Twin Lakes, I would encounter as many as 500 tiger swallowtails, *Papilio glaucus* (Papilionidae), on any given day during their flight season. In the following two years, I was lucky to encounter 50 individuals per day, a tenfold decrease in abundance. Moreover, the abundance of almost every species that occurred in the same habitats at the same time had declined drastically from one year to the next. What had changed?

What changed in the second year was the spraying of the local forest with *Bt* (*Bacillus thuringiensis*, a biological control agent) to control tree

Many butterfly species are remarkably specific in their choice of larval host plants. This plain tiger or African wanderer, *Danaus chrysippus* (Nymphalidae), will only accept plants in the milkweed (Asclepiadaceae) or dogbane (Apocynaceae) families. Habitat losses directly affect host-plant availability and thus impact butterfly survival and reproduction.

Butterflies, like this regal fritillary, *Speyeria idalia* (Nymphalidae), which once had expansive ranges are now quarantined to the few small surviving remnants of their prairie habitat. The spiral of decline often grows much steeper as the numbers of butterflies decline.

defoliation by gypsy moths (*Lymantria dispar*; Lymantriidae), an introduced pest, around a lake frequented by summer vacationers. One of the local cottagers' associations had privately contracted for *Bt* spraying to protect the appearance of their trees. The problem, however, soon became evident: the control agent affected all of the caterpillars that were feeding at the time of spraying, not just the gypsy-moth caterpillars. I later learned, too, that the aerial spraying had occurred on a breezy day, thus broadcasting the pesticide much farther than was originally intended. The butterfly populations had not begun to recover by the third year, despite a cessation of the spring pesticide spraying.

The irony is that, while the spraying did help to control the gypsy-moth defoliation in the spring, it failed to control the tent caterpillars (*Malacosoma* sp., Lasiocampidae) that subsequently did a pretty good job of defoliating the trees in the early summer. This simple example illustrates how a combination of causes may multiply the potential for harm. In this particular case, there was competition for habitat between butterflies and people (not to mention a misplaced value system that favored appearance over substance), the occurrence of an introduced exotic and competing pest insect, and the misapplication and misuse of a non-specific pesticide. Together they illustrate the ultimate futility—to the detriment of the butterflies and other beneficial Lepidoptera—of trying to exert this kind of control over the environment.

HABITAT LOSS

Despite the multitude of hazards that butterflies face in their everyday lives, the most prevalent and devastating factor in butterfly decline is loss, damage and fragmentation of their habitat. If a habitat changes sufficiently that necessary resources are not available, then butterflies have three choices: adapt to the new conditions, move to a different location or go extinct. The close association between butterflies and their host plants underscores the fragility of their connection to habitat parameters. Remember that one of the most important factors in butterfly population sizes is the ability of females to find a sufficient number of acceptable host plants on which to lay their eggs. As habitats contract or are detrimentally altered, the number of suitable hosts declines. It is this primary connection between butterflies and their host plants that makes butterflies good indicators of habitat quality.

Of course, butterflies vary in their abundance from place to place and from time to time, especially at the edges of their range, and their habitats are similarly dynamic and change with time. Some change in the availability and suitability of butterfly host plants—and with it, the size of a particular population, or of a particular habitat, and thus the occurrence of

Our impact on butterflies extends well beyond habitat degradation, fragmentation or outright loss, as this red admiral, *Vanessa atalanta* (Nymphalidae), perched on a warning sign, reminds us.

Please DO NOT Spray Herbicides or Pesticides Near This Building
Federally Listed Endangered Species of Insects Are Being Cultured And May Be Affected

a population—is natural. The main differences between natural dynamics and undesirable unnatural (or even undesirable natural) changes are the scale of the habitat alterations and the rate at which they occur. Natural changes occur, for the most part, over time spans long enough to allow butterflies to adapt to new conditions; but, when changes occur rapidly, butterflies lose that option and must relocate to suitable habitat or die. Exceptions, such as severe weather or other catastrophic events, do occur, of course, but their relative scarcity and localization mean that entire species are rarely endangered. One of the goals of conservation should always be to minimize the unnatural changes while simultaneously allowing natural dynamics and normal evolutionary changes to continue unabated.

Further, as habitats become fragmented or degraded, population sizes decline. Small, restricted populations are far more prone to endangerment and extirpation from events that would have been far less catastrophic to a larger, more expansive population. Local, rare species may be affected by small alterations to habitats and are devastated by seemingly minor "catastrophes," while broadly distributed, common species are more resilient to minor habitat changes and less likely to be adversely affected by all but the largest of catastrophes. As habitats become more and more

The impact of our activities on the "unseen" life stages of butterflies is reflected in our apparent impact on their adult stages. Here a queen, *Danaus gilippus* caterpillar (Nymphalidae), has succumbed to a pathogen that may have originated in a laboratory.

Endangered butterflies, like the many races of the Apollo, *Parnassius apollo* (Papilionidae), may have become endangered by our actions but it is important to remember that, like this endangered butterfly caught in a spider's web, they are still subject to all of the same sources of mortality that common butterflies experience.

patchy, the likelihood that populations may persist only if there is a sufficient level of immigration increases drastically. Extinction becomes the norm rather than the exception, fewer potential sources of colonists remain, and the last few butterflies in the last remaining habitat "islands" become more and more vulnerable to natural enemies and other natural causes of endangerment.

THE HAND OF MAN

It is nearly impossible to overemphasize the effects that human population growth is having on gradual habitat loss, fragmentation and degradation because these are so prevalent and persistent. Still, there are a few other causes of butterfly decline and endangerment that are the result of our direct or indirect intervention in their lives. One of these, currently rare but becoming more common, is deliberate extirpation. There are very few butterflies that

GLAUCOPSYCHE XERCES XERCES - BDV.

The premier insect conservation organization in North America, the Xerces Society, took its name from the extinct Xerces blue, *Glaucopsyche xerces* (Lycaenidae). The only xerces blues that you will ever see are specimens like these in museum collections.

are considered pests (e.g., the cabbage or small white butterfly, *Pieris rapae*, Pieridae, on cabbage crops; the alfalfa or orange sulfur, *Colias eurytheme*, Pieridae, on alfalfa), so they are rarely direct targets of extirpation efforts. More often than not, endangerment and destruction result from the indirect effects of deliberate efforts against other species. These are often manifested through pesticide or biological control efforts involving *Bacillus thuringiensis* (*Bt*) or other agents, but may also include transference of natural enemies from a pest species to a non-target species after the target species declines as a result of the control efforts.

One recent example of the potential for indirect extirpation is especially informative. We have recently become capable of genetically engineering crops. The goal of these efforts is to increase the yield, or at the least maintain the current yield, of a particular crop by controlling the amount of insect herbivory that the crop receives. One recent success in this field, the transgenic engineering of genes from *Bt* into corn (*Zea maize*), has become problematic in butterfly conservation. The problem is that the incorporation of the toxin from *Bt* is not confined to the vegetative tissue, as was intended, but also shows up in the pollen. Corn is a wind-pollinated species, that is, extremely large quantities of pollen are produced and dispersed to the female flowers by breezes. Much of the pollen never lands

OPPOSITE BOTTOM: Butterfly specimens are commonly used as decorative *objets d'art*. The species used are generally abundant and common but large numbers are collected or reared for this purpose. The problem is where do we draw the line between endangered and common and what moral dilemmas are faced by considering the trade in rare versus abundant species? Do we have the right to use such specimens to simply decorate our own lives?

on female flowers but deposits on the leaves of other plants that are located downwind. Pollen from so-called *Bt* corn has been shown to kill the larvae of monarch butterflies, *Danaus plexippus* (Nymphalidae), when it becomes deposited on the leaves of their obligate milkweed host plants (*Asclepias* sp.; Asclepiadaceae).

Another direct effect of humans on butterfly populations is that of overcollecting or overexploitation. A few species (or subspecies) have been purportedly collected to the point of extinction. One example is the endangered status of the many local variants and subspecies of the apollo butterfly, *Parnassius apollo* (Papilionidae), in Europe and western Asia. Distinctive geographic variations of the Apollo made it a prime target for collectors, and it was the first invertebrate to have its trading monitored by the Convention on International Trade in Endangered Species (CITES). However, it should be noted that, while there are numerous local ordinances prohibiting collection of the Apollo, charges of overcollecting are not supported by data. It is likely that the most threatening problem facing the Apollo and other Parnassians is habitat loss, fragmentation and degradation—which collection prohibitions do nothing to safeguard.

A few attempts have been made to assess the direct effects of collecting on butterfly populations. In one such attempt the deliberate extirpation of a local population of a North American checkerspot butterfly was not successful. There is little doubt that, in a few instances, collection prohibitions are necessary and a number of collection "codes" that entreat hobbyist collectors to collect responsibly now exist. Rare, local species that are under severe pressure from habitat loss or fragmentation are especially vulnerable to overcollecting. It is not the hobbyist collector, most of whom, in my experience, do act responsibly and limit their take to one or two specimens, or the researchers studying butterfly biology that we must worry about, however. Substantial numbers of commercial collectors, especially in the tropics, do exert great pressure on some rare species that are highly valued by dedicated or hardcore collectors; collect large numbers of generally common species that are used as tourist souvenirs or in "art" objects; or collect, farm and transport living caterpillars, pupae or adults for the ever-expanding number of butterfly houses and zoos.

A relatively new kind of overexploitation is the release of living butterflies at special events such as weddings and grand openings, or as advertising gimmicks. You would think that the release of live butterflies would be a good thing—after all, wouldn't this just increase the number of butterflies? The problem is not that releases occur (although I find the exploitation of living organisms for the express amusement of people personally distasteful) but that no one pays much attention to the source of the butterflies that are released. Species that are generally involved in live releases in North America include giant swallowtail (*Papilio cresphontes*; Papilionidae), painted lady (*Vanessa cardui*; Nymphalidae), American painted lady (*Vanessa virginiensis*; Nymphalidae), red admiral (*Vanessa atalanta*; Nymphalidae), mourning cloak (*Nymphalis antiopa*, Nymphalidae), gulf fritillary (*Agraulis vanillae*; Nymphalidae), zebra (*Heliconius charithonius*; Nymphalidae), and the monarch (*Danaus plexippus*; Nymphalidae). The minimum criteria for releases should be that butterflies reared from local populations be used, but this is rarely the case.

Part of the problem is that some of these species (e.g., red admirals, giant swallowtails, gulf fritillaries and zebras) are not usually found over much of North America. The potential for introducing butterflies that do not normally occur in an area is very high. At the least, researchers may misconstrue these releases as extralimital "distribution records," but, at the worst, it has the potential to upset the ecology of local species. Even if the species occurs locally, the mixing of populations from two widely separated geographic areas may have drastic effects on local populations. For example, monarchs from western populations, reared under artificial conditions and released in the fall, are not likely to be physiologically prepared to migrate even if they could orient to a destination that is different from that imprinted in their genetic makeup. Similarly, the potential for transporting diseases or parasites between butterfly populations is high. This is of special concern for monarchs since western individuals are likely to be infected by a Neogregarine protozoan parasite (*Ophryocystis electroscirrha*) that is less predominate in the eastern population.

OPPOSITE: There is little doubt that some species, like the zebra swallowtail, *Eurytides marcellus* (Papilionidae), are especially charismatic. Recent legislation in Ontario, Canada, has given this species "special protection" despite the fact that it is really just a rare stray and is not in need of protection anywhere within its normal range.

PROTECTIVE MEASURES

The conservation of butterflies began, as most such initiatives do, at the grass-roots level. As species began to decline in numbers or go extinct, a few well-intentioned researchers became alarmed and, through the various entomological and lepidopterological societies to which they belonged, began efforts to protect specific species. New organizations such as the Committee for the Protection of British Lepidoptera (followed by the British Butterfly Conservation Society, now called Butterfly Conservation) and the Xerces Society in North America (named for the extinct Xerces blue butterfly, *Glaucopsyche xerces*, Lycaenidae) were formed for the express purpose of conservation. Organizations such as the International Unions for the Conservation of Nature and Natural Resources (IUCN), or simply the World Conservation Union, began assembling and publishing objective assessments of the needs for butterfly conservation in "Red Data Books." These international examples were quickly applied on a more local scale as burgeoning interest in butterflies eventually forced governments to extend their endangered-species programs and legislation to specific butterfly (and now other insect) species.

The 1988 IUCN Butterfly Red Data Book listed some 332 taxa of concern: 12 were extinct, 37 endangered, 81 vulnerable, 119 rare, and the remainder considered status indeterminate or insufficiently known. Numerically they include 142 Nymphalids, 85 Papilionids, 79 Lycaenids, 21 Hesperiids and only 5 Pierids; however, as a proportion of the number of species of these groups, these figures are remarkably low (2 percent or less) for all except the Papilionids. Almost 15 percent of swallowtails are listed in the 1988 Red Data Book. Whether this is due to the relatively large size, or notability or desirability, of the swallowtails, or to some inherent "endangerability" of the taxa, is unknown. Lycaenids are often considered unusually prone to endangerment as a result of their small size, extremely local distributions and complex life history; however, if this is actually the case, then the IUCN lists are biased (a real possibility).

Categorization of species into general-risk categories such as "endangered," "threatened" and "vulnerable," while subjective, has focused study and initial conservation efforts. While the IUCN has no legal or political status, its efforts became valuable guides for countries and local governments to begin designation of protective status for butterflies within their area. Soon, countries were cooperating by recognizing and restricting trade in internationally endangered species, and monitoring the trade of threatened and vulnerable species, under CITES. Of course, simply assembling lists of species does nothing to protect or conserve the species in and of itself. This is one of the main criticisms leveled at endangered-species legislation by scientists and researchers: prohibitions on collecting and trade without study, habitat protection and management, and continual clarification of their status and vulnerability leads to the false impression that species are "conserved." Further, protective legislation is frequently unevenly enforced, when it is enforced at all, resulting in confusion and inadequate protection, and may present a real danger by creating problems it was meant to solve by artificially inflating the value of specimens and increasing the danger of unscrupulous collecting of listed species.

In many instances, it appears that species names have been "picked out of a hat" or randomly or haphazardly selected without real attention to the specific needs of the listed species. Such ill-advised legislation has recently

The Karner blue, *Lycaeides melissa samuelis* (Lycaenidae), is rare in all but a few remnant populations throughout its northeastern North America range (left, male; right, female). The extirpation of the Karner blue in Ontario, Canada provides some useful lessons in butterfly conservation planning.

been initiated in Ontario, Canada. The new Specially Protected Invertebrates category of the recently proclaimed Fish and Wildlife Conservation Act lists such common butterflies as the black and Canadian tiger swallowtails, *Papilio polyxenes* and *P. canadensis* (Papilionidae). It lists the Karner blue, *Lycaeides melissa samuelis* (Lycaenidae), as "specially protected" when it is already extirpated from the province, and is also already covered under existing endangered-species legislation. In another case, it confuses the issue by again listing the West Virginia white, *Pieris virginiensis* (Pieridae), originally listed as endangered in Ontario in 1976 and subsequently removed from the endangered list in 1990. In yet another, it lists the zebra swallowtail, *Eurytides marcellus* (Papilionidae), which is nothing more than a rare stray and casual immigrant, as requiring "special protection."

The Act prohibits collecting of Specially Protected Invertebrates for any purpose and prohibits keeping of these taxa in captivity, propagating

The caterpillars of the Karner blue, *Lycaeides melissa samuelis* (Lycaenidae), are tended by ants but do not absolutely require their protection since they feed on chemically defended lupine, *Lupinus perennis* (Leguminosae), that contain noxious alkaloids. Nevertheless, their survival is better when ants are present than it is when they are absent.

them, using them in educational programs, or displaying them in zoos without a license. The legislation interferes with ongoing studies such as monarch-migration tagging, life-history documentation, the educational value of a teacher-rearing live caterpillars in a classroom, and educating the general public by offering them the chance to get "up close and personal" with local butterflies in zoos and butterfly houses. In short, it actively interferes with many of the valuable activities undertaken by amateur lepidopterists. Most glaringly, the legislation offers no habitat protection and no means for ensuring funding or providing directions for studies of the biology and ecology of included species (in fact, it threatens to bury new research in mountains of needless red tape). Further, it needlessly interferes with ongoing conservation plans and scientific studies, and offers no means to amend the list, to remove a listed species, without enacting still further legislation.

This legislation (and other similar legislation in Australia and many other countries) emphasizes that simply listing species does nothing to protect or conserve them because few, if any, measures are taken other than the grand "token gesture" of listing. Such lists do nothing but prohibit collecting or study, although these actions are rarely harmful, and may actually increase the risk to listed taxa. Worse still, prohibitions change with political venue: what is prohibited in one region is not prohibited in another. The goal of any conservation legislation should be to promote study, not prohibit it. Legislation should increase public and political awareness of the plight of rare or valuable species and should facilitate the gathering of the information needed to devise a suitable conservation strategy and action plan. Habitat preservation, restoration and protection are necessary components of all such plans.

Selected Case Studies

I've chosen the following six case studies to illustrate some of the major problems faced by butterflies, and some of the real and potential solutions that have been (or can be) used to moderate their decline or endangerment.

A lone male Karner blue, *Lycaeides melissa samuelis* (Lycaenidae), perches waiting for a female that never arrives. This photo, taken on July 9, 1988, is of one of the last Karner blues ever seen in Ontario: they were declared extirpated, or locally extinct, in 1989.

THE EXTIRPATION OF THE KARNER BLUE FROM ONTARIO, CANADA

The Karner blue butterfly (*Lycaeides melissa samuelis*; Lycaenidae) is an example of a "classic" rare species—that is, one in which individuals have small restricted distributions or geographic range and narrow habitat specificity—of the northeastern United States and southeastern Canada. The Karner blue is federally endangered in the northeastern United States (Indiana, Michigan, Minnesota, New Hampshire, New York, Ohio and Wisconsin) and is considered extirpated or locally extinct from Ontario, the only region where it occurred in Canada. In Ontario, it was known to exist at six sites around the end of the nineteenth century, but only two of these locations persisted into the 1980s. The habitat of the Karner blue in Ontario is characterized as Black Oak Savannah—short-grass prairie with interspersed copses of oaks and pines—and is itself considered threatened, currently occupying less than 0.02 percent of its former range in Canada.

The Karner blue uses lupine, *Lupinus perennis* (Leguminosae), as its obligate host plant, associates with ants that defend the larvae from predators, and requires the availability of ample nectar resources as adults. It has two broods per year, with the progeny of the second brood overwintering and producing a spring first brood that produces, without diapause, a second summer brood. The Karner blue exhibits a metapopulation structure. Population studies were conducted at both sites in Ontario in 1984, and then again in 1986. At the more populated site there were estimated to be 100 first-brood adults and 850 second-brood adults in 1984, and 300 first-brood and 920 second-brood adults in 1986. The low population sizes of the first brood are thought to be due to overwintering losses. Three years later, only one adult was seen during the flight period of the second brood; none was encountered in 1990. The population had gone from moderate to high population levels to zero in only three or four years. Why such a drastic decline?

In the late 1930s and early 1940s, some errant biologists assessed the

Like the Karner blue, the frosted elfin, *Incisalia irus* (Lycaenidae), also depends on lupine hosts. It has not been seen in Ontario since 1989 and is likely also extirpated. Habitat restoration for the Karner blue will undoubtedly also aid the frosted elfin.

Black Oak Savannah habitat around the southeast shore of Lake Huron as "degraded pine forest" since the bulk of Ontario was, or at least had been, covered in white/red pine forests. A massive effort culminated in the planting of millions of pine trees. The decline of the Karner blue began with this massive habitat change. The planting effort, together with the interruption of the natural fire regime that had acted to keep the savannah open, resulted in the development of a closed forest canopy that the lupines could not endure. Other habitat losses due to competition between humans and butterflies for prime lakefront properties also occurred. However, while habitat fragmentation and degradation were contributing factors that resulted in the slow decline of Karner blue population numbers, and extinctions of local satellite populations, the factor most responsible for their extirpation from Ontario is the occurrence of an extended drought in 1987–89. The drought caused the early senescence of the lupine so that the second-brood caterpillars were unable to complete their development.

Restoration efforts for the habitat (opening the canopy through prescribed burning, brush and selective tree removal, planting lupines and nectar sources) have begun, and efforts have been made to generate multiple satellite habitats with corridors to suit the metapopulation dynamics of the Karner blue. Restoration efforts have, however, encountered problems: one of the key habitats is a provincial park that carries more than eight times its real carrying capacity in white-tailed deer (*Odocoileus virginianus*; Cervidae: Mammalia). As soon as lupines or vital adult nectar plants begin to germinate in the areas opened by restoration work, the deer eat them. It only takes a couple of years of such heavy herbivory to completely deplete the soil seed bank if left unchecked. This problem has hampered ongoing plans to reintroduce the Karner blue to restored habitats and has been compounded by arguments over deer culling methods, times and participants. Another anticipated problem will be in acquiring reintroduction stock, because the Karner blue is federally endangered, thus protected, in the northeastern United States, the only potential source of colonists. Recent Ontario legislation also now requires that government representatives approve any reintroduction of Specially Protected Invertebrates.

The large blue, *Maculinea arion* (Lycaenidae), disappeared from Britain in the late 1970s due to a combination of inadequate knowledge of its life history and subsequent habitat mismanagement. This one was photographed in the Netherlands.

What lessons can be learned from the extirpation of the Karner blue in Ontario? First, even moderately sized populations can decline sharply in short periods of time, especially when abrogated by unusual weather conditions. However, it is important to also realize that the Karner blue did persist for an extended period of time at what proved to be dangerously low densities, in isolated pockets of habitat. A second lesson, therefore, is that, at some level, rare species may persist for long periods of time without our intervention. Could small-scale rehabilitation of their habitat have saved them before they were extirpated? Evidence suggests that it could have, since considerable increases in lupine growth results from simply opening the canopy. A third lesson is that we must know the ecology and biological requirements of an organism thoroughly before intervening—we need detailed information on population structure, resource requirements, life-history parameters, dispersal abilities, and so on. As we will shortly learn,

269

The missing piece of the life history puzzle of the large blue was its symbiotic relationship with particular species of ants and the ants dependence on particular grasses. Here, the caterpillar of a similar species, Reakirt's blue, *Hemiargus isola* (Lycaenidae), is carried by an ant.

beginning conservation efforts without a good understanding of the organism may do more harm than good.

THE EXTIRPATION OF THE LARGE BLUE FROM BRITAIN

The large blue, *Maculinea arion* (Lycaenidae), was recognized as being in danger of becoming extinct in Britain as early as the 1880s. Progressive isolation of increasingly smaller colonies led to their decline from around thirty locales in the 1950s to only two in the mid-1970s. Some of the colonies are known to have succumbed to land-use changes such as farming, sand-and-gravel extraction and urbanization; however, other colonies disappeared for no obvious reason from apparently suitable habitats. By the time the butterfly had been lost from all but the last few sites, active management for its conservation was deemed necessary. Management strategies included nominating sites as nature reserves, fencing them and removing grazing livestock. These strategies yielded dismal results, and finally much-needed biology and ecology studies were conducted, eventually culminating in captive rearing and controlled release of caterpillars into suitable former habitats. After a great deal of attention to the problem, especially in the last few years of its existence, the large blue became extinct in Britain in 1979.

The problem with the early management strategies came down to a woefully inadequate understanding of the complexity of the problem. The large blue has a complex life history that we now know is not that uncommon among Lycaenid butterflies. It uses only a specific larval host plant, wild thyme (*Thymus praecox*; Labiatae), but also depends on the protection of attending ants (*Myrmica* sp.; Hymenoptera). Where the large blue differs from many ant-attended Lycaenids is that it feeds on its host plant only when it is young. As early as 1915, it was known that older caterpillars drop off of the host, are collected by the ants and carried into the ant nest, where the caterpillars become carnivorous and begin feeding on ant larvae. The real problem, and the unknown fragment of the butterfly's life history, is that the most common protecting host ant prefers short-grass, grazed habitats. When nature reserve management suspended grazing, longer grasses crowded out the host plants, and the attendant ants

BOTTOM: **Complex life histories, like that of the large blue, *Maculinea arion* (Lycaenidae)—shown here ovipositing on its larval host plant, wild thyme, *Thymus* sp. (Labiatae) in the Netherlands—make complete knowledge of the biology of conservation target species absolutely essential.**

271

The endangered status of the Homerus swallowtail, *Papilio homerus* (Papilionidae), endemic to Jamaica, has been recognized for many years but only recently have efforts been made towards its conservation. An adult specimen shown on a phonecard illustrates the first step: make people aware of the problem.

quickly disappeared. By the time the ecological requirements of the large blue became sufficiently well known, the species had already declined to a single site. Habitat management quickly increased the number of ant nests, but severe overcrowding of large blue caterpillars in the relatively few persisting ant nests led to their death.

The decline of the large blue in Britain is no doubt due in large part to habitat loss and fragmentation, isolating potentially interbreeding colonies into a decreasing spiral of abundance due to continuing habitat degradation. In this particular case, reserves that were set up to protect the species from perceived overcollecting were mismanaged because of a lack of a crucial piece of information—not about the butterfly itself, but of the habitat requirements of a co-occurring species upon which it depended. This stresses the need for management strategies and conservation plans to have complete knowledge not only of the species, but of the interactions of the species with its habitat and the other organisms that co-occur in it. On a happier note, the large blue was reintroduced to its last known habitat, which had been maintained for the possibility since the extirpation of the species, in 1983. Three years later, a full-scale reintroduction of some 300 caterpillars in the territories of the ants' nests was attempted and a viable population was established. Restoration of other former habitats continues, and further reintroductions are planned; however, the original British race will never be seen again.

THE DECLINE OF THE HOMERUS SWALLOWTAIL IN JAMAICA

The Homerus swallowtail, *Papilio homerus* (Papilionidae), is the largest butterfly in the Americas and is considered one of the four most-endangered swallowtails in the world by the IUCN. Specimens of this species have sold on the black market for as much as $1,500 (U.S.) and it is listed in Appendix 1 of CITES as one of only four butterfly species for which *all* trade in specimens is strictly forbidden. Homerus is endemic to the small Caribbean island of Jamaica. It once ranged over more than half of the island but is now confined to two isolated, rapidly diminishing populations. The eastern population (from which virtually all museum specimens were collected) is confined to the slopes of the valley at the juncture of the Blue Mountains and the John Crow Range. The "western" population is found in the forbidding and rugged Cockpit Country, a series of limestone outcrops punctuated by deep sinkholes or pits.

Typical Homerus habitat is wet limestone or lower-montane rainforest, where their obligate larval host plants, trees of *Hernandia* sp. (Hernandiaceae), occur. The forest has a low canopy, rarely exceeding 40 feet (12 m) in height, and high annual rainfall of 79 inches (200 cm) with the accompanying high humidity. The life cycle varies from 63 to 78 days, including about 45 days as caterpillars, from egg oviposition to pupal eclosure. The larval stage is very sensitive to changes in humidity, and current forest clearing in its remaining habitat, resulting in decreased humidity retention in the forest, is of significant conservation concern. Forest reserves that are intended to preserve the watersheds

Research into the biology of the Homerus swallowtail, *Papilio homerus* (Papilionidae), has revealed that the immature stages of this butterfly, such as the captive caterpillar shown here, are subject to extensive mortality from parasites and fungal and bacterial pathogens. Butterfly "farming" would greatly benefit this species by protecting the immature stages from these mortality sources.

Without relatively large tracts of habitat in which the butterflies can live, the release of farmed butterflies will fail. Habitat restoration of severely degraded "forests," and protection of the remaining forest through the formation of national parks, is needed to ensure the survival of the Homerus swallowtail, *Papilio homerus* (Papilionidoe).

inhabited by Homerus have been established; however, enforcement has been non-existent and there is little to prevent the local population from cutting down trees.

Population abundances of Homerus have never been large, but have declined dramatically in recent years. From the turn of the last century through the mid-1960s, it was possible to see as many as 45 to 50 adults on a single trip, but by 1986 four seasoned, experienced lepidopterists were, at the height of the flight season, able to find only one adult and several larvae during "an entire day of careful observation." Fragmentation of the habitat through subsistence agriculture has contributed greatly to their endangerment, as has pressure from overzealous collectors, although they are currently not the main threats. A commercial development company formed in 1979 has been cutting 5,000 acres (2,000 ha) per year of rainforest in order to plant fast-growing pines that are intended to make the island country self-sufficient in wood production. Evidence is accumulating quickly that, without the formation and enforcement of a national park or biological reserve, the eastern population will cease to exist in only a few years.

Along with much-needed habitat protection and restoration, the Homerus swallowtail would benefit from intensive population studies to determine its current abundance and distribution. Similarly, a biological assessment of the critical features of the life history is needed. (For example, small hymenopterous parasitoids cause remarkable mortality of eggs, with about 77 percent of eggs yielding from 10 to 18 minute wasps, while a further 10 percent succumbed to fungal pathogens and bacterial infections.) Controlled captive-rearing to relieve commercial-collecting pressure and supplement population sizes would also be beneficial. After the devastation of Hurricane Gilbert in 1988, the pine plantations have not been replanted. The rainforest and the larval host plants have recovered quickly and are now more abundant than they were before the hurricane. The Blue Mountain/John Crow Mountain National Park is slowly becoming a reality, but enforcement to prevent the illegal trade of poached specimens and the fragmentation of lower-elevation habitats by subsistence farming, as well as continued study of the factors limiting population density, are still needed.

FARMING ENDANGERED BIRDWING BUTTERFLIES FOR CONSERVATION

As we've learned, butterfly populations often suffer extreme mortality in their immature stages. Mortality of as much as, or greater than, 99 percent (meaning that only 1 or 2 eggs of every 100 laid survive to become butterflies) is common. What happens if the butterfly is relatively rare, subject to pressure from habitat loss due to subsistence resource use by local peoples, and is greatly desired by collectors? In species such as the Homerus swallowtail (as discussed in the previous case history) or the world's largest butterflies, the birdwing (*Ornithoptera* sp. and *Troides* sp.; Papilionidae) of the Oriental and Australian regions, it means that the already-fragile population of adults cannot replace themselves. Let's say, for the sake of argument, that a female butterfly (of a fictional species) is capable of laying 500 eggs. Under optimal conditions, that is, when the female lays her entire complement of eggs, only 5 of these eggs will survive to become butterflies. It's far more likely that she will not be able to lay

The birdwing butterflies, like this *Ornithoptera victoria* (Papilionidae), endemic to the Solomon Islands, are spectacular both in appearance and size. These qualities have made them the object of intense collection, to the point of poaching, by collectors.

them all as a result of host-plant availability limits, restricted flight time or predation (this includes collection by human "predators").

What effect would we have if we collected the female and brought her into captivity? Let's say that she has already been able to lay 60 percent of her complement under optimum conditions, eventually yielding three adults. If we are sufficiently knowledgeable of the life history and potential mortality sources of the immature stages of the species, then we should be able to do significantly better than they would normally do in nature. We should be able to protect better than 75 percent of the remaining 200 eggs, eventually yielding some 150 butterflies. If we release these into the wild, then we have increased the female's potential fecundity by a factor of 30. Even if we were to sell 50 of the reared specimens (which is our source of funding for continuing conservation efforts and which we are able to guarantee are in perfect condition, a significant benefit to collectors) and keep 10 butterflies for captive-rearing purposes, we have increased the population size by a factor of 18. These are the essential principles behind butterfly farming.

Butterfly farming accomplishes several desirable goals simultaneously. Controlled rearing of immature stages satisfies the demand for perfect specimens, lowers the price of poached specimens because they are not as rare as they once were, nor as perfect and unblemished, and protects the immature stages from normal mortality sources. It also provides a significant source of adults with which to boost the abundance of the local population. Butterfly farming is sufficiently low-tech that it can easily be carried on by indigenous peoples (albeit, under government supervision). It provides another means of making a respectable living and further reduces unsustainable pressure on the habitat. The benefits soon overflow into ecotourism, other sustainable sideline industries such as art objects, and, taken together, offers an effective means of raising funds for protecting tropical rainforest.

Butterfly farming was pioneered in Papua New Guinea under the Australian Administration following the Second World War. The basic technique of planting larval host plants, mainly *Aristolochia* sp. (Aristolochiaceae), near the forest where wild females colonized them was pioneered by poachers and butterfly "pirates." The techniques have subsequently been refined to include many innovations, such as "sleeving" entire plants to protect immatures and farmers' rotating collecting and re-release of propagation stock to promote recovery of local populations. Similarly, old garden plots that are past their prime production, are perfect sites for these "butterfly factories" because the host plants are often secondary successional species of regrowth communities, and this promotes habitat conservation. Provided that there are adequate controls to ensure a high-quality product, with the necessary infrastructure to ensure sustainability, butterfly farming is, for some charismatic species, a win-win situation.

Butterfly farming accomplishes a number of desirable goals including protecting immature stages such as this caterpillar of *Ornithoptera victoria* (Papilionidae) from natural mortality sources that may limit population growth rate.

GLOBAL WARMING AND BUTTERFLY RANGE

One of the purported consequences of our technology is the increase in the emission of gases that have modified our atmosphere to make it more

Here we see a dozen pupae of *Ornithoptera victoria* (Papilionidae) hanging from the roof of a butterfly farmer's home. This protects the pupae from parasites as well as allowing the farmer to monitor their health and emergence.

retentive of heat, the so-called greenhouse effect. That the mean temperature of the world is increasing is inarguable; however, its cause is the subject of some debate. Regardless of why the temperature is increasing, we should consider the consequences of global warming on plants and other animals, and what effect it might have on butterflies. Theoretically, as the planet warms up, the distributions of plants and animals, especially those like butterflies that are sensitive to such changes, may shift toward the poles. For example, for a plant at the southern extreme of its range a change of only a degree or so may mean the difference between an early death due to senescence of sensitive tissue and the possibility for setting seed. At the opposite extreme, the plant may be more likely to complete setting seed before the end of the growing season.

The problem is that detecting subtle shifts in the distribution of most plants is hampered by a dearth of historical knowledge about their former distribution. We do, however, have excellent historical data, via museum specimens and published accounts, of organisms that are extremely sensitive to changes in distribution of some specific plants as well as being directly sensitive to thermal regimes: butterflies. Butterfly researcher Camille Parmesan, in conjunction with many colleagues, has recently shown that, in fact, twenty-two of thirty-five species of non-migratory

European butterflies have ranges that have shifted northwards by 22 to 150 miles (35 to 240 km) over the last 100 years. In contrast, only one species range has expanded southward, while the remaining twelve species have had no discernible change in range. The majority of the northward shifts, about two-thirds of the twenty-two species, were, in reality, northward-range extensions because the southern ranges did not also contract northward, but nine of the twenty-two species' ranges shifted northward in their entirety.

The crucial benefit of butterfly farming is that it allows us to supplement natural populations by releasing captive-reared butterflies, such as this male *Ornithoptera victoria* (Papilionidae), that have been protected from mortality in their immature stages.

OPPOSITE BOTTOM: Butterfly farming is economically self-sustaining through the sale of perfect, unblemished specimens, such as the female (upper left) and male (upper right) of *Ornithoptera victoria* (Papilionidae). Poachers rarely, if ever, obtain specimens as fresh, thus providing another benefit of farming: decreased poaching rates.

As the researchers note, the magnitude of the range shifts are about five to fifty times the distances flown by colonizing butterflies in single colonization events. This suggests that the sequential establishment of new populations is responsible for the northward-range expansions. They discount the possibility that changing land-use patterns are responsible because, among other reasons, habitat loss has actually been greater in northern countries. Further, the increase in mean European temperature, about 1.5°F (0.8°C), over the last century has resulted in a mean northward shift of climatic isotherms of about 75 miles (120 km). This is an excellent approximation of the mean northward-range shift in the butterflies. In previous research, Dr. Camille Parmesan reported a similar phenomena in Edith's checkerspot, *Euphydryas editha* (Nymphalidae), where a mean northward-range shift of 58 miles (92 km) corresponded quite closely to the 66-mile (105-km) northward shift of climatic isotherms in North America.

As the researchers note, "consistency across taxa and continents indicates that butterfly species in the northern hemisphere are shifting generally northwards in response to a common environmental change." The interesting question comes with consideration of the relatively mild warming of the twentieth century in comparison with 3.8 to 8.3°F (2.1 to 4.6°C) increase predicted for this century. Such drastic warming will undoubtedly become a major force in the factors that determine butterfly distributions in the near future. Will north-temperate butterflies be capable of colonizing new habitat across highly fragmented landscapes of a people-dominated world? Probably not; only the most efficient and capable colonizers will be able to persist. What will these temperature changes mean to distributions of tropical butterflies? Only time will tell...

THE MIGRATION OF THE MONARCH: AN "ENDANGERED PHENOMENON"

The monarch butterfly, *Danaus plexippus* (Nymphalidae), can be found in many places around the world. In most, but not all, of those places it undergoes a seasonal migration. In North America the monarch is a dispersing migrant that colonizes the continent each year to breed, repopulating its entire range from its overwintering grounds. There are

The consequences of global warming are not limited to species with complex life histories but can also be seen in the northward range shift of the common ringlet, *Aphantopus hyperantus* (Nymphalidae). The range shifts are complete, that is, both the southern and the northern boundaries have been shifted north by as much as 150 miles (240 km).

two distinct populations: one found west of the Rocky Mountains, which overwinters in California, and a much larger eastern population, which overwinters in central Mexico. The continent-wide breeding distribution of the monarch is determined largely by the distribution of its obligate larval host plants, the milkweeds (*Asclepias* sp.; Asclepiadaceae). Due to its monumental migration in eastern North America, travelling up to 2,500 miles (4,000 km) from its northern breeding grounds to its overwintering range in Mexico, it is the best current example of what has come to be known as an "endangered phenomenon."

Beginning in the late summer/early fall, butterflies of the eastern population emerge in a state of reproductive diapause. Driven by some unknown "instinct," they begin to fly south or southwest, depending on their point of origin, and eventually begin to aggregate in overnight roosts. Their numbers gradually increase as more and more individuals are funneled along the migration flyways, through Texas and into northern Mexico to their overwintering site west of Mexico City (see map on page 286). A few individuals fly over the Gulf of Mexico, while others in Florida are non-migratory. The terminus of their long migratory flight is the Oyamel Fir forests (*Abies religiosa*; Pinaceae) of the high peaks of the Transverse Neovolcanic Belt of central Mexico.

Once the butterflies arrive at the overwintering site, in massive roosts with individuals numbering in the hundreds of millions, they enter a dormancy period. The roost sites are essentially similar to the boreal ecosystems of northern Canada due to the great height, up to 12,000 feet (3,600 m), of the mountain peaks. Cool temperatures that promote the butterfly's state of reproductive arrest and reduce activity levels, without

A few species, like the pearly heath, *Coenonympha arcania* (Nymphalidae), have stable ranges, that is, their ranges have not shifted northward. This suggests they have not yet been affected by global warming.

283

The North American migration of the monarch butterfly, *Danaus plexippus* (Nymphalidae), is monumental and without peer. While the monarch itself seems common and secure, appearances can be deceptive. In fact, the monarch is a threatened species and its migration has been deemed an "endangered phenomenon." Here we see a mixed group of males and females (note the presence of androconial patches on the hindwings) sunning themselves on Spanish moss in Mexico.

being life-threatening or preventing movement entirely, characterize the sites. Thus butterflies are able to survive short, infrequent cold periods but are also able to take advantage of warm days. The roosts are active from November through early March.

In the early spring, while still in hibernation, the butterflies complete their development and become sexually mature. They mate in the late spring and the females begin the trek northward. They generally fly far enough to find host plants on which to lay their eggs and then die, although some have been recorded to fly about 2,000 miles (3100 km) north. It is this subsequent generation that continues the journey north, laying eggs as they go, joined by a second and third generation, until they have literally recolonized all of eastern North America. Their northward limit is coincident with the northern limit of the range of their milkweed host plants (*Asclepias* sp.). In the monarch's case, the northward expansion of the species range is dispersal to take advantage of habitat as it becomes suitable.

All of the fall migrants that overwinter in Mexico are produced at the northernmost portions of their range because their milkweed host plants are unable to persist in the hotter, drier climate of the south. There is little doubt that the clearing of forests for farmland over the last two centuries

O P P O S I T E : **The extinction of southern populations and colonization of new northern habitats by the Edith's checkerspot,** *Euphydryas editha* **(Nymphalidae), have echoed the range shifts of European butterflies. This photo is of a mating pair of** *E. editha aurilacus* **from Gold Lake, California.**

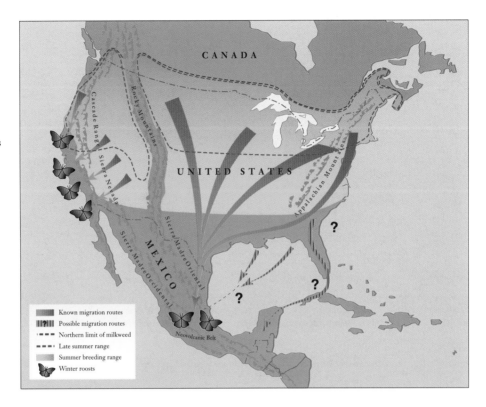

The migration of the Monarch butterfly, *Danaus plexippus* (Nymphalidae). Individuals from their late-summer range in Canada must travel up to 2,500 miles (4,000 km) to reach the overwintering grounds in central Mexico. Modified from Brower, 1995.

OPPOSITE: On their southward migration, monarch butterflies, *Danaus plexippus* (Nymphalidae), fly across the Gulf of Mexico, contrary to expectation. Here an overnight roost has formed on a rope of an offshore oil-drilling platform.

have greatly aided the expansion of milkweeds, especially the common milkweed, *A. syriaca*, in the east, and the showy milkweed, *A. speciosa*, in the west, thus increasing the available range of the monarch. For example, there has been a demonstrable increase in the abundance and northern distribution of monarchs in Ontario, over the last fifty years. However, monarch researcher Lincoln Brower fears that the monarch could become extirpated in North America in less than twenty years if mitigating actions are not undertaken now.

The most important conservation issue facing eastern monarchs is the ongoing degradation and destruction of their vital overwintering roosts in the mountains of central Mexico. Gradual clearing of the roost sites by indigenous peoples is altering the microclimate needed to ensure the survival of the overwintering butterflies. A catastrophic event here, after the changes that have taken place in their roosts over the last few decades, has a very real potential to largely eradicate the monarch from eastern North America. Similar pressure, and the potential for calamity, is

On sunny days at their central Mexico overwintering roosts, the air can be alive with monarch butterflies, *Danaus plexippus* (Nymphalidae). The overwintering roosts of the eastern monarch butterfly population are threatened by habitat changes caused by man and, because *all* of the butterflies are there at once, the monarch butterfly is also threatened as a consequence.

occurring in the encroachment of humanity on the overwintering groves of the western population in California. After the colonies of overwintering butterflies break apart in the early spring, their progeny continue north. They follow the availability of their milkweed host plants as the season progresses, until the majority of individuals are found only at higher latitudes (and higher altitudes in the west).

Conservation issues that may affect their breeding distribution in the coming years include the effects of global warming and concomitant increases in carbon dioxide and low-level ozone, genetically engineered crops such as *Bt* corn that broadcast toxins onto nearby host plants, and weed-control legislation and programs that have direct impacts on host-plant availability. Weed-control programs also have indirect effects on the habitat as a whole due to the prevalence of herbicide and pesticide spraying, and the spread of invasive alien plant species that alter open habitats and

288

may, in some instances, compete as inappropriate larval hosts. The prevalence and virulence of alien invasive fire ants in Texas may also be putting significant pressure on numbers of first brood progeny, thus decreasing the number of northward-dispersing migrants. Still, the most pressing need is to protect the overwintering sites in Mexico and California.

International cooperation between Mexico, the United States, and Canada is essential to ensure the continuation of the "endangered phenomenon" that is the migration of the monarch butterfly. Cooperation is necessary to protect both the overwintering sites in Mexico and California and their spring and autumn migratory pathways through the United States. The protection of these pathways has a direct impact on the numbers of monarchs that return to breed each spring and, in turn, conservation efforts in the north will have far-reaching effects on recruitment to the overwintering roosts. Unilateral conservation efforts by any one country will be ineffective in conserving this endangered phenomenon. Thankfully, a concerted international effort is under way, although its success is by no means assured.

What Can I Do?

One of the most intriguing aspects of butterflies for me is the role that they have played in the study of a surprising variety of life sciences. For example, the study of the genetics of mimicry in an African swallowtail led directly to the elucidation of the inheritance of the *Rh* blood factor, and possible ways to avoid its lethal effects, in humans. Much of what we now know about the effects of insect herbivory on plant growth and development (e.g., botany and chemistry) is due to the study of butterflies. Similarly, our understandings of evolutionary change (e.g., mimicry), population structure and dynamics (e.g., metapopulations), animal behavior (e.g., courtship and mating; oviposition), biogeography (e.g., of islands; disjunct distributions) and community biology (e.g., tritrophic interactions) have benefited immeasurably from the study of butterflies. The modern-day reality bears out the prediction of nineteenth-century author and naturalist H.W. Bates's comment that "the study of butterflies—creatures selected as the types of airiness and frivolity—instead of being despised, will some day be valued as one of the most important branches of Biological Science."

Entomologists that study other groups of insects have disparagingly told me that "too many people are studying butterflies" but I don't believe it for a minute. While it is true that our perceptions color our interests—how else can we explain that more than three-quarters of all biologists study animals, with better than 75 percent of those studying mammals that constitute much less than 1 percent of all life on this planet—there is still a surprising amount that is not known about butterflies. Pick up virtually any recent field guide for anywhere in the world and you will find that the larval host plants or life histories of some species are still unknown. Further, too much of what we know of the behavior of butterflies is based on only a few species (an insufficient sample size from which to draw true generalities) and we know virtually nothing about some subjects, such as the incidence and prevalence of larval mimicry. Pick just about any question of butterfly biology and ecology and you will discover that there is still much to learn. In my view, there are too few people studying butterflies!

This is where you, as an amateur lepidopterist, can help. Contrary to popular belief, "amateur" is *not* a derogatory term but is, in fact, a complimentary one. "Amateur" roughly translates as "for the love of," and it wonderfully describes every amateur lepidopterist I know. The many photographers that have contributed their beautiful work to this book are a striking example. Think about this: One of the reasons that the conservation of butterflies is possible is because we have a great deal of taxonomic, geographic, historical abundance and biological information about them. Specimens in museums and other collections, field notes, life-history rearing notes, letters and other personal publications over the last hundred years or so, largely the work of amateurs, have made much of what we may now contemplate possible. Knowledge is cumulative, and every scrap, regardless of its source, is precious. Here's what you can do to help.

While habitat degradation at their overwintering grounds threatens the monarch butterfly, *Danaus plexippus* (Nymphalidae), so do actions and policies such as weed control legislation, herbicide and pesticide spray programs, and the spread of genetically engineered or alien invasive plant species in their breeding grounds.

WATCHING, OBSERVING AND STUDYING BUTTERFLIES

One of the most enjoyable aspects of studying butterflies is that it can be done almost anywhere. An abbreviated list, borrowed from Robert M. Pyle's wonderful *Handbook for Butterfly Watchers*, includes bogs, university campuses, canyons, cemeteries, deserts, fields, gardens (public and private), hilltops, marshes, meadows, orchards, parks, pastures, prairies, power, pipe and railway right-of-ways, roadsides, trails, tundra, vacant lots and your backyard. Study activities could include watching, listing, counting, surveying, mapping, observing behavior, teaching, learning or collecting. You can do these by yourself or with a friend or group of almost any size on nature walks; in your backyard; during your vacation; at picnics; or while visiting local gardens, parks and natural areas.

Your activities can help to document the presence or absence of

butterflies at various times of the year in the locations that you visit most
often. You could watch for and observe the various behaviors that
butterflies perform, such as puddling and feeding, courtship, mating and
mate-carrying, resting, basking and oviposition or egg laying. You could
take part in, or initiate, the creation of a community butterfly reserve with a
local naturalists' club, interested business or other group. Activities that
you would have to undertake would include listing and counting the
number of species and individuals that occur there and surveying and
mapping the vegetation communities. You might also want to research the
history of the area to discover what species occurred there in the past or
what species occur only in surrounding areas. What actions could you
take to attract that species? While you might become the local expert or
guide to the reserve, it might be a good idea to seek out the help of local
biologists, extension services or government agencies.

Regardless of what kind of activity you choose, or where you undertake
it, remember to keep a field notebook or diary, take pictures, draw, or
otherwise record what you see and do. Can you think of some way that you
might measure butterfly behavior? How might you quantify and monitor

292

LEFT: Studies of the spot patterns of the meadow brown, *Maniola jurtina* (Nymphalidae), have been instrumental in advancing our knowledge of evolution and population genetics.

OPPOSITE: Studies of the genetics of sex-limited mimicry in the African mocker swallowtail, *Papilio dardanus* (Papilionidae), were instrumental in recognizing the *Rh* blood factor in humans. Here we see an array of mimetic females (top row, left to right: ssp. *cenea*, ssp. *hippocoonoides*, ssp. *dorippoides* and ssp. *trophonius*) with their various models (center row, left to right: *Amauris albimaculata*, *A. niavius*, *Danaus chrysippus dorippus* and *D. c. aegyptius*; all Nymphalidae). Males also vary from place to place but do not exhibit the mimicry of their females (bottom row, left to right: ssp. *cenea*; ssp. *dardanus*; ssp. *antinorii*). The specimen at the bottom right is a non-mimetic female of ssp. *antinorii*.

changes in the species composition or abundance through a season? Are the patterns you discover within a year or season repeated in the following year or season? Answers to questions like these are well worth investigating. Most people don't think about it very much, but knowledge is only partially learning. The rest is teaching. If something is worth knowing, then it is worth communicating to others. Write a short article for the local naturalists' magazine or journal, or a letter to the local nature columnist at the newspaper. It's another activity that you can enjoy.

REARING AND LIFE-HISTORY STUDIES

The next time you find an unfamiliar caterpillar, stop and observe it. There are surprisingly few guides to caterpillars, so it's quite likely that you won't be able to identify it; however, you should, with a little practice, be able to determine what family or group it belongs to. Is it feeding on the plant that it's on? What plant is it? Is the plant common in the vicinity? Are there other larvae like this one on other plants nearby? From here what you do will pretty much depend on how actively you want to pursue these questions. A low-involvement strategy might include revisiting the site every few days to check on the larvae, verifying its survival, document (notes, drawings, photos) any color or pattern changes, feeding pattern, type and extent of damage to the host plant, and so on. Benefits of monitoring this sort of thing in the wild rather than in captivity include

Population studies might entail capturing, marking, releasing and then recapturing individuals to obtain estimates of population size and to study population dynamics. Here we see a marked individual of Queen Alexandra's sulfur, *Colias christina* (Pieridae).

294

Watching butterflies can have its own rewards. Here a mating pair of dark, winter buckeyes, *Junonia coenia* (Nymphalidae), perch on my finger and open their wings to the weak winter sun.

gathering information on population sizes, potential mortality sources, and documenting the "natural" life history of the species. The problem with this strategy is that you may miss the chrysalis stage, and thus never discover what it was, if the caterpillar(s) wander away from the host to pupate.

A slightly more involved strategy might include putting a muslin or net sleeve around a portion of the plant, ensuring that there is enough tissue for the caterpillar to eat, to protect the caterpillar(s) from predators and other potential mortality sources. You may have to "resleeve" the larvae on another portion of the plant on return visits—caterpillars can eat

Making a collection, while frowned on by some, is still a valid way of studying butterflies—some species simply cannot be differentiated on sight. This is a group of butterflies, all patrolling species, which I collected for my undergraduate thesis in Ontario. The butterflies are: LEFT (top to bottom): *Glaucopsyche lygdamus* (Lycaenidae), *Papilio canadensis* (Papilionidae), *Ancyloxypha numitor* (Hesperiidae), *Speyeria cybele*, *Speyeria atlantis* (Nymphalidae). CENTER: *Pieris rapae. Pieris napi* (Pieridae), *Speyeria aphrodite* (Nymphalidae), *Poanes viator (left)*, *Thymelicus lineola* (right; both Hesperiidae), *Megisto cymela* (Nymphalidae). RIGHT: *Euchloe olympia, Colias philodice* (Pieridae), *Clossiana selene, Phyciodes tharos, Coenonympha inornata, Cercyonis pegala* (Nymphalidae).

prodigious amounts of plant tissue! In this way you can ensure its survival and also document the pupal stage, since the caterpillar cannot wander away. Once the chrysalis has formed and hardened up, it can be removed and kept until it ecloses. The mature adult stage should allow you to identify the species. Keep in mind that if you are doing this sort of thing in a temperate region in the fall, or a tropical region approaching the dry season, the caterpillar or pupa may be an overwintering or diapause stage and might need particular conditions to ensure survival.

The ultimate would require that you remove the caterpillar from the site and rear it in captivity. This allows you to fully document the complete life history of the organism through notes, drawings and photographs. Keep in mind that color and pattern changes, sizes and similar attributes may be affected by rearing in unnatural conditions. It's the most labor-intensive since you must become the sole provider for your new charge—fresh host-plant tissue, in large amounts in the last couple of instars, will be required, so make sure that you have ready access to a source of food acceptable to the larvae. The chances are pretty good that what you rear might be a moth species, since moths outnumber butterflies by as many as ten to one, or that what you find out might already be known. On the other hand, it might be a species for which the life history is completely unknown, or you might notice something that no one else has. In any event, keep meticulous records and notes, documenting everything that you did.

HABITAT RESTORATION AND BUTTERFLY GARDENING

One of the "saving graces" of butterfly conservation is that they are not very large. Small creatures such as butterflies can often, but not always, benefit from small-scale efforts to ameliorate the damage to or loss of their

Rearing butterflies from eggs, caterpillars or pupae collected in the field is a great way to learn about the life cycle of butterflies. The Metropolitan Toronto Zoo has been rearing the eastern tailed blue, *Everes comyntas* (Lycaenidae), as a way of working out the protocols in preparation for rearing endangered Karner blues, *Lycaeides melissa samuelis* (Lycaenidae), for potential reintroduction in Ontario.

297

Many butterflies can be easily reared in greenhouses or appropriately sized cages. Here is a group of rearing cages from my studies of the life history of the Mexican fritillary, *Euptoieta hegesia* (Nymphalidae), when I was at York University in Toronto, Canada.

habitat. One example is to turn your sterile, grass-covered backyard into an island of butterfly habitat; a garden for the benefit of butterflies. It's surprisingly easy to set up a backyard sanctuary and, thankfully, people are becoming less enamored of lawns and more inclined to garden for wildlife. If your neighbors are doing, or already have done, something similar, then you're already well on your way to establishing a small network of butterfly habitats.

Gardening for butterflies, whether it be in a backyard sanctuary or a large public space, requires that you provide attractants such as the flowers of nectar plants as well as conditions that will provide the necessities of life so that the butterflies will stay. These might include providing an array of potential butterfly host plants, areas of sunshine for basking, perches to rest on, shelter from strong winds or weather, and, of necessity, avoiding the use of all artificial pesticides. When choosing your site, and your nectar and larval food plants, keep seasonality considerations in mind. Decide whether you want something small, simple and easy to keep up, or to fill a complex, large space that will require considerable labor and time to manage. When given a choice between local wildflowers and host plants versus exotic and difficult-to-maintain species, always opt for the local species. Your local butterflies have a history with the local wildflowers and host plants, so it makes some sense to use them wherever possible.

Without doubt the most commonly used nectar sources by the widest

Gardening to attract butterflies is an excellent way to observe the community of butterflies in your area up-close and personal. Here we see a group of silver-spotted skippers (*Epargyreus clarus*; Hesperiidae) with monarchs (*Danaus plexippus*, Nymphalidae) and a single great-spangled fritillary (*Speyeria cybele*, Nymphalidae) visiting a blazing star (*Liatris* sp., Compositae).

variety of butterflies are composites, that is, members of the aster or daisy family. First, there are more species of composites than there are of almost any other kind of plants; and, second, they are often the most common kinds of flowers blooming when butterflies are about. Keep an eye out for the kinds that are used most often by the local butterflies and try to incorporate them into your garden. Some of the most attractive composites do not resemble daisies at all—for example, *Eupatorium* sp. or *Liatris* sp.— so butterfly watchers and gardeners quickly become fairly accomplished botanists. Other butterfly favorites, regardless of location but always

Butterfly milkweed, *Asclepias tuberosa* (Asclepiadaceae), is a favorite nectar source. Here a mixed group of Lycaenids, including American coppers (*Lycaena phleas*) and coral and banded hairstreaks (*Harkenclenus titus* and *Satyrium calanus*), visit the brilliant orange flowers of this attractive species.

assuming that it is possible or desirable to incorporate them into your garden space, include a variety of verbenas, such as *Verbena*, *Lantana* and *Pentas* sp. (Verbenaceae); milkweeds (*Asclepias* sp., Asclepiadaceae); and butterfly bush, *Buddleia* sp. and varieties (Loganiaceae).

Restoring damaged habitats is a worthwhile endeavor but should not to be undertaken by the faint of heart: it requires a lot of careful consideration, knowledge and work. That being said, creating a community butterfly reserve by rehabilitating a damaged habitat is another way that you can get involved with butterfly conservation. Perhaps a local organization has a plot of land that could benefit from the creation of a butterfly "garden," either formal or informal and more natural. Again, research the local species of butterflies, their favorite nectar sources and larval host plants. Observe their behavior in other natural habitat nearby. Is it possible, without damaging other aspects of the habitat, to provide similar conditions and resources through rehabilitation? Is there a way for the butterflies to travel between habitat patches? Habitat restoration is as much an art as a science, but there are tried-and-true methods that work and others that don't. Again, knowledge is the key.

Explore your area throughout the seasons to find out which species are especially attractive to the butterflies and try to incorporate those species into your garden. In central Texas, a favorite of a great many species, including the American painted lady (*Vanessa virginiensis*, Nymphalidae; left) and the great purple hairstreak (*Atlides halesus*, Lycaenidae; right) is the Texas groundsel or black-eyed susan, *Rudbeckia hirta* (Compositae).

Some flowers and plants, like this flossflower, *Eupatorium greggii* (Compositae) being mobbed by a group of male queen butterflies, *Danaus gilippus* (Nymphalidae), are attractive not only for their nectar but because of their chemistry. This particular plant contains compounds that the male Queens will process into sex pheromones.

TEACH YOUR CHILDREN WELL

Here, finally, is what I personally think is the most important contribution that any one person can make to the conservation of butterflies or any other species or spaces: teach your children to respect nature. Teach them the value of the "three Cs" (courtesy, consideration and caring) in addition to the "three Rs" (reduce, reuse and recycle). Try not to dispel the sense of wonder that all children seem to have for insects and all life around them. It might seem hard to be fascinated by the hornet at your picnic table, or not to scream "Kill it" at anything even vaguely insect-like, but children learn by example. Show some interest when they come home with a beetle in a bottle or decide that they want an ant farm for their birthday. I'm not asking you to love cockroaches, I'm not particularly fond of them myself, but to realize that they have a place in the grand scheme of life. Butterflies, the flying flowers and model citizens of the insect world, are a wonderful place to start.

Turk's cap hibiscus, *Malvaviscus drummondii* (Malvaceae), does not a have typical butterfly flower but is very attractive to a wide variety of hummingbirds as well as many sulfurs including this cloudless sulfur, *Phebis sennae* (Pieridae).

Appendix

RESOURCES

It's typical for natural history books to include a short section devoted to additional resources for the reader. The problem is, these lists are often out of date before the book hits the bookshelves! Thankfully, the advent of the Internet and the World Wide Web means that this never has to happen again. Rather than include the resource material here, I've chosen to set up a web site (www.aworldforbutterflies.com) where readers can find this kind of information—and more.

The web site will not only provide resource listings, but also live links to the online presence of these resources (where they exist). The web site also provides the reader with additional resource material such as endangered species lists; links to species treatments on sites all over the world; other butterfly and moth sites worldwide (including those maintained by many of the photographers in this book); and updates to the bibliography, glossary and text to keep the book current and useful for you, the reader. The web site will also include essays by myself and guest authors on subjects as varied as the etymology of butterfly names; why butterfly releases are a problem for conservation; more case studies of endangered butterflies; and butterfly gardening.

Please drop by and leave me a note, suggestion, criticism or whatever. I look forward to hearing from you.

Phil Schappert
April 2000

Glossary

Abdomen — The third, most posterior, major body division or tagma of insects.

Abiotic — Non-living components of an ecosystem.

Aedeagus — The penis of a male insect.

Aerial — Occurring in the air.

Aestivate — A dormancy period through a dry or summer season that is a regular feature of the life cycle. (also written as estivate)

Anal fold — The portion of the hindwings that folds against the abdomen in a butterfly at rest.

Androconium — Specialized, highly modified scales, usually on the wings, that produce chemical compounds that act as sex pheromones, aphrodisiacs or attractants. (plural Androconia)

Antenna — A segmented sensory organ, found in pairs, above the mouthparts on the head of an insect. Clubbed in butterflies, generally tapering or filiform in moths. (plural Antennae)

Apex — The tip of a wing.

Aphrodisiac — A male-emitted pheromone that causes a female to prepare for copulation.

Aposematism — Warning coloration that is supported by unpalatability or some defense, e.g. chemistry.

Arctic — Non-forested regions north of the temperate coniferous forest of the northern hemisphere.

Austral — The temperate and subtemperate zones of the southern hemisphere.

Automimicry — Mimicry of one's own species in species that vary in palatability due to the presence/absence or strength of some defense.

Barrier — An abiotic or biotic feature that restricts the movement of individuals from one location to another.

Basal — Towards the base (as in the part of the wing closest to the body).

Basking — A method of modifying body temperature or thermoregulating depending on the sun.

Batesian mimicry — Mimicry of an unpalatable model by a palatable mimic.

Biogeography — Study of the distribution of organisms.

Biotic — Living components of an ecosystem.

Binomial nomenclature — The system of naming organisms with two names, one generic and one specific.

Bivoltine — Having two generally discrete generations or broods in each year or season.

Brood — The even-aged offspring of the females of a single species.

Bursa copulatrix — Part of the female genitalia that stores the male's spermatophore.

Camouflage — To imitate, or appear to be, the background.

Caterpillar — The second life-history stage of Lepidoptera. Stage at which growth occurs. See also larva.

Cell — An area of the wing that is enclosed by veins, e.g., a discal cell.

Chitin — The compound, a nitrogenous polysaccharide, that is the major component of the exoskeleton of insects.

Chrysalis — The third life-history stage of Lepidoptera. Stage during which the bulk of metamorphosis occurs. Interchangable with chrysalid. See also pupa.

Circumpolar — A term meaning found all around the polar region.

Claspers — Paired organs of the male abdomen that are used to clasp the female during copulation.

Cocoon — The casing, usually silk, around a chrysalis or pupa.

Coevolution — The evolution of two or more species in close ecological relationship to each other. Generally assumed to mean reciprocal evolutionary changes in interacting species.

Colony — A geographically discrete population or subpopulation of butterflies with determinable boundaries that is separated from other populations.

Common | A term used to describe an organism that is abundant, widely distributed, and often encountered.

Community | The assemblage of organisms that interact with each other in some defined habitat.

Compound eye | An eye made up of separate facets or light-gathering units or ommatidia.

Concave | Curving inward.

Congeneric | Species from the same genus.

Conspecific | Individuals of the same species.

Convex | Curving outward.

Coprophilous | Butterflies that seek excrement as a food resource.

Corpus bursae | Part of the female genitalia that receives the male's spermataphore.

Corridor | A route that allows for the dispersal of individuals from one place to another.

Cosmopolitan | Occurring all over the world, e.g. on essentially all continents

Costa | The forward or leading edge of a butterflies wing.

Costal fold | The area of the costal margin that contains androconial scales in some butterfly species.

Coxa | Basal segment, closest to the body, of an insect leg.

Cremaster | Hooked structure at the posterior end of a chrysalis used to attach it to a silken pad.

Crepuscular | Active at the interface between day and night, e.g. dusk or dawn.

Crochets | Hooks on the prolegs of caterpillars.

Crypsis | The combination of color, pattern and structure that allow an organism to conceal itself by camouflage.

Cuticle | The outer layer of the epidermis/integument.

Diapause | A period of inactivity and arrested development.

Dimorphism | A single species that may have two different forms or appearances.

Disjunct | Widely separated populations or a discontinuous range.

Disk | Central portion of a butterfly's wing, e.g., discal.

Dispersal | Movements by individuals as part of their daily activities the sum of which are not necessarily directional.

Disruptive coloration | A color pattern that helps to break up the outline of the body in order to make the shape less recognizable.

Distal | The portion of an appendage that is farthest from the body.

Diversity | An ecological term with several meanings. Usually refers to the number of species present in some defined habitat but also refers to the equitability or similarity in abundance of the species.

Dormancy | A period of inactivity.

Dorsal | Upper surface of a body or wing.

Ecdysis | The shedding of an old cuticle during molting.

Eclose (eclosion) | The emergence of the imago or adult butterfly from the chrysalis or pupa. Sometimes also used to refer to the hatching of a caterpillar or larva from the egg.

Ecology | The study of the factors that determine the distribution and abundance of organisms.

Ecosystem | A biological community in relation to its physical environment.

Egg | The first life-history stage of Lepidoptera and other insects in which the zygote develops into a caterpillar or larva.

Emigrate | To permanently leave a region or area.

Endemic | Limited to a specific area, occurring nowhere else.

Entomophagous | Feeding on insects.

Exoskeleton | An outer skeleton as opposed to an endoskeleton or internal skeleton.

Extant | Now living.

Extinct | Having no surviving individuals or populations anywhere.

Extirpated | Having no surviving individuals or populations in an area where they formerly occurred.

Eyespot | A pattern on a wing that resembles an eye.

Femur | The third segment of a leg between the tibia and trochanter.

Flagellum | The antennal segments beyond the scape.

Forewing | The anterior pair of wings.

Fossil | A remnant, impression or other trace of an organism from the past.

Frass | The excrement or droppings of caterpillars.

Frenulum | A wing coupling mechanism where bristles in the costal margin of the hindwing interlock with a region of the anal margin of the forewing.

Frons | The triangular patch on the forehead between the eyes.

Galeae | Outer lobes of the maxillae that make up the proboscis.

Generation | A discrete but complete life history, e.g. adult to adult via eggs, caterpillars and pupae.

Genitalia | Copulatory organs.

Genus | A taxonomic category in which all species share some defined trait that is not shared by other genera.

Girdle | A band of silk around the thorax that is used to hold some pupae upright.

Gynandromorph | An individual that has both male and female characteristics.

Habitat | The place where an organism normally lives.

Haemolymph	The body fluid that is the insect equivalent of blood. (also written Hemolymph)	Mandibles	Paired chewing mouthparts of a caterpillar.
		Margin	The edge of a wing.
Hairpencil	A specialized androconial organ of butterflies used to disseminate pheromones.	Maxillae	Paired mouthparts immediately behind the mandibles.
Haustellum	The coiled mouthpart that allows adult butterflies to suck up liquid nourishment. Also called the proboscis.	Meconium	Waste material from pupation, usually pigmented, that is released before a butterfly's first flight.
Head	The first, most anterior, major body division or tagma of insects.	Megafauna	Relatively large (in comparison to the average) organisms.
Herbivore	An animal that feeds exclusively on plants.	Melanic	Having excess dark pigment.
Heterocera	All Lepidoptera that are not Rhopalocera, i.e. moths.	Mesothorax	The second or middle thoracic segment from which the forewings arise.
Hibernation	A dormancy period through a wet or winter season. Also called overwintering in temperate regions.	Metamorphosis	Change in form during development as in the change between a caterpillar and a butterfly.
Hibernaculum	A protective structure built by a caterpillar in which to hibernate or aestivate.	Metapopulation	A collection of populations that exchange individuals.
Hilltopping	A butterfly behavior used by males to find mates, often at landmarks or hills.	Metathorax	The third, most posterior, thoracic segment from which the hindwings arise.
Hindwing	The rear pair of wings.	Microlepidoptera	An ill-defined group of families most of which contain small moths.
Holarctic	Occurring in both the Nearctic and Palearctic realms.	Micropyle	Tiny opening in the egg through which it was fertilized.
Host plant	The particular food plant of a caterpillar.	Migrant	A participant in a migration.
Hyaline	Glossy, shiny, translucent, transparent.	Migrate	A change in location via directed dispersal by all, or a large proportion, of a population.
Hybrid	The result of a cross between dissimilar parents.	Mimetic	An individual that mimics another individual.
Imago (imagine)	The fourth and final life-history stage of Lepidoptera. Stage at which reproduction occurs. Also called the adult or butterfly. (plural Imagines)	Mimicry	A resemblance between individuals that provides some benefit to one or both, e.g. a resemblance between palatable and unpalatable butterflies that protects the palatable individuals from predators.
Imaginal disks	Regions of undifferentiated cells from zygote through the larval stage from which arise the structures of the adult.	Molt	The shedding of the exoskeleton that allows caterpillars to grow.
Immature	All life history stages before the reproductive imago or adult stage.	Monophagy	Being able to use only one kind of food, e.g. a species that accepts only a single host.
Immigrate	To permanently move to a new region.	Monophyletic	A group of taxa descended from, and including, their common ancestor.
Inbreeding	Mating of close relatives, leads to increase in genetic defects.	Monotypic	Having a single form, e.g. a single species in a taxon.
Indicator species	A species that is characteristic of particular habitats or ecological conditions where a change in the habitat/conditions is reflected by changes in abundance of the species.	Morph	A single appearance or combination of body form, shape or color.
Intraspecific	Within species.	Müllerian mimicry	A mimetic system wherein all participants are unpalatable and share a single morph.
Instar	Developmental stage between successive molts in an insect.	Multivoltine	Having multiple (three or more) discrete generations per year or season.
Interspecific	Between species.	Muscular thermogenesis	Shivering to generate heat in the muscles.
Labial palps	Paired jointed sensory appendages arising from the mouthparts of an insect.	Mutation	Heritable changes that differ from that most commonly encountered.
Larva	The second life-history stage of Lepidoptera. Stage at which growth occurs. See also caterpillar.	Myrmocophily	Literally, "ant loving," as in the majority of Lycaenids.
Lepidoptera	The insect order containing the moths, skippers and butterflies.		
Lunule	A crescent-shaped mark.		
Maculation	Markings (spots, bars, etc.) on a butterfly's wings.		

Nearctic | Temperate and arctic North America.

Nectar guides | Markings on flowers, sometimes invisible/ultraviolet, that guide insects to nectaries.

Necrophagous | Feeding on dead animal matter.

Neotropic | Tropical North, Central and South America.

Ocellus | Small, single-facetted, simple eye. (plural Ocelli)

Oligophagy | Being able to use only a few kinds of food, e.g. a species that feeds on a group of closely-related hosts.

Ommatidium | A single facet or unit of a compound eye.

Osmeterium | A brightly colored extrusible odor-producing organ used as a defense by Papilionid butterfly caterpillars.

Ovaries | The egg-producing organs of a female butterfly.

Ovarioles | An individual egg-producing portion of the ovaries; in butterflies there are four ovarioles in each of the two ovaries.

Overwinter | To hibernate.

Oviposition | The process by which a female butterfly chooses a site to lay eggs. Also used to describe the act of egg laying.

Ovum | A single egg. (plural Ova)

Palearctic | Temperate and arctic Europe and Asia.

Palpus | One of a pair of appendages found beside the proboscis, arising from the maxilla or labium, that serve a sensory function. See also labial palps. (plural Palpi or palps)

Pantropic | A term meaning found all around the tropics.

Parasite | An organism that lives off of another organism but does not kill it.

Parasitioid | An organism that kills another organism by living off of it.

Patrol | An active mate location strategy characterized by flying to seek potential mates.

Pedicel | The antennal segment between the scape and the flagellum.

Perch | A passive mate location strategy characterized by waiting at landmark sites for the passing of potential mates.

Pharate | Stage of development where a new form is still enclosed within an old form, e.g. a butterfly seen through the transparent pupal case just before eclosure.

Phenology | Study of the timing of natural events.

Pheromones | Specialized chemical compounds that promote behavioral responses by other individuals.

Photoperiod | The length of the day/night cycle.

Pleistocene | The geological epoch, beginning about one million years ago, in which recent glaciation occurred.

Polymorphism | Having several distinct forms or morphs.

Polyphagy | Being able to use many kinds of food, e.g. a species that is able to feed on several unrelated plants is polyphagous.

Polyphenism | A polymorphism that is determined by environmental conditions.

Polyphyletic | A group of taxa containing more than one common ancestor.

Population | An interbreeding group of individuals of the same species that are separated in space or time from other groups of the same species.

Predator | An organism that eats another organism.

Prepupa | A resting stage within the last larval instar prior to pupation.

Prey | An organism that is eaten by another organism.

Proboscis | The coiled, straw-like sucking tube mouthparts of a butterfly. See also Haustellum.

Prolegs | The fleshy abdominal legs of caterpillars.

Protandry | The appearance or maturation of males before females.

Prothorax | The first, most anterior, thoracic segment (does not have wings).

Proximal | The portion of an appendage that is closest to the body.

Pupa | The developmental stage between a larva (caterpillar) and an imago (adult butterfly). See also Chrysalis. (plural Pupae or pupas)

Race | A distinctive population within a species that may be geographically limited or co-occur with another species morph. Equivalent to a variety, sometimes considered equivalent to a subspecies.

Rare | Term used to describe a species that is not abundant, narrowly distributed, and infrequently encountered (any one or a combination of all three).

Refuge | An area that has remained unchanged while areas around it have changed markedly, often serving as a refuge for species with specific habitat requirements.

Relict | A population that is stranded and no longer able to interbreed with individuals from the main range of a species.

Rhopalocera | The butterflies, Papilionoidea and Hesperiioidea, together with their common ancestors, the butterfly-moths of the Hedyloidea (or, potentially, the Castnoidea). As distinct from the Heterocera.

Roost | A gathering place of resting butterflies.

Scale | A flattened plate-like hair that is loosely attached to the wing; together the scales provide the color and pattern of the wings.

Scape | The basal segment of an antenna.

Scent scales | Specialized, highly modified scales, usually on the wings, that produce chemical compounds that act as sex pheromones, aphrodisiacs or attractants. Also called androconial scales.

Segment Structural units of invertebrate bodies, as in the segments of caterpillars, antennae, etc.

Seta A moveable sensory hair. (plural Setae)

Sex patch A patch of androconial scales visible on the wings. Also known as stigmata or brands.

Sibling species Two or more closely related species, usually from the same genus.

Speciation Process by which a single species gives rise to two or more species.

Species Any group of interbreeding organisms that are differentiated from other such reproductive groups. Also a taxonomic category in which all organisms of the same species are considered different from all other species.

Spermatophore A package containing sperm, salts and nutrients that is deposited by a male within a female's body during copulation.

Sphragis A hard structure secreted by a male to cover the end of a females abdomen and prevent her from mating again.

Spinneret The organ on the head of a caterpillar responsible for secreting silk.

Spiracles Openings along the abdomen through which air enters and leaves the insect body.

Stadium A single stage or instar, as in the prepupal stadium.

Stigma A patch of androconial scales visible on the wings. (plural Stigmata)

Stray An individual that is found far outside its usual range but is not a common emigrant.

Sub A prefix meaning below or under, as in a subfamily (between family and genus).

Subspecies A distinctive subset of a species, may be geographic in origin. Sometimes considered a variety or race.

Super A prefix meaning above or over, as in a superfamily (between family and order).

Symbiosis Organisms living in close association.

Tagma A distinct body region (e.g. head, thorax, or abdomen). (plural Tagmata)

Tarsus The most distal end of the butterfly leg, has a pair of claws for clinging and sensing substrates.

Tarsomeres The segments that make up the tarsus, usually five in number.

Taxon An individual unit in a taxonomic classification, e.g. a species, a genus or any other identifiable group. (plural Taxa)

Tectonic Any process involved in the production or deformation of the earth's crust.

Temperate An area with a mean annual temperature of between 10°C and 13°C (50°F and 55°F).

Teneral Period after eclosion during which the butterfly is incapable of flight.

Territory A living space that enhances either the survival or the reproduction of an individual.

Thermoregulation The process of regulating body temperature.

Thorax The second, center, major body division or tagma of the insect body, contains the bulk of the locomotory muscles, the legs and the wings.

Tibia The fourth segment of an insect leg, between the tarsus and the femur.

Tornus Outer angle of an insect wing.

Trachea Internal tubes that allow air to diffuse into the insect body and tissues. (plural Tracheae)

Trochanter Segment of the insect leg between the femur and the coxa.

Tropical An area with a mean annual temperature above 25°C (75°F) where no freezing occurs.

Tropics The latitudinal region between the Tropic of Cancer, 23.5°N latitude, and the Tropic of Capricorn, 23.5°S latitude.

Truncate Appearing to be clipped or missing the tip of a converging object.

Tubercle A bump or knob on a caterpillar's body.

Type Taxonomic term for the individual upon which a species description is based.

Ultraviolet Wavelengths of light that are beyond the human visual spectrum but visible to some insects.

Univoltine Having one generation per year.

Vagility Ability to move or be moved from one place to another.

Valvae Male claspers that are used to grasp the external genitalia of the female.

Venation Pattern of veins that constitute the structural support of the insect wing.

Ventral Opposite of dorsal, the undersurface of an object.

Warning coloration Colors used to advertise unpalatability, regardless of the palatability of the advertiser. Usually combinations of black with white, red, orange or yellow, often in alternating bands.

Zygote The diploid fusion of gametes of males and females, e.g. sperm and egg.

Bibliography

My intent in this bibliography is to provide you with both literature sources for the major topics that I discuss in the text as well as "jumping off points" into the vast, accumulates literature on butterfly biologoy, evolution, ecology and conservation. Many of the books, articles and papers listed here serve not only as topical references for the written text but are themselves classic reports of studies, experiments and investigations into the biology of butterlies. They are worth seeking out and I hope that you enjoy reading them as much as I have.

BOOKS

Ackery, P. R. and Vane-Wright, R. I. *Milkweed Butterflies, their Cladistics and Biology*. London: British Museum of Natural History, 1984.

Bates, H. W. *The Naturalist on the River Amazons*. 2nd ed., London: Murray, 1864.

Brewer, J. and Sandved, K. B. *Butterflies*. New York: Harry N. Abrams, 1978.

—. and Winter, D. *Butterflies and Moths: A Companion to your Field Guide*. New York: Phalarope Books, 1986.

Brooks, M.. M. and Knight, C. *A Complete Guide to British Butterflies*. London: Jonathan Cape Ltd., 1982.

Brown, F. M. and Heineman, B. *Jamaica and its Butterflies*. London: E. W. Classey Ltd., 1972.

Brown, J. H. and Lomolino, M. V. *Biogeography*, 2nd edition. Sunderland: Sinauer Associates, Inc., 1998.

Carter, D. J. *Butterflies and Moths*. London: Eyewitness Handbooks, Dorling Kindersley Ltd., 1992.

Caterpillars: Ecological and Evolutionary Constraints on Foraging. eds. Stamp, N. E. and Casey, T. M., New York: Chapman & Hall, 1993.

Collins, N. M. and Morris, M. G. *Threatened Swallowtail Butterflies of the World*. Gland and Cambridge: IUCN Red Data Book, 1985.

Common, I. F. B. and Waterhouse, D. F. *Butterflies of Australia*. Revised edition. Sydney: Angus & Robertson, 1981.

DeVries, P. J. *The Butterflies of Costa Rica and their Natural History: Papilionidae, Pieridae, Nymphalidae*. Princeton: Princeton University Press, 1987.

Douglas, M. M. *The Lives of Butterflies*. Ann Arbor: University of Michigan Press, 1986.

Eaton, J. L. *Lepidopteran Anatomy*. New York: John Wiley and Sons, 1988.

Emmel, T. C.; Minno, M. C. and Drummon, B. A. *Florissant Butterflies: A Guide to the Fossil and Present-Day Species of Central Colorado*. Palo Alto: Stanford University Press, 1992.

Grace, E. S. *The Nature of Monarch Butterflies: Beauty Takes Flight*. Vancouver: Greystone Books, 1997.

Hanski , I. *Metapopulation Ecology*. Oxford: Oxford University Press, 1999.

Henning, G. A.; Henning, S. F.; Joannou, J. G. and Woodhall, S. E. *Living Butterflies of Southern Africa: Biology, Ecology and Conservation*. Vol. 1: Hesperiidae, Papilionidae and Pieridae of South Africa. Hatfield: Umdaus Press, 1997.

Holmes, A. M.; Hess, Q. F.; Tasker, R. R. and Hanks, A. J. *The Ontario Butterfly Atlas*. Toronto: Toronto Entomologists' Association, 1991.

Layberry, R. A.; Hall, P. W. and Lafontaine. J. D. *The Butterflies of Canada*. Toronto: University of Toronto Press, 1998.

Lewis, H. L. *Butterflies of the World*. London: George G. Harrap, 1974.

New, T. R. *Butterfly Conservation*. Melbourne: Oxford University Press, 1991.

Nijhout, H. F. *The Devolpment and Evolution of Butterfly Wing Patterns*. Washington: Smithsonian Institution Press, 1991.

Opler, P. A. and Krizek, G. O. *Butterflies East of the Great Plains: An Illustrated Natural History*. Baltimore: Johns Hopkins University Press, 1984.

Owen, D. F. *Tropical Butterflies: The Ecology and Behavior of Butterflies in the Tropics with Special Reference to African Species*. Oxford: Clarendon Press, 1971.

—. *Camouflage and Mimicry*. Chicago: University of Chicago Press, 1980.

Pennington's Butterflies of Southern Africa. eds. Henning, G. A.; Pringle, E. L. L. and Ball, J. B., 2nd ed., Cape Town: Struik Publishing, 1994

Perspectives on Insect Conservation. eds., Gaston, K. J.; New, T. R. and Samways, M. J., Hampshire: Intercept Ltd., 1993.

Pollard, E. and Yates, T. J. *Monitoring Butterflies for Ecology and Conservation*. London: Chapman & Hall, 1993.

Preston-Mafham, R. and Preston-Mafham, K. *Butterflies of the World*. New York: Facts on File Publications, 1988.

Pyle, R. M. *The Audubon Society Handbook for Butterfly Watchers*. New York: Charles Scribner's Sons, 1984.

Samways, M. J. *Insect Conservation Biology*. London: Chapman & Hall, 1994.

Sbordoni, V. and Forestiero, S. *Butterflies of the World*. New York: Crescent Books, 1985.

Schwartz, A. *The Butterflies of Hispaniola*. Gainesville: University of Florida Press, 1989.

Scoble, M. J. *The Lepidoptera: Form, Function and Diversity*. Oxford: Oxford University Press, 1992.

Scott, J. A. *The Butterflies of North America: A Natural History and Field Guide*. Palo Alto: Stanford University Press, 1986.

Smart, P. *The Illustrated Encyclopedia of the Butterfly World*. Essex: Salamander Books, 1975.

Smith, D. S.; Miller, L. D. and Miller J. Y. *The Butterflies of the West Indies and South Florida*. Oxford: Oxford University Press, 1994.

Stokes, D. L.; Stokes, L. Q. and Williams, E. *The Butterfly Book*. Boston: Little, Brown and Co., 1991.

Strong, D. R.; Lawton, J. H. and Southwood, T. R. E. *Insects on Plants: Community Patterns and Mechanisms*. Cambridge: Harvard University Press, 1984.

The Biology of Butterflies. eds. Vane-Wright, R. I. and Ackery, P. R., London: Academic Press, 1984.

The Ecology of Butterflies in Britain. ed. Dennis, R. L. H. Oxford: Oxford University Press, 1992.

Tyler, H. A.; Brown, Jr., K. S. and Wilson, K. H. *Swallowtail Butterflies of the Americas*. Gainesville: Scientific Publishers, 1994.

Urquhart, F. A. *The Monarch Butterfly: International Traveller*. Chicago: Nelson-Hall, 1987.

Watson, A.; Whalley, P. E. S. and Duckworth, W. D. *The Dictionary of Butterflies and Moths in Colour*. London: Peerage Books, 1975.

Whalley, P. E. S. *Butterfly and Moth*. London: Eyewitness Books, 1988.

Wickler, W. *Mimicry in Plants and Animals*. New York: McGraw-Hill, 1968.

ARTICLES AND PAPERS

Ackery, P. R. "Systematic and Faunistic Studies on Butterflies." in: *The Biology of Butterflies*. eds. Vane-Wright, R. I. and Ackery, P. R. 9-21. London: Academic Press, 1984.

—. "Hostplants and Classification: A Review of Nymphalid Butterflies." *Biological Journal of the Linnean Society* 33 (1988): 95-203.

Adler, P. H. and Pearson, D. L. "Why do Male Butterflies Visit Mud Puddles?" *Canadian Journal of Zoology* 60 (1982): 322-325.

Aiello, A. "*Adelpha* (Nymphalidae): Deception on the Wing." *Psyche* 91 (1984): 1-45.

Alcock, J. "Leks and Hilltopping in Insects." *Journal of Natural History* 21 (1987): 319-328.

Alonso-Meija, A. and Marquez, M. "Dragonfly Predation on Butterflies in a Tropical Dry Forest." *Biotropica* 26 (1994): 341-344.

Arnold, R. A. "Ecological Studies of Six Endangered Butterflies (Lepidoptera: Lycaenidae): Island Biogeography, Patch Dynamics and the Design of Nature Preserves." *Entomology* 99 (1983): 1-161.

Aronson, A. and Wu, D. "Specificity *In Vivo* and *In Vitro* of *Bacillus Thuringiensis* Delta-endotoxins Active in Lepidoptera." in: *New Directions in Biological Control: Alternatives for Suppressing Agricultural Pests and Diseases*, eds., Baker, R. R. and Dunn, P. E., 547-559. Woods Hole: Alan R. Liss, Inc., 1990.

Atsatt, P. R. "Lycaenid Butterflies and Ants: Selection for Enemy-Free Space." *American Naturalist* 118 (1981): 638-654.

Austad, S. N.; Jones, W. T. and Waser, P. M. "Territorial Defence in Speckled Wood Butterflies: Why does the Resident Always Win?" *Animal Behavior* 27 (1970): 960-961.

Baker, R. R. "Bird Predation as a Selective Pressure on the Immature Stages of the Cabbage Butterflies, *Pieris Rapae* and *P. Brassicae*." *Journal of Zoology* 162 (1970): 43-59.

—. "Territorial Behaviour of the Nymphalid Butterflies, *Aglais Urticae* and *Inachis Io*." *Journal of Animal Ecology* 41 (1972): 453-469.

—. "Insect Territoriality." *Annual Review of Entomology* 28 (1983): 65-89.

—. "The Dilemma: When and How to Go or Stay." in: *The Biology of Butterflies*, eds. Vane-Wright, R. I. and Ackery, P. R., 279-296. London: Academic Press, 1984.

Bartholomew, G. A. A Matter of Size: An Examination of Endothermy in Insects and Terrestrial Vertebrates." in: *Insect Thermoregulation*, ed. Heinrich, B., 45-78. New York: Wiley & Sons, 1981.

Beccaloni, G. W. and Gaston, K. J. "Predicting the Species Richness of Neotropical Forest Butterflies: Ithomiinae (Lepidoptera: Nymphalidae) as Indicators." *Biological Conservation* 71 (1995): 77-86.

Benson, W. W. "Resource Partitioning in Passion Vine Butterflies." *Evolution* 32 (1978): 493-518.

—. Brown, Jr., K. S. and Gilbert, L. E. "Coevolution of Plants and Herbivores: Passion Flower Butterflies." *Evolution* 29 (1975): 659-680.

Berenbaum, M. R. "Coumarins and Caterpillars: A Case for Coevolution." *Evolution* 37 (1983): 163-179.

—. "Aposematism and Mimicry in Caterpillars." *Journal of the Lepidopterists' Society* 49 (1995): 386-396.

Bernard, G. D. "Red-Absorbing Visual Pigment of Butterflies." *Science* 203 (1979): 1125-1127.

Blau, W. S. "The Effect of Environmental Disturbance on a Tropical Butterfly Population." *Ecology* 61 (1980): 1005-1012.

Boggs, C. L. "Reproductive Strategies of Female Butterflies: Variation In and Constraints On Fecundity." *Ecological Entomology* 11 (1986): 7-15.

—. "Ecology of Nectar and Pollen Feeding in Lepidoptera." in: *Nutritional Ecology of Insects, Mites, Spiders, and Related Invertebrates,* eds. Slansky, Jr., F. and Rodriguez, J. G., 369-391. New York: Wiley & Sons, 1987.

—. and Jackson, L.A. "Mud Puddling by Butterflies is Not a Simple Matter." *Ecological Entomology* 16 (1991): 123-127.

Boppré, M. "Chemically Mediated Interactions Between Butterflies." in: *The Biology of Butterflies,* eds., Vane-Wright, R. I. and Ackery, P. R., 259-275. London: Academic Press, 1984.

Bowers, M. D. "Plant Allelochemistry and Mimicry." in: *Novel Aspects of Insect-Plant Interactions,* eds., Barbosa, P. and Letourneau, D. K., 273-311. New York: Wiley & Sons, 1988.

—. "Aposematic Caterpillars: Life Styles of the Warningly-Coloured and Unpalatable." in: *Caterpillars: Ecological and Evolutionary Constraints on Foraging.,* eds., Stamp, N. E. and Casey, T. M., 331-371. New York: Chapman and Hall, 1993.

—. Brown, I. L. and Wheye, D. "Bird Predation as a Selective Agent in a Butterfly Population." *Evolution* 39 (1985): 93-103.

—. and Puttick, G. M. "Response of Generalist and Specialist Insects to Qualitative Allelochemical Variation." *Journal of Chemical Ecology* 14 (1988): 319-334.

Brakefield, P. M. "The Ecological Genetics of Quantitative Characters of *Maniola Jurtina* and Other Butterflies." in: *The Biology of Butterflies,* eds., Vane-Wright, R. I. and Ackery, P. R., 167-190. London: Academic Press, 1984.

—. and Larsen, T. B. "The Evolutionary Significance of Dry and Wet Season Forms in Some Tropical Butterflies." *Biological Journal of the Linnean Society* 22 (1984): 1-12.

Brewer, J. "Butterfly Gardening." *Xerces Society Self-help Sheet* No. 7 (1982): 1-16.

Brower, L. P. "Ecological Chemistry." *Scientific American* 220 (1969): 22-29.

—. "Monarch Migration." *Natural History* 86 (1977): 41-53.

—. "Chemical Defense in Butterflies." in: *The Biology of Butterflies,* eds., Vane-Wright, R. I. and Ackery, P. R., 109-134. London: Academic Press, 1984.

—. "Understanding and Misunderstanding the Migration of the Monarch Butterfly (Nymphalidae) in North America: 1857-1995." *Journal of the Lepidopterists' Society* 49 (1995): 304-385.

—. Brower, J. V. and Cranston, F. P. "Courtship Behavior of the Queen Butterfly, *Danaus Gilippus Berenice.*" *Zoologica* (NY) 50 (1965): 1-39.

—. McEvoy, P. B.; Williamson, K. L. and Flannery, M. A. "Variation in Cardiac Glycoside Content of Monarch Butterflies from Natural Populations in Eastern North America." *Science* 177 (1972): 426-429.

—. and Malcolm, S. B. "Endangered Phenomena." *Wings* 14(2) (1989): 3-9.

Brown, J. H. "On the Relationship Between Abundance and Distribution of Species." *American Naturalist* 124 (1984): 255-279.

Brown, Jr., K. S. "The Biology of *Heliconius* and Related Genera." *Annual Review of Entomology* 26 (1981): 427-456.

—. "Historical and Ecological Factors in the Biogeography of Aposematic Neotropical Butterflies." *American Zoologist* 22 (1982): 453-471.

—. "Mimicry, Aposematism and Crypsis in Neotropical Lepidoptera: The Importance of Dual Signals." *Bulletin de la Société Zoologique de France* 113 (1988): 83-101.

—.; Sheppard, P. M. and Turner, J. R. G. "Quaternary Refugia in Tropical America: Evidence from Race Formation in *Heliconius* Butterflies." *Proceedings of the Royal Society, London* B 187 (1974): 369-378.

—. and Francini, R. B. "Evolutionary Strategies of Chemical Defense in Aposematic Butterflies: Cyanogenesis in Asteraceae-Feeding American Acraeinae." *Chemoecology* 1 (1990): 52-56.

—.; Trigo, J. R.; Francini, R. B.; Barros de Morais, A. B. and Motta, P. C. "Aposematic Insects on Toxic Host Plants: Coevolution, Colonization and Chemical Emancipation." in: *Plant-Animal Interactions: Evolutionary Ecology in Tropical and Temperate Regions,* eds., Price, P. W.; Lewinsohn, T. M.: Fernandes, G. W. and Benson, W. W., 375-402. New York: Wiley & Sons, 1991.

Caldas, A. "Population Ecology of *Anaea Ryphea* (Nymphalidae): Immatures at Campinas." *Brazil. Journal of the Lepidopterists' Society* 49 (1995): 234-245.

Calvert, W. H.; Zuchowski, W. and Brower, L. P. "Monarch Butterfly Conservation: Interactions of Cold Weather, Forest Thinning and Storms on the Survival of Overwintering Monarch Butterflies (*Danaus plexippus* L.)" *Mexico.* Atala 9 (1984): 2-6.

Cappuccino, N. and Kareiva, P. "Coping With a Capricious Environment: A Population Study of a Rare Pierid Butterfly." *Ecology* 66 (1985): 152-161.

Chai, P. "Wing Coloration of Free-Flying Neotropical Butterflies as a Signal Learned by a Specialized Avian Predator." *Biotropica* 20 (1988): 20-30.

—. and Srygley, R. B. "Predation and the Flight, Morphology, and Temperature of Neotropical Rain-Forest Butterflies. *American Naturalist* 135 (1990): 748-765.

Chew, F. S. "The Effects of Introduced Mustards (Cruciferae) On Some Native North American Cabbage Butterflies (Lepidoptera: Pieridae)." *Atala* 5 (1977): 13-19.

—. and Robbins, R. K. "Egg-Laying in Butterflies." in: *The Biology of Butterflies.* eds., Vane-Wright, R. I. and Ackery, P. R., 65-79. London: Academic Press, 1984.

—. and Courtney, S. P. "Plant Apparency and Evolutionary Escape From Insect Herbivory." *American Naturalist* 138 (1991): 729-750.

Clarke, C. A. and Sheppard, P. M. "The Evolution of Mimicry in the Butterfly *Papilio Dardanus*." *Heredity* 14 (1960): 163-173.

Clench, H. K. "Behavioral Thermoregulation in Butterflies." *Ecology* 47 (1966): 1021-1034.

Courtney, S. P. "The Evolution of Egg Clustering by Butterflies and Other Insects." *American Naturalist* 123 (1984): 276-281.

—. "The Ecology of Pierid Butterflies: Dynamics and Interactions." *Advances in Ecological Research* 15 (1989): 51-131.

—. and Anderson, K. "Behaviour Around Encounter Sites." *Behavioural Ecology & Sociobiology* 19 (1986): 241-248.

—. and Chew, F. S. "Co-Existence and Host Use by a Large Community of Pierid Butterflies: Habitat is the Templet." *Oecologia* 71 (1987): 210-220.

Crawley, M. J. "Insect Herbivores and Plant Population Dynamics." *Annual Review of Entomology* 34 (1989): 531-64.

Davies, N. B. "Territorial Defence in the Speckled Wood Butterfly (*Pararge Aegeria*): The Resident Always Wins." *Animal Behaviour* 26 (1978): 138-147.

Davis, R. H. and Nahrstedt, A. "Biosynthesis of Cyanogenic Glycosides in Butterflies and Moths." *Insect Biochemistry* 17 (1987): 689-693.

Dempster, J. P. "The Natural Control of Populations of Butterflies and Moths." *Biological Review* 58 (1983): 461-481.

—. "The Natural Enemies of Butterflies." in: *The Biology of Butterflies.* eds.,Vane-Wright, R. I. and Ackery, P. R., 97-104. London: Academic Press, 1984.

DeVries, P. J. "Pollen-Feeding Rainforest *Parides* and *Battus* Butterflies in Costa Rica." *Biotropica* 11 (1979): 237-238.

—. "Patterns of Butterfly Diversity and Promising Topics in Natural History and Ecology." in: *LaSelva: Ecology and Natural History of a Neotropical Rainforest.*, eds., McDade, L. A.; Bawa, K. S.; Hespenheide, H. A. and Hartshorn, G. S., 187-194. Chicago: University of Chicago Press, 1994.

—. and Baker, I. "Butterfly Exploitation of an Ant-Plant Mutualism: Adding Insult to Herbivory." *Journal of the New York Entomological Society* 97 (1989): 332-340.

Douglas, M. M. "Hot Butterflies." *Natural History* 88 (1978): 56-65.

—. and Grula, J. W. "Thermoregulatory Adaptations Allowing Ecological Range Expansion by the Pierid Butterfly, *Nathalis Iole* Boisduval." *Evolution* 32 (1979): 776-783.

Durden, C. J. and Rose, H. "Butterflies From the Middle Eocene: The Earliest Occurrence of Fossil Papilionoidea (Lepidoptera)." *Pearce-Sellards Series* 29 (1978): 1-25.

Ehrlich, P. R. The Structure and Dynamics of Butterfly Populations." in: *The Biology of Butterflies.*, eds., Vane-Wright, R. I. and Ackery, P. R., 25-40. London: Academic Press, 1984.

—. "Population Biology of Checkerspot Butterflies and the Preservation of Global Biodiversity." *Oikos* 63 (1992): 6-12.

—. and Ehrlich, A. H. "Lizard Predation on Tropical Butterflies." *Journal of the Lepidopterists' Society* 36 (1982): 148-152.

—. and Gilbert, L. E. "Population Structure and Dynamics of the Tropical Butterfly *Heliconius Ethilla*." *Biotropica* 5 (1973): 69-82.

—. and Murphy, D. D. "Conservation Lessons From Long-Term Studies of Checkerspot Butterflies." *Conservation Biology* 1 (1987): 122-131.

—. and Raven, P. H. "Butterflies and Plants: A Study in Coevolution." *Evolution* 18 (1964): 586-608.

—. and Raven, P. H. "Butterflies and Plants." *Scientific American* 216 (1967): 104-113.

Emmel, T. C. and Austin, G. T. "The Tropical Rain Forest Butterfly Fauna of Rondonia, Brazil: Species Diversity and Conservation." *Tropical Lepidoptera* 1 (1990): 1-12.

—. and Garraway, E. "Ecology and Conservation Biology of the Homerus Swallowtail in Jamaica (Lepidoptera: Papilionidae)." *Tropical Lepidoptera* 1 (1990): 63-76.

Endler, J. A. "An Overview of the Relationships Between Mimicry and Crypsis." *Biological Journal of the Linnean Society* 16 (1981): 25-31.

Erhardt, A. "Diurnal Lepidoptera: Sensitive Indicators of Cultivated and Abandoned Grassland." *Journal of Applied Ecology* 22 (1985): 849-862.

Findlay, R.; Young, M. R. and Findlay, J. A. "Orientation Behaviour in the Grayling Butterfly: Thermoregulation or Crypsis?" *Ecological Entomology* 8 (1983): 145-153.

Freitas, A. V. L. "Biology and Population Dynamics of *Placidula Euryanassa*, a Relict Ithomiine Butterfly (Nymphalidae: Ithomiinae)." *Journal of the Lepidopterists' Society* 47 (1993): 87-105.

Gall, L. F. "Measuring the Size of Lepidopteran Populations." *Journal of Research on the Lepidoptera* 24 (1985): 97-116.

Garraway, E.; Bailey, A. J. A. and Emmel, T.C. "Contribution to the Ecology and Conservation Biology of the Endangered *Papilio Homerus* (Lepidoptera: Papilionidae)." *Tropical Lepidoptera* 4 (1993): 83-91.

Gilbert, L. E. "Pollen Feeding and Reproductive Biology of *Heliconius* Butterflies." *Proceedings of the National Academy of Science*, USA 69 (1972): 1403-1407.

—. "Ecological Consequences of a Coevolved Mutualism Between Butterflies and Plants." in: *Coevolution of Animals and Plants.*, eds.,

Gilbert, L. E. and Raven, P. H., 210-240. Austin: University of Texas Press, 1975.

—. "Postmating Female Odor in *Heliconius* Butterflies: A Male-Contributed Antiaphrodisiac?" *Science* 193 (1976): 419-420.

—. "The Coevolution of a Butterfly and a Vine." *Scientific American* 247 (1982): 110-121.

—. "Coevolution and Mimicry." in: *Coevolution.*, eds., Futuyma, D. J. and Slatkin, M., 263-281. Boston: Sinauer Assoc., 1983.

—. "The Biology of Butterfly Communities." in: *The Biology of Butterflies.*, eds., Vane-Wright, R. I. and Ackery, P. R., 41-54. London: Academic Press, 1984.

—. "Biodiversity of a Central American *Heliconius* Community: Pattern, Process, and Problems." in: *Plant-Animal Interactions: Evolutionary Ecology in Tropical and Temperate Regions.*, eds., Price, P. W.; Lewinsohn, T.M.; Fernandes, G.W. and Benson, W. W., 41-54. New York: Wiley & Sons, 1991.

—. and Singer, M. C. "Butterfly Ecology." *Annual Review of Ecology and Systematics* 6 (1975): 365-397.

Gilchrist, G. W. "The Consequences of Sexual Dimorphism in Body Size for Butterfly Flight and Thermoregulation." *Functional Ecology* 4 (1990): 475-487.

Harrison, S.; Quinn, J. F.; Baughman, J. F.; Murphy, D. D. and Ehrlich, P.R. "Estimating the Effects of Scientific Study on Two Butterfly Populations." *American Naturalist* 137 (1991): 227-243.

Hazel, W. N. "The Genetic Basis of Pupal Colour Dimorphism and its Maintenance by Natural Selection in *Papilio polyxenes* (Papilionidae: Lepidoptera)." *Heredity* 38 (1977): 227-236.

Heinrich, B. "Thermoregulation and Flight Activity of a Satyrine, *Coenonympha Inornata* (Lepidoptera: Satyridae)." *Ecology* 67 (1986): 593-597.

Heppner, J. B. "Faunal Regions and the Diversity of Lepidoptera." *Tropical Lepidoptera 2, Supplement* 1 (1991): 1-85.

Huheey, J. E. "Warning Coloration and Mimicry." in: *Chemical Ecology of Insects.*, eds., Bell, W. J. and Carde, R. T., 257-297. London: Chapman and Hall, 1984.

Karlsson, B. "Resource Allocation and Mating Systems in Butterflies." *Evolution* 49 (1995): 955-961.

Kellert, S. R. "Why Save Butterflies?" *Defenders* Fall (1993): 8, 41.

Kevan, P. G. and Shorthouse, J. D. "Behavioural Thermoregulation by High Arctic Butterflies." *Arctic* 23 (1970): 268-279.

Kingsolver, J. G. "Butterfly Thermoregulation: Organismic Mechanisms and Population Consequences." *Journal of Research on the Lepidoptera* 24 (1985): 1-20.

—. "Butterfly Engineering." *Scientific American* 253, August (1985): 106-113.

—. "Predation, Thermoregulation, and Wing Color in Pierid Butterflies." *Oecologia* 73 (1987): 301-306.

—. "Weather and the Population Dynamics of Insects: Integrating Physiological and Population Ecology." *Physiological Zoology* 62 (1989): 314-334.

Kitching, R. L. and Zalucki, M. P. "Observations on the Ecology of *Euploea Core Corinna* (Nymphalidae) With Special Reference to an Overwintering Population." *Journal of the Lepidopterists' Society* 35 (1981): 106-119.

Larsen, T. B. "Butterfly Mass Transit." *Natural History* 102 (6) (1993): 30-39.

—. "Butterflies as Indicator Species in Africa." *Tropical Lepidoptera News*, September 3 (1996): 1, 3-4.

Lederhouse, R. C.; Ayres, M. P. and Scriber, J. M. "Adult Nutrition Affects Male Virility in *Papilio Glaucus* L." *Functional Ecology* 4 (1990): 743-751.

Legg, G. "A Note on the Diversity of World Lepidoptera (Rhopalocera)." *Biological Journal of the Linnean Society* 10 (1978): 343-347.

Lemon, E. K. "Butterflies Are Free." *Wildlife Review*, Spring (1985): 7-10.

Mallet, J. "Gregarious Roosting and Home Range in *Heliconius* Butterflies." *National Geographic Research* 2 (1986): 198-215.

—. and Gilbert, L. E. "Why Are There So Many Mimicry Rings? Correlations Between Habitat, Behaviour and Mimicry in *Heliconius* Butterflies." *Biological Journal of the Linnean Society* 55 (1995): 159-180.

Marden, J. H. "Newton's Second Law of Butterflies." *Natural History* 1/92 (1992): 54-61.

Marshall, L.D. "Male Nutrient Investment in the Lepidoptera: What Nutrients Should Males Invest?" *American Naturalist* 120 (1982): 273-279.

Mattson, W. J. and Scriber, J. M. "Nutritional Ecology of Insect Folivores of Woody Plants: Nitrogen, Water, Fiber, and Mineral Considerations." in: *Nutritional Ecology of Insects, Mites, Spiders, and Related Invertebrates.*, eds., Slansky, Jr., F. and Rodriguez, J. G., 105-146. New York: Wiley & Sons, 1987.

Miller, L. D. and Miller, J. Y. "The Biogeography of West Indian Butterflies (Lepidoptera: Papilionoidea, Hesperioidea): A Vicariance Model." in: *Biogeography of the West Indies.*, ed., Woods, C.A., 229-262. Gainesville: Sandhill Crane Press, 1989.

Moore, S. D. "Male-Biased Mortality in the Butterfly *Euphydryas Editha*: A Novel Cost of Mate Acquisition." *American Naturalist* 130 (1987): 306-309.

—. "Patterns of Juvenile Mortality Within an Oligophagous Insect Population." *Ecology* 70 (1989): 1726-1737.

Morris, M. G. "Changing Attitudes to Nature Conservation: The Entomological Perspective." *Biological Journal of the Linnean Society* 32 (1987): 213-223.

Murphy, D. D. "California's Vanishing Butterflies." *Defenders*, Fall (1993): 17-21.

New, T. R. "Conservation of Butterflies in Australia." *Journal of Research on the Lepidoptera* 29 (1992): 237-253.

Odendaal, F. J.; Iwasa, Y. and Ehrlich, P. R. "Duration of Female Availability and its Effect on Butterfly Mating Systems." *American Naturalist* 125 (1985): 673-678.

—. ; Turchin, P. and Stermitz, F. R. "Influence of Host-Plant Density and Male Harassment on the Distribution of Female *Euphydryas Anicia* (Nymphalidae)." *Oecologia* 78 (1989): 283-288.

Owen, D. F. and Smith, D. A. S. "Interpopulation Variation and Selective Predation in the Meadow Brown Butterfly, *Maniola Jurtina* (L.) (Lepidoptera: Satyridae) in the Canary Islands." *Biological Journal of the Linnean Society* 39 (1990): 251-267.

Packer, L. P. "Extirpation of the Karner Blue Butterfly in Ontario." in: *Karner Blue Butterfly: A Symbol of a Vanishing Landscape.*, eds., Andow, D. A.; Baker, R. J. and Lane, C. P., 143-151. St. Paul: University of Minnesota, 1994.

Papageorgis, C. "Mimicry in Neotropical Butterflies." *American Scientist* 63 (1975): 522-532.

Parmesan, C. "Climate and Species' Range." *Nature* 382 (1996): 765-766.

—. et al. "Poleward Shifts in Geographical Ranges of Butterfly Species Associated with Regional Warming." *Nature* 399 (1999): 579-583.

Parsons, M. J. "Butterfly Farming and Conservation in the Indo-Australian Region."
Tropical Lepidoptera 3, Supplement 1 (1992): 1-62.

Pierce, N. E. "The Evolution and Biogeography of Associations Between Lycaenid Butterflies and Ants." in: *Oxford Surveys in Evolutionary Biology.*, Volume 4. eds., Harvey, P. H. and Partridge, L., 89-116. Oxford: Oxford University Press, 1987.

—. and Mead, P. S. "Parasitoids as Selective Agents in the Symbiosis Between Lycaenid Butterfly Larvae and Ants." *Science* 211 (1981): 1185-1187.

Pivnick, K. A. and McNeil, J. N. "Mate Location and Mating Behavior of *Thymelicus lineola* (Lepidoptera: Hesperiidae)." *Annals of the Entomological Society of America* 78 (1985): 651-656.

—. and McNeil, J. N. "Sexual Differences in the Thermoregulation of *Thymelicus Lineola* Adults (Lepidoptera: Hesperiidae)." *Ecology* 67 (1986): 1024-1035.

—. and McNeil, J. N. "Puddling in Butterflies: Sodium Affects Reproductive Success in *Thymelicus Lineola*." *Physiological Entomology* 12 (1987): 461-472.

—. and McNeil, J. N. "Diel Patterns of Activity of *Thymelicus Lineola* Adults (Lepidoptera: Hesperiidae) in Relation to Weather." *Ecological Entomology* 12 (1987): 197-207.

Polcyn, D. M. and Chappell, M. A. "Analysis of Heat Transfer in *Vanessa* Butterflies: Effects of Wing Position and Orientation to Wind and Light." *Physiological Zoology* 59 (1986): 706-716.

Pollard, E. "Temperature, Rainfall and Butterfly Numbers." *Journal of Applied Ecology* 25 (1988): 819-828.

Pyle, R. M. "A History of Lepidoptera Conservation, With Special Reference to its Remingtonian Debt." *Journal of the Lepidopterists' Society* 49 (1995): 397-411.

—.; Bentzien, M. and Opler, P. A. "Insect Conservation." *Annual Review of Entomology* 26 (1981): 233-258.

Rausher, M. D. "Larval Habitat Suitability and Oviposition Preference in Three Related Butterflies." *Ecology* 60 (1979): 503-511.

Rawlins, J. E. "Thermoregulation by the Black Swallowtail Butterfly, *Papilio polyxenes* (Lepidoptera: Papilionidae)." *Ecology* 61 (1980): 345-357.

Ray, T. S. "Antbutterflies: Butterflies that Follow Army Ants to Feed on Antbird Droppings." *Science* 210 (1980): 1147-1148.

Ritland, D. B. "Variation in Palatability of Queen Butterflies (*Danaus Gilippus*) and Implications Regarding Mimicry." *Ecology* 75 (1994): 732-746.

—. and Brower, L. P. "The Viceroy Butterfly is not a Batesian Mimic." *Nature* 350 (1991): 497-498.

Robbins, R. K. "The Lycaenid "False Head" Hypothesis: Historical Review and Quantitative Analysis." *Journal of the Lepidopterists' Society* 34 (1980): 194-208.

—. "The "False Head" Hypothesis: Predation and Wing Pattern Variation of Lycaenid Butterflies." *American Naturalist* 118 (1981): 770-775.

—. "How Many Butterfly Species?" *News of the Lepidopterists' Society* (1982): 40-41.

Ross, G. N. "Butterflies Descend on Offshore Rigs." *Louisiana Environmentalist* 2(5) (1994): 12-15.

—. "Monarchs Offshore in the Gulf of Mexico." *Holarctic Lepidoptera* 5 (1998): 52.

Rutowski, R. R. "Sexual Selection and the Evolution of Butterfly Mating Behavior." *Journal of Research on the Lepidoptera* 23 (1984): 125-142.

—. "Mating Strategies of Butterflies." *Scientific American* 279(1) (1998): 64-69.

Rutowski, R. L.; Newton, M. and Schaefer, J. "Interspecific Variation in the Size of the Nutrient Investment Made by Male Butterflies During Copulation." *Evolution* 37 (1983): 708-713.

—.; Alcock, J. and Carey, M. "Hilltopping in the Pipevine Swallowtail Butterfly (*Battus Philenor*)." *Ethology* 82 (1989): 244-254.

Schappert, P. J. and Shore, J. S. "Ecology, Population Biology and Mortality of *Euptoieta Hegesia* Cramer (Nymphalidae) in Jamaica." *Journal of the Lepidopterists' Society* 52 (1998): 9-39.

—. "Effects of Cyanogenesis Polymorphism in *Turnera Ulmifolia* on *Euptoieta Hegesia* and Potential *Anolis* Predators." *Journal of Chemical Ecology* 25 (1999): 1455-1479.

Scoble, M. J. and Aiello, A. "Moth-Like Butterflies (Hedylidae: Lepidoptera): A Summary, With Comments on the Egg." *Journal of Natural History* 24 (1990): 159-164.

Scott, J. A. "Hilltopping as a Mating Mechanism to Aid the Survival of Low Density Species." *Journal of Research on the Lepidoptera* 7 (1970): 191-204.

—. "Mating of Butterflies." *Journal of Research on the Lepidoptera* 11 (1970): 99-127.

—. "Lifespan of Butterflies." *Journal of Research on the Lepidoptera* 12 (1973): 225-230.

—. "Mate-Locating Behavior of Butterflies." *American Midland Naturalist* 91 (1974): 103-117.

Scriber, J. M. "Latitudinal Gradients in Larval Feeding Specialization of the World Papilionidae (Lepidoptera)." *Psyche* 80 (1973): 355-373.

—. "Effects of Leaf-Water Supplementation Upon Post-Ingestive Nutritional Indices of Forb-, Shrub-, Vine-, and Tree-Feeding Lepidoptera." *Entomologia Experimentalis et Applicata* 25 (1979): 240-252.

—. and Feeny, P. "Growth of Herbivorous Caterpillars in Relation to Feeding Specialization and to the Growth Form of their Food Plants." *Ecology* 60 (1979): 829-850.

Shapiro, A. M. "Seasonal Polyphenism." *Evolutionary Biology* 9 (1976): 259-333.

—. "The Pierid Red Egg Syndrome." *American Naturalist* 117 (1981): 276-294.

Sheppard, P. M. "Some Contributions to Population Genetics Resulting from the Study of the Lepidoptera." *Advances in Genetics* 10 (1961): 165-216.

Shields, O. "Hilltopping." *Journal of Research on the Lepidoptera* 6 (1967): 69-178.

—. "Fossil Butterflies and the Evolution of Lepidoptera." *Journal of Research on the Lepidoptera* 15 (1976): 132-143.

—. "World Numbers of Butterflies." *Journal of the Lepidopterists' Society* 43 (1989): 178-183.

Shreeve, T. G. and Dennis, R. L. H. "The Development of Butterfly Settling Posture: The Role of Predators, Climate, Hostplant-Habitat and Phylogeny." *Biological Journal of the Linnean Society* 45 (1992): 57-69.

Sibatani, A. "Decline and Conservation of Butterflies in Japan." *Journal of Research on the Lepidoptera* 29 (1992): 305-315.

Sikes, D. S. and Ivie, M. A. "Predation of *Anetia Briarea* Godart (Nymphalidae: Danainae) at Aggregation Sites: A Potential Threat to the Survival of a Rare Montaine Butterfly in the Dominican Republic." *Journal of the Lepidopterists' Society* 49 (1995): 223-233.

Silberglied, R. E. "Visual Communication and Sexual Selection Among Butterflies." in: *The Biology of Butterflies*., eds., Vane-Wright, R. I. and Ackery, P. R., 207-223. London: Academic Press, 1984.

—.; Aiello, A. and Lamas, G. "Neotropical Butterflies of the Genus *Anartia*: Systematics, Life Histories and General Biology (Lepidoptera: Nymphalidae)." *Psyche* 86 (1979): 219-260.

Singer, M. C. "Complex Components of Habitat Suitability Within a Butterfly Colony." *Science* 176 (1972): 75-77.

—. "Sexual Selection for Small Size in Male Butterflies." *American Naturalist* 119 (1982): 440-443.

—. "Butterfly-Hostplant Relationships: Host Quality, Adult Choice and Larval Success." in: *The Biology of Butterflies*., eds., Vane-Wright, R. I. and Ackery, P. R., 81-88. London: Academic Press, 1984.

Slansky, Jr., F. "Phagism Relationships Among Butterflies." *Journal of the New York Entomological Society* 84 (1976): 91-105.

Stamp, N. E. "Egg Deposition Patterns in Butterflies: Why do Some Species Cluster their Eggs Rather than Deposit them Singly?" *American Naturalist* 115 (1980): 367-380.

—. and Bowers, M. D. "Phenology of Nutritional Differences Between New and Mature Leaves and its Effect on Caterpillar Growth." *Ecological Entomology* 15 (1990): 447-454.

Swengel, A. B. and Swengel, S. R. "Co-Occurrence of Prairie and Barrens Butterflies: Applications to Ecosystem Conservation." *Journal of Insect Conservation* 1 (1997): 131-144.

Thomas, C. D. and Mallorie, H. C. "Rarity, Species Richness and Conservation: Butterflies of the Atlas Mountains in Morocco." *Biological Conservation 33* (1985): 95-117.

Thomas, J. A. "The Conservation of Butterflies in Temperate Countries: Past Efforts and Lessons for the Future." in: *The Biology of Butterflies*., eds., Vane-Wright, R. I. and Ackery, P. R., London: Academic Press, 1984.

Thompson, J. N. "Selection Pressures on Phytophagous Insects Feeding on Small Host Plants." *Oikos* 40 (1983): 438-444.

—. and Pellmyr, O. "Evolution of Oviposition Behaviour and Host Preference in Lepidoptera." *Annual Review of Entomology* 36 (1991): 65-89.

Turner, J. R. G. "A Tale of Two Butterflies." *Natural History* 84 (2) (1975): 28-37.

—. "Why Male Butterflies are Non-Mimetic: Natural Selection, Sexual Selection, Group Selection, Modification and Sieving." *Biological Journal of the Linnean Society* 10 (1978): 385-432.

—. "Mimicry: The Palatability Spectrum and its Consequences." in: *The Biology of Butterflies*., eds.,Vane-Wright, R. I. and Ackery, P. R., 141-161. London: Academic Press, London, 1984.

Vane-Wright, R. I. "Ecological and Behavioral Origins of Diversity in Butterflies." in: *Diversity of Insect Faunas*., eds., Mound, L. A. and Waloff, N., 56-70. Oxford: Blackwell Scientific, 1978.

Vasconcellos-Neto, J. and Lewinsohn, T. H. "Discrimination and Release of Unpalatable Butterflies by *Nephila Clavipes*, a Neotropical Orb-Weaving Spider." *Ecological Entomology* 9 (1984): 337-344.

Weiss, S. B.; Murphy, D. D. and White, R. R. "Sun, Slope and Butterflies: Topographic Determinants of Habitat Quality for *Euphydryas Editha*." *Ecology* 69 (1988): 1486-1496.

—.; —.; "Montane Butterfly Distributions and the Potential Impact of Global Warming." *Wings* 15 (1) (1990): 3-7.

Whalley, P. "A Review of the Current Fossil Evidence of Lepidoptera in the Mesozoic." *Biological Journal of the Linnean Society* 28 (1988): 253-271.

Wheye, D. and Ehrlich, P. R. "The Use of Fluorescent Pigments to Study Insect Behaviour: Investigating Mating Patterns in a Butterfly Population." *Ecological Entomology* 10 (1985): 231-234.

White, R. R. "The Trouble with Butterflies." *Journal of Research on the Lepidoptera* 25 (1987): 207-212.

Wickman, P. O. "Sexual Selection and Butterfly Design—A Comparative Study." *Evolution* 46 (1992): 1525-1536.

Wiklund, C. and Fagerstrom, T. "Why do Males Emerge Before Females? A Hypothesis to Explain the Incidence of Protandry in Butterflies." *Oecologia* 31 (1977): 153-158.

—. and Ahrberg, C. "Host Plants, Nectar Source Plants, and Habitat Selection of Males and Females of *Anthocharis Cardamines* (Lepidoptera)." *Oikos* 31 (1978): 169-183.

Wilcox, B. A. and Murphy, D. D. "Conservation Strategy: The Effects of Fragmentation on Extinction." *American Naturalist* 125 (1985): 879-887.

Wilson, E. O. "The Little Things that Run the World (The Importance and Conservation of Invertebrates)." *Conservation Biology* 1 (1987): 344-346.

Wourms, M. K. and Wasserman, F. E. "Bird Predation on Lepidoptera and the Reliability of Beak-Marks in Determining Predation Pressure." *Journal of the Lepidopterists' Society* 39 (1985): 239–261.

Photo and Illustration Credits

James K. Adams p. 167 (both)

Corel Photo p. 31 (Larvae plate; *E. dirtea*). Copyright © 2000 Phil Schappert and licensors. All rights reserved.

Corina Brdar / Greg Taylor p. 294

Márcio Zikán Cardoso pp. 32, 126, 209 (b).

Peng Chai pp. 31 (Larvae plate; *D. darius*, *O. tamarindi* and *Z. itys*), 33 (Pupae plate; *A. melanthe* and *O. tamarindi*), 79, 131 (t), 145, 162 (b),

Chris Durden pp. 42, 51, 60, 204.

Alana M. Edwards pp. 205, 237

Jeff M. Fengler pp. 30 (Eggs plate; all but *Limenitis* sp. and *P. interrogationis*), 31 (Larvae plate; all but *D. darius*, *E. atala*, *O. tamarindi*, *P. polyxenes* and *Z. itys*), 33 (Pupae plate; all but *A. melanthe*, *C. tutia* and *O. tamarindi*), 38 (both), 64, 69, 81, 118, 128 (b), 131 (b), 134, 135 (t), 137 (t), 160 (t), 165 (b), 186 (t), 223 (b), 260

Lawrence E. Gilbert pp. 33 (Pupae plate; *C. tutia*), 99, 139, 181, 220, 226, 241, 242, 292

Nelson Guda pp. 10 (t), 49, 76, 96, 168, 214

William T. Hark pp. 46, 71 (t), 188 (t), 216 (t)

Durrell D. Kapan pp. 78, 195 (t),

Tooru Kawabe p. 193 (b)

Oleg Kosterin pp. 17, 28 (all), 29 (all), 65, 73, 83, 101, 140, 191, 198 (t), 200 (t), 208, 213, 231, 243, 259

George O. Krizek pp. 15, 57

Takashi Kumon pp. 13, 61, 125, 159, 234

John F. Landers pp. 68, 103, 150, 178

Torben Larsen pp. 111, 137 (b), 180

Mario Maier pp. 14, 19 (both), 120 (t), 193 (t), 194 (b), 211, 230, 281, 282, 283

David A. Millard pp. Title page, 9 (t), 24 (upper four), 25 (t), 30 (Eggs plate; *Limenitis* sp.), 31 (Larvae plate; *P. polyxenes*), 45, 136, 270 (t)

Patti Murray pp. 16, 24 (b), 25 (lower three), 30 (Eggs plate; *P. interrogationis*), 31 (Larvae plate; *E. atala*), 41, 70 (t), 75, 86, 119, 143, 144, 148, 158 (t), 172, 179, 183, 185 (t), 192, 197, 200 (b), 249, 288, 300

Paul Opler pp. 62, 109, 257

Camille Parmesan / Michael Singer p. 284

Kenelm W. Philip p. 121 (t)

Emil M. Pignetti, Jr. p. 147

Michael A. Quinn pp. 35, 58 (b), 59, 151, 188 (b), 199, 216 (b), 223 (upper two), 232, 233, 255, 301 (b)

Hub. Reumkens pp. 67 (b), 104, 154 (b), 236, 239, 246, 256 (t), 269, 293

Gary Noel Ross pp. 130, 161, 162 (t), 163, 185 (b), 186 (b), 187 (both), 227, 285, 287, 299

Phil Schappert pp. 9 (b), 10 (m), 22, 23, 26, 27, 30 (t), 34, 44, 66, 67 (t), 70 (b, 77, 80, 88, 90, 91, 97, 108, 120 (b), 121 (b), 122, 124, 127, 128 (t), 132 (both), 133, 135 (lower four), 138, 141, 146, 149, 153 (both), 154 (t), 156, 158 (b), 160 (b), 166, 169 (both), 171 (both), 173, 174 (both), 175, 176, 177, 182, 189, 190, 195 (b), 201 (t), 202 (both), 203, 206, 207 (both), 209 (t), 210, 215, 217 (all), 218, 222 (both), 224, 228 (b), 235 (all), 240, 244, 250, 256 (b), 266, 272, 273, 274, 291, 295, 296, 297, 298, 301 (upper two), 302

Leroy Simon p. 129

Andrei Sourakov pp. 39, 71 (b), 74, 164, 165 (t), 228 (t), 245, 254, 276, 277, 278 (both), 279

Ann B. Swengel pp. 10 (b), 114, 252, 263 (both), 264

Richard Tanner p. 170

John Tennent pp. Frontispiece, 201 (b), 251

Norbert Ullman pp. 72, 221

Jayne Yack p. 58 (t)

Cor Zonneveld pp. 63, 142 (both), 157, 194 (t), 198 (b), 212, 219, 229, 270 (b)

Illustrations: pp. 36, 84, 85, 92, 94, 98, 286

Lightfoot Art and Design Inc.

Index

A

Acraea leucographa
(Nymphalidae), 86
Acraeinae, 78, 79, 87, 95
Actinote (Nymphalidae):
anteas, 99; ozomene, 78
Adelpha melanthe
(Nymphalidae), 33
adult butterfly, 21-22, 36-
38; crypsis in, 155, 166-
168; eclosure of, 150-152;
food of, 190-198; mating
behavior in, 215-221;
predators of, 156-166;
reproduction, 152-155;
survival of, 152-155
aestivation, 109-110
aggregations, 199-204
Aglais urticae (Nymphalidae),
208
Agraulis vanillae
(Nymphalidae), 129, 130,
141, 147, 153, 163, 175,
215, 261
Amathusinae, 79
Amauris (Nymphalidae):
albi maculata, 293; niavius,
293
Anaea andria (Nymphalidae),
215, 215, 218, 219, 220
Anartia (Nymphalidae):
amathea, 73; jatrophe, 149
Anclyoxypha numitor
(Hesperiidae), 296
Anetia briarea (Nymphalidae),
204
Anolis sp. (Squamata;
Iguanidae), 129, 130-132,
164

antennae, 34, 36, 38, 151-152,
227, 229
Anteos (Pieridae): maerula, 67;
sp., 216
Anthocharis (Pieridae):
cardamines, 132, 142;
midea, 33, 108
anti-aphrodisiac, 241-242
ants, 75, 118, 120, 137, 138-
139, 139, 152, 270, 271
Apatura irus (Nymphalidae),
219
Aphantopus hyperantus
(Nymphalidae), 282
aphytophagy, 73, 118
Aporia crataegi (Pieridae), 140,
190, 200, 230
aposematism, 134-135, 155;
See also warning coloration
Araschnia levana
(Nymphalidae), 18, 247
Arawacus sito (Lycaenidae;
Riodininae), 168, 169
Archaeolopsis, 50-51
Archonias (Pieridae); eurytele,
99; tereas, 99
Argiope aurantia (Araneae;
Araneidae), 154
Argynnini/Argynninae, 77, 87,
129
Argynnis paphia
(Nymphalidae), 15, 230
Arhopala pseudocentaurus
(Lycaenidae), 137
Ascia monuste (Pieridae), 31,
127, 206, 206
Asterocampa (Nymphalidae):
clyton, 129, 151, 161;
leilia, 224, 234-235, 235;

sp., 220
Atlides balesus (Lycaenidae),
301
automimicry, 182

B

Bacillus thuringiensis; See Bt.
Baronia brevicornis
(Papilionidae; Baroniinae), 51,
64
basking, See thermoregulation
Bates, Henry W., 179, 290
Battus (Papilionidae): philenor,
135, 182, 183, 184-188,
185, 186; polydamus, 174;
sp., 175
biogeography, 82-84
body: fluid, See haemolymph;
form and structure, 29-38;
temperature, 206-215
Boloria titania (Nymphalidae),
199
Brassolinae, 76, 78, 79
Brephidium exilis
(Lycaenidae), 70
Bt (Bacillus thuringiensis),
251-253, 257, 258, 288
butterflies: classification of, 51-
56; geographic distribution
of, 84-85, 89; observation
of, 291-294; origin of, 50-
51; as predators of plants,
106-107; rearing of, 294-
297; range of, 105, 275-
277, 278-280; study of,
291-294, See also lepi
dopterology
Butterfly Conservation
(organization), 262

butterfly: farming of, 275-277;
gardening for, 297-301
butterfly-moths, 21, 40, 56,
59-60

C

Calephelis virginiensis
(Lycaenidae), 69
Caligo (Nymphalidae): atreus,
76, 170; sp., 169-170
Calycopis cecrops
(Lycaenidae), 68
camouflage, See crypsis
cannibalism, 124
carnivory, 71, 118
Carterocephalus palaemon
(Hesperiidae), 63
case studies: butterfly farming,
275-277; extirpation of
Karner blue, 266-271;
extirpation of large blue,
271-273; global warming
and butterfly range, 277-
280; Homerus swallowtail,
273-275; monarch
migration, 280-289
Castnia licus (Castniidae), 57
Castniidae/Castnioidea, 40,
56, 57-59, 87, 89
caterpillar, 21, 23, 26, 28, 31,
31-33, 49, 116, 123-140
Catopsilia florella (Pieridae),
111
Celastrina (Lycaenidae): ladon,
212; sp., 145
Ceratinia (Nymphalidae):
diona, 181; fenestella, 181,
tutia, 33
Cercyonis pegala

(Nymphalidae), 296
Charaxes (Nymphalidae):
eupale, 74; jasius, 193
Charaxinae, 74, 78
Chlorostrymon simaethis
(Lycaenidae), 171
Chlosyne lacinia
(Nymphalidae), 136
Choaspes benjaminii
(Hesperiidae), 61
chrysalis, 21, 27, 33, 34-36, 40,
49, 117, 141-149, 141, 142,
143
CITES; See Convention on
International Trade in
Endangered Species
(CITES)
Cithaerias menander
(Nymphalidae), 215
Clossiana selene
(Nymphalidae), 296
Coeliadinae, 61
Coenonympha (Nymphalidae):
arcania, 283; inornata, 192,
209, 296
Coliadinae, 67-68, 67
Colias (Pieridae): australis,
230; cesonia, 216;
christina, 294; erate, 234;
eurytheme, 31, 46, 257;
philodice, 296; sp., 233
Colobura dirce (Nymphalidae),
169
color, 130-135, 151-152; see
also warning coloration
Committee for the Protection
of British Lepidoptera, 262
commonness, 103-106
confusion displays, 202, 203-
204
conservation: 45-47, 93, 102,
115, 262-265, 288-289;
and alien species, 249; and
habitat loss, 252, 253-256;
and protective measures in,
262-265
continental drift, 85, 86-88
Convention on International
Trade in Endangered
Species (CITES), 258, 263,
273
copulation, 238-243; See also
courtship, reproduction
Cossoidea, 59
courtship: 222, 223, 225-235;
pheromones and, 225, 228;
rejection posture and, 229,
230; species specific behav

iors, 228-230; success, 225,
238
crypsis, 145-147, 155, 166-168,
169-173
Cupido minimus (Lycaenidae),
258

D
Damora sagana
(Nymphalidae), 28/29
Danainae, 80-81, 80
Danaus (Nymphalidae):
chrysippus aegyptius 293;
chrysippus dorippus, 293;
chrysippus, 180, 251;
eresimus, 182; gilippus, 31,
175, 179, 182, 199, 230-
233, 232, 233, 255, 301;
plexippus, 81, 107, 112,
175-176, 177, 178, 178,
179, 198, 204, 204, 205,
237, 258, 261, 280-289,
285, 286, 288, 291, 299
Diaethria cemdrera
(Nymphalidae), 40
diapause, 23, 109-113
Dichorragia nesimachus
(Nymphalidae), 192
Dismorphia (Pieridae):
amphiona, 99; eunoe, 99;
praxinoe, 181; theucharila,
99
Dismorphiinae, 67, 68
dispersal, 107, 109-113
diversity, 54-56; and conservation, 47; and continental
drift, 86-88; and island
biogeography theory, 89-
93,92; and rainforest
refugia,93-99; study of, 42,
96-97; of wing pattern, 21,
36; by zoogeographic
regions, 89
dormancy, 109-110
Dynastor darius
(Nymphalidae), 31
Dysschemia jansonius
(Arctiidae; Pericopinae), 99

E
eclosure, 28-29
egg(s): 21-26, 29-30, 30, 49,
116, 117-123, 119, 143;
red-egg syndrome in, 123,
132
endangered-species legislation,
263-265
endangerment, causes of, 250-

253, 256-261; natural
threats, 250-251
Enodia anthedon
(Nymphalidae), 222, 223
Epargyreus clarus
(Hesperiidae), 131, 299
Erebia pronoe (Nymphalidae),
194
Eresia (Nymphalidae): coela,
99; mechanitis, 99; philyra,
181
Euchloe olympia (Pieridae),
66, 122, 123, 296
Euides (Nymphalidae):
isabella, 166; zorcaon, 181
Eumaeus atala (Lycaenidae),
16, 31
Euphaedra neophron
(Nymphalidae), 197
Euphydryas (Nymphalidae):
editha bayensis, 105, 244-
247, 280, 285; gilletti, 119;
maturna, 194; phaeton,
137; sp., 112, 138
Euptoieta (Nymphalidae):
claudia, 120, 128, 128;
hegesia, 22, 23, 23-28, 26,
27, 30, 53, 121, 124, 132,
133, 138, 152, 167, 176,
298
Eurema (Pieridae): lisa, 222,
233; mexicana, 216;
nicippe, 15; sp., 230
Eurytides (Papilionidae):
euryleon, 99; marcellus,
33, 64, 261, 264
Euschemon rafflesia
(Hesperiidae), 50
Euthalia dirtea (Nymphalidae),
31
Everes comyntas (Lycaenidae),
297
eyepots, 169-172, 170, 172
eyes, 36, 151-152

F
false head, 168, 171, 171-173
Feniseca tarquinius
(Lycaenidae), 71, 118, 118
Fixsenia favonius (Lycaenidae),
217
"flash and conceal" strategy,
167-168
flight: during courtship, 227-
228, 230-233; forward,
212; fuel for, 116, 192;
temperature for, 207-208;
time available for, 189-190

food, 124, 125-128, 190-198;
alternative sources, 192-
196, 193-195, 197, 198,
203, 245; flowers, 190-192
fossils, 50-51
frass, 129

G
Galbula ruficauda
(Galbulidae), 163
Glaucopsyche (Lycaenidae):
alexis, 280; lygdamus, 296;
xerces, 257, 262
glaciation, 88, 94
global warming, 277-280
Gondwanaland, 85, 87
Graphium antiphates
(Papilionidae), 201
gregrarious, 125, 135-138, 136,
140
Greta diaphana
(Nymphalidae), 245

H
habitat: fragmentation, 93,
105, 274; loss, 253-256;
management, 271-272;
preference, 82, 105, 113-
115; restoration, 268, 297-
301
haemolymph, 28, 37
Hamadryas (Nymphalidae):
amphycloe, 165; sp., 166
Harkenclenus titus
(Lycaenidae), 300
haustellum; See proboscis
Hedylidae/ Hedyloidea, 40, 56,
59-60, 89
Heliconiinae, 77, 79-80, 95,
176, 182-183
Heliconius (Nymphalidae):
charithonia, 32, 33, 34, 35,
148, 149, 173, 173, 205,
261; erato, 95, 96, 98, 225,
242; ethilla, 244-247;
hecalasia, 240; hecale,
99; hewitsoni, 99, 127;
ismenius, 99; melpomene,
95, 97, 98, 209, 240, 245;
numata, 77; pachinius, 99;
sp., 206, 238; telchinia, 181
Hemiargus isola (Lycaenidae),
270
Hesperia sp. (Hesperiidae), 145
Hesperioidea/Hesperiidae/
Hesperinae, 21, 38, 56, 60-
62, 62, 89, 128
Heteropterinae, 61, 62

Heterocera, 21
hibernation, 109-110
Hipparchia (Nymphalidae):
    autonoe, 213; semele, 145,
    156, 229
Historis odius (Nymphalidae),
    221
Hylephila phyleus
    (Hesperiidae), 59
Hypoleria cassotis
    (Nymphalidae), 79
Hypolimnas misippus
    (Nymphalidae), 180
Hypothyris euclea
    (Nymphalidae), 99

I
Idea leucone (Nymphalidae),
    80
imago/imagine; See adult
    butterfly
Incisalia irus (Lycaenidae), 114,
    267
instar, 27, 35
International Union for the
    Conservation of Nature
    and Natural Resources
    (IUCN), 262, 273
island biogeography theory,
    89-93, 92
Issoria lathonia
    (Nymphalidae), 229
Ithomiinae, 79, 79, 80, 227

J
Jalmenus evagorus
    (Lycaenidae), 145
Juditha molpe (Lycaenidae),
    139
Junonia coenia (Nymphalidae),
    176, 177, 228, 295

K
Kallima inachus
    (Nymphalidae), 166
Karanasa regeli
    (Nymphalidae), 82

L
larva/larvae, 26-27, 135-137;
    see also caterpillar
Laurasia, 87
lepidopterology, 13, 21, 41-44
Leptidea sinapsis (Pieridae), 67
Leptininae, 71
Leptotes perkinsae
    (Lycaenidae), 90
Libellula sp. (Odonata;

Libellulidae), 161
Libytheana bachmanii
    (Nymphalidae), 81,107,
    108, 233-234, 234
Libytheinae, 63, 81, 81
life cycle, 22-29; studying,
    294-297
Limenitini, 78
Limenitis (Nymphalidae):
    archippus, 145, 177, 178,
    179; arthemis arthemis,
    188, 188; arthemis
    astyanax, 31, 186, 188;
    populi, 194
Lycaeides melissa samuelis
    (Lycaenidae), 106, 263,
    264, 266-271, 297
Lycaena (Lycaenidae): dorcas,
    102; hyllus, 70; phleas, 300
Lycaenidae/Lycaeninae, 62,
    63, 68-75, 70, 137, 142,
    145, 212, 220, 238
Lycaeninae, 73
Lycorea (Nymphalidae):
    atergatis, 181; cleobaea,
    228
Lymantria dispar (Lycaenidae),
    250, 252

M
Macrosoma (Castniidae):
    heliconiaria, 58, 59; sp., 59
Maculinea (Lycaenidae): alcon,
    239; arion, 118, 269, 271,
    271-273
Malacosoma sp.
    (Lasiocampidae), 253
Maniola jurtina
    (Nymphalidae), 293
mates: patrolling for, 217-218,
    219, 227; perching for,
    215, 218, 220-221, 227
mating behavior:
    mate-carrying, 238-239;
    mate-locating, 217-221;
    mate-discrimination, 221;
    of pupae, 148, 225, 238,
    240, 242; signal-response
    chain, 225; and
    sperm-precedence,
    241-243
Mechanitis (Nymphalidae):
    doryssus, 181; sp., 145,
    145-147
meconium, 28, 147, 152, 176
Megathyminae, 61-62
Megathymus streckeri
    (Hesperiidae), 62

Megisto cymela
    (Nymphalidae), 296
Melanargia russiae
    (Nymphalidae), 73
Melinaea (Nymphalidae):
    ethra, 99; imitata, 181;
    cinxia, 101; trivia, 211
Melitaeini, 78
metamorphosis, 20, 21, 26, 35,
    110, 142
metapopulation, 101, 103
migration, 109-113, 280-289;
    estimating size of, 107
Miletinae, 71, 73
Mimeresia libentina
    (Lycaenidae), 71
mimicry: 95-96, 289;
    automimicry, 182;
    Batesian, 179-180, 180;
    geographic, 184, 188;
    monarch-viceroy system,
    281-182; Müllerian, 182;
    pipevine swallowtail
    system, 178-188;
    sex-limited, 184, 186, 187
    mineral salts, 196,
    199-204, 200-202
Misumena vatia (Araneae;
    Thomisidae), 156
Mitoura grynea (Lycaenidae),
    31, 33
molt, 27, 33, 142
Morphinae, 75, 78-79
Morpho (Nymphalidae):
    cypris, 220; peleides, 75,
    163; sp., 220
mortality rates, 155, 275
moths, 21, 38-40, 48, 49-50
Mylothria malenka (Pieridae),
    181
Myrmica sp. (Hymenoptera;
    Formicidae), 118, 271

N
Napeogenes peredia
    (Nymphalidae), 99
nitrogen, need for, 196;
    See also mineral salts
nomenclaure, 36, 51-56;
    binomial, 52-54; common
    names, 54; Linnean
    system, 52-54
Nymphalidae/ Nymphalinae,
    62, 63, 73, 75-81, 95, 169,
    212, 238
Nymphalis (Nymphalidae):
    antiopa, 54, 110, 207, 208,
    211, 261; milberti, 110;

vaualbum, 110, 195

O
Odocoileus virginianus
    (Mammalia; Cervidae), 268
Oecophylla sp. (Hymenoptera;
    Formincinae), 137
Oeneis (Nymphalidae):
    macounii, 108; uhleri, 108,
    109; sp., 108
Oleria paula (Nymphalidae),
    99
Opsiphanes tamarindi
    (Nymphalidae), 31, 33, 49
Ornithoptera (Papilionidae):
    sp., 64, 275; victoria, 277,
    278, 279
osmeterium, 134-135, 135
ova/ovum; See egg
ovarian dynamics, 244-247
overcollection/over-
    exploitation, 106, 258-261,
    264-265
oviposition, 23, 116, 120, 122,
    123, 127, 174, 189, 244-
    247, 245, 247

P
Pangea, 86-87
Papilio (Papilionidae):
    androgeus, 200; cana-
    densis, 170,250, 264, 296;
    cresphontes, 133, 223, 261;
    dardanus, 293; glaucus,
    172, 184-185, 185, 186,
    251; homerus, 272, 273,
    273-275, 274; machaon,
    121; polyxenes, 31, 143,
    144, 162, 183, 185, 215-
    216, 216, 264; troilus, 23,
    24/25, 31, 134, 134-135,
    135, 185; xuthus, 125
Papilionoidea/Papilionidae/
    Papilioninae, 21, 40, 51,
    56, 60, 62, 63-81, 89, 142,
    145, 238
parasitoids, 128-129, 128, 131,
    144
Parides arcas (Papilionidae), 99
Parnara guttata (Hesperiidae),
    158
Parnassiinae, 64-65
Parnassius (Papilionidae):
    actius, 17; apollo, 106, 120,
    256, 258; eversmanni, 65,
    242; sp., 242
Parthenos sylvia
    (Nymphalidae), 44

pheromones, 198, 199, 225, 227, 241-242
Phocides urania (Hesperiidae), 58
Phoebis (Pieridae): argante, 200; philea, 33; sennae, 222, 302; sp., 216
Phyciodes (Nymphalidae): (Antillea) proclea, 91; tharos, 201, 202, 296
Phymata sp. (Hemiptera; Phymatidae), 158
Pieridae/Pierinae, 60, 62, 65-68, 66, 142, 145, 238
Pieris (Pieridae): napi, 105, 296; rapae, 102, 103, 112, 158, 203, 257, 296; virginiensis, 102, 210
pipevine swallowtail mimicry system, 184-188
plants: chemistry of, 174-176, 181, 183, 184, 185; as food, 48-49, 125-128; as predators, 156, 156, 158; sequestration from, 174-176
Poanes viator (Hesperiidae), 296
Polistes sp. (Hymenoptera), 129, 162
Polites (Hesperiidae): mystic, 189, 190; peckius, 33
Polygonia (Nymphalidae): c-album, 198; comma, 31; interrogationis, 45, 165, 220; sp., 134, 166
Polyommatinae, 69, 70
Polyommatus icarus (Lycaenidae), 236
Pompeius verna (Hesperiidae), 150
Pontia protodice (Pieridae), 108
population: biology, 82-84, 100-115; dynamics, 106-109; human growth in, 256; outbreaks, 107-108; size, 105-108, 253-254; structure, 101-103
Praepapilio sp. (Papilionidae), 51
predators: avoidance of, 125, 130-139, 145-147, 155, 164, 170, 173; of butterflies, 153-154, 156, 158, 160, 161, 162-163, 164; foraging strategies of, 128; of eggs, 120, 121;

kinds of, 106-107, 128-129, 133, 155, 156-166, 178-179; of larvae, 130, 138; and population size, 106
prepupal stadium, 27, 143
proboscis, 36, 151, 151-152
prolegs, 32, 49
Promachus binei (Diptera; Asilidae), 163
protection; See conservation
Protogonius cecrops (Nymphalidae), 181
Pseudopontia paradoxa (Pieridae), 68
Pseudopontiinae, 68
puddling, 199-204, 216-217
pupa/pupae; See chrysalis
Pyrginae, 50, 60-61, 62
Pyronia tithonus (Nymphalidae), 154
Pyrrhocalles jamiacensis (Hesperiidae), 88
Pyrrhogyra neaerea (Nymphalidae), 131
Pyrrhopyge araxes (Hesperiidae), 60
Pyrrhopyginae, 61

R
rainforest refugia, 93-99, 94
Rana pipiens (Anura; Ranidae), 202
rare: definitions of, 105; life stages, 155; rarity, 103-106
refugia; See rainforest refugia
release of living butterflies, 261
reproduction, 150, 152-155, 225, 238-242; See also courtship
Rhabdodryas trite, 200
Rhopalocera, 21, 54, 56-57, 60
Riodininae, 51, 68-69, 69, 138
Rondonia, 57, 97
roost: fidelity, 206; sites, 204-206, 286, 204-205

S
salt, See mineral salts
Satyrinae, 51, 73, 77, 78, 127, 238
Satyrium calanus (Lycaenidae), 300
seasonality, 108-109
sensory capabilities, 151-152
Sericinus montela (Papilionidae), 13
Sesioidea, 59

silk, 130, 138, 142
Solenopsis invicta (Hymenoptera; Formicidae), 152
source/sink dynamics, 101
speciation, 88
spermatophore, 196-198, 239
Speryeria (Nymphalidae): cybele, 129, 296, 299; aphrodite, 203, 296; atlantis, 296; diana, 185, 187; idalia, 252
sphragis, 242, 243
spiracles, 32, 34, 37
Strymon melinus (Lycaenidae), 172, 220
survival, 152-155

T
taxonomy, 51-56
Tellervinae, 80
Tenodera aridifolia (Orthoptera; Mantidae), 158
territoriality, 217, 218-219, 221-225, 238; and courtship, 234-235
territory: floaters, 224; holders, 224; location of, 223-224; and male-male interactions, 235-238, 237; and mate-locating behavior, 217, 218-219
Theclinae, 68, 69
thermoregulation: 164, 206-215; basking, 207-211; and body size, 211-215, 213, 215; heat gain/loss, 211-213; shivering or thermogenesis, 209-209
Thymelicus (Hesperiidae): lineola, 160, 202, 249, 296; sp., 145
Thymus sp. (Labiatae), 118, 271
Tithorea hippothous (Nymphalidae), 181
Tomarus ballus (Lycaenidae), 212
transgenic plants, 257
Trapezitinae, 61, 62
Troides sp. (Papilionidae), 275

U
Urania leilus (Uraniidae), 39
Urbanus proteus (Hesperiidae), 31

V
Vanessa (Nymphalidae): atalanta, 110, 254, 261; cardui, 112, 147, 167, 168, 261; virginiensis, 110, 128, 261, 301
Vespula sp; Hymenoptera, 129

W
warning coloration, 134-135, 136, 155, 166, 167-168, 173-174, 178; see also color
white-tailed deer, 268
wing: color and pattern of, 20, 21, 36, 37, 39, 164; coupling mechanism, 39, 50; muscles, 208-209; position of, 39; scales on, 20, 21, 37, 48; size of, 37; veins, 36, 37; wave, 230, 230
World Conservation Union, 262

X
Xerces Society, 262

Z
Zaretis itys (Nymphalidae), 31
Zelus longipes (Hemiptera; Reduviidae), 130
zoogeographic regions, 84, 84, 89
Zygaenoidea, 59